JOHN O'LEARY

A STUDY IN IRISH SEPARATISM

MARCUS BOURKE

JOHN O'LEARY

A STUDY IN IRISH SEPARATISM

ANVIL BOOKS LIMITED
5 Rock Street Tralee

First published in mcmlxvii
by Anvil Books Limited
5 Rock Street Tralee
Printed in the Republic of Ireland by
The Kerryman Limited Tralee
All rights reserved

© 1967 by Marcus Bourke

TO ALL OTHER RESEARCH WORKERS IN
MODERN IRISH HISTORY

ACKNOWLEDGMENTS

For their co-operation and patience over a period of several years I wish to thank the staff of the National Library of Ireland (particularly Messrs. T. P. O'Neill, A. MacLochlainn, M. Breen and J. Scully), and Breandán Mac Giolla Coille and Brighid MacGrath of the State Paper Office.

For permission to inspect records in their custody I am indebted to the Bishop of Kildare and Leighlin, Most Rev. Dr. P. J. Lennon (then President of St. Patrick's College, Carlow); Rev. J. Hackett, DD, Tipperary, and the Registrar of the Erasmus Smith Schools.

For permission to quote from a poem by W. B. Yeats, and to use a sketch by J. B. Yeats (senior), I am indebted to Senator Michael Yeats; and for permission to quote from the letters of the late Matthew Harris MP, I wish to thank Ulick O'Connor BL.

For their assistance in supplying photostats or other documentary material, in replying to queries and in giving access to publications not available elsewhere, I wish to thank the librarians or archivists of Trinity College, Dublin; New York City Public Library (Newspaper Division); British Museum Newspaper Library; Boston College Library, Massachusetts; Chicago Public Library (Newspaper Service); Catholic University of America, Washington; Cork Historical and Archaeological Society; the County Library, Thurles; and Dublin Corporation (Central Library, Pearse Street).

For assistance in tracing the origin of the O'Leary family in Tipperary, I am grateful to Messrs. Michael Fitzpatrick, James and Michael Kirby and Séamus O Ceallaigh, all of that town.

For information and advice generally on the IRB I am indebted to the late Piaras Beaslai (Dublin), Ernest Blythe (Dublin), Bulmer Hobson (Castleconnell), Denis MacCullough (Dublin), the late Dr. P. J. McCartan (Greystones), Walter McGrath (Cork), Seán O Lúing (Dublin), and the late Desmond Ryan (Dublin).

Finally, the following kindly assisted my research with replies to queries or with information on miscellaneous topics: Mrs. Bronson Alberry (London), Desmond Bell SC (Dublin), Rev. P. J. Bruen CC (Loughrea), Miss Maureen and Mr. Norman Carew (formerly of Kilkenny and now of Fleet, Hampshire, and Elanora, New South Wales, respectively), John T. Collins (Cork), Rev. W. D'Arcy OFM CONV. (New York), James Delehanty (Kilkenny), Henry Fottrell (Dublin), the late District Justice D. Gleeson (Nenagh), the late Miss Florence Hackett (Kilkenny), Cahir Healy, ex-MP (Fermanagh); the late James Hurley (Cork), the late District Justice M. J. Lennon (Dublin), James Maher (Mullinahone), Archbishop David Mathew (London), Canon T. Maguire (Fermanagh), Rev. Prof. F. X. Martin OSA (Dublin), Ald. C. M. Milligan (Bangor), the late Seán S. O hEigeartaigh (Dublin), and Rev. A. O'Reilly SJ (Galway).

Marcus Bourke, Dublin, October 1967.

CONTENTS

ILLUSTRATIONS

ACKNOWLEDGMENTS

Nationalist and Leinster Times, Clonmel (Nos. 2 & 3); State Paper Office, Dublin (Nos. 4 & 22); Catholic University of America (No. 7); *Radio Times* Hulton Picture Library (Nos. 9-12); Mrs. M. Quinlan, Monkstown, Dublin (No. 20); Anne & Michael Yeats (Nos. 26 & 28); Ald. C. M. Milligan, Bangor (No. 27); *Kilkenny People,* Kilkenny, and James Maher, Mullinahone (No. 30).

CHAPTER ONE

1

WHEN YOU STAND AT THE JUNCTION of Main Street and Davis Street you are in the heart of Tipperary town. Half-a-mile or so to the east the road to Cashel climbs over the Hill of Crogue; nearer to the centre of the town lies the old quarter known as The Spiddal. To the right as you face the towering range of the nearby Galtees your view ends a short distance up O'Brien Street, the western continuation of Main Street. Down in front of you, at the foot of steeply-falling Bridge Street, sprawl the cattle yard and the railway station, with the old military barracks beyond them again.

However, while the area of Tipperary town has probably doubled in the past 130 years or so, official statistics show that its population has fallen in the same period by nearly thirty per cent, from 7,000 in 1831 to little over 5,000 in 1961. And if allowance were made for the subsequent steady fall in the value of the pound sterling, this town would doubtless be found to have been a more prosperous business centre for the enterprising local merchants of a century-and-a-quarter ago than it is for their successors today.

In those pre-Famine days the rich natural resources of the

surrounding countryside (officially claimed in 1846 to be 'the most fertile and luxuriant tract of land under the dominion of the British crown') were fully, not to say ruthlessly, exploited by a large, decadent, expensive-living class of big estate-owners. The area's reputation for agrarian outrages did not deter 'a considerable number of gentry' from residing in the many 'pleasant villas' scattered round the vicinity. 'The soil everywhere is rich, but especially so around Tipperary town', says an official commentary of a decade or so later.

On and out of this soil lived at subsistence level a tenant peasantry whose numbers grew steadily from year to year; in squalid hovels resided the descendants of the original owners of the land, separated from starvation by their potato crop alone, and ready to take the law into their own hands to protect their interest. It was arising out of a killing by some of these same tenants only a few years later that an Under-Secretary for Ireland, in a statement of which the first part is as often misquoted as is the second overlooked, reminded the magistrates of Tipperary that 'property has its duties as well as its rights; to the neglect of these duties in times past is mainly to be ascribed that diseased state of society in which such crimes take their rise'.[1]

Of public buildings, Tipperary around 1830 boasted a newly-erected Protestant church, a Methodist meeting-house, an endowed Protestant boys' school, a jail and courthouse, a hospital (whence in all probability the name Spiddal), and several reputable 'inns and posting establishments'. The recently emancipated Catholics had in the early 1820s commenced work on a magnificent new parish church, which would not be completed for another quarter of a century; their thirst for learning they partly satisfied at half-a-dozen or so private elementary daily schools. In all, nearly 1,200 families occupied close on 1,100 private dwellings.

Several small industries which have long since disappeared also flourished. 'The general appearance of the town' was 'clean and agreeable'; 'a busy retail trade and a good weekly market' indicated a thriving local commercial life. All the evidence supports the view that, in those days at any rate, the shopkeepers of Tipperary were appreciably 'better off than elsewhere'. Such, indeed, was the prosperity of the town in the early decades of the nineteenth century that it appears to have attracted from other towns in the area enterprising merchants eager to make their fortune there.

Amongst these was one John O'Leary (senior), who by the early 1820s—if not considerably earlier—was in business in Main Street as a butter buyer, wool comber and leather seller. O'Leary was then, as it still is today, essentially a north Cork or Kerry surname; we have it on the authority of the second son of John O'Leary (senior) that his own 'immediate forbears' came from Cork.[2] Moreover, the knowledge that among the O'Learys' closest friends in Tipperary were William Bible the pawnbroker, and Jeremiah Dowling the cabinet-maker (both also of Main Street), points to the possibility that the O'Leary family had its immediate origins in the town of Fermoy, where the Bibles were also grocers and the Dowlings drapers. Another lifelong business connection of the O'Learys was the Rice family, grocers and publicans in Fermoy and leather sellers in the nearby village of Kilworth.

Nor was John O'Leary (senior) apparently the only member of the family to move northwards. Since Arthur was a family name, it is not unlikely that Arthur O'Leary, a leather-seller of Cahir in the early 1820s, was a brother. It is certain that William O'Leary, soon to set up in Main Street, Tipperary, too, as a general dealer in hardware, ironmongery, seed and timber, was a younger brother. So was Jeremiah M. O'Leary, a bank manager in Loughrea, county Galway from about 1845.[3] Dennis F. O'Leary, a wine and spirit merchant a decade or so later in Clonmel, may have been another relation, for Clonmel was the home town of the Kings, tanners and butchers, of whom at least two were to marry into the O'Leary family before the middle of the century.

Even at a distance of over a century it is evident that the two O'Leary brothers, John (senior) and William, were shrewd business-men whose affairs in Tipperary soon prospered. At his death, just before the middle of the century, John (who married three times), and his wife between them were middle landlords of upwards of thirty houses in the town. In addition, they had property in the village of Lattin and a farm in Ballinilard on the western approaches to the town. Unlike John, William resided, not over his shop, but in a spacious modern residence in the select Derby Terrace adjoin-ing the new Catholic church;[4] when he died in 1877, he left his second wife amply provided for, for the remaining twenty-four years of her life.

By 1827 John O'Leary (senior) had become a widower for the first time and was the father of four children—Daniel, Eliza, Margaret and Kate. Dan, the eldest, must have been approaching manhood then; by 1830 his name no longer appears on the roll of a local secondary school, and some time after he emigrated. On 25 November 1827, in the parish church in Tipperary, John O'Leary (senior) re-married, his bride being Margaret Ryan, presumably from the locality.

Of the three witnesses, the last to sign the register was Margaret Dwyer, who was destined thirteen years later to become the third wife of John O'Leary (senior). The Dwyers were a well-to-do farming family from the townland of Kyle—on whose land a field is still locally known as 'the widow Leary's field'. 'Respectable, prosperous people, highly esteemed by their neighbours but not distinguished in any way' was how an acquaintance of the O'Learys described them around the turn of the century.[5] A fair description it seems to have been.

Upon his arrival in Tipperary John O'Leary (senior) first set up business in 16 West Main Street. Later he moved across the street to Number 23 where, like his successors the Kielys today, he became a successful grocer and publican. Number 16, a tall, plain, three-storied building, is now part of the site of Number 54, which is occupied by Kissane's pharmacy; the lane behind, opening on to Davis Street, is called O'Leary's Arch to this day.

It was in this house on 23 July 1830 that Margaret O'Leary's first child and her husband's second son, John, the future leader of the Fenian movement, was born. Within three years two other children arrived. On 22 October 1831 Ellen was born, and on 6 July 1833 came Arthur. Both John and Ellen had priests as godfathers, John's godfather being the Rev. Edmond Cummins and Ellen's the Rev. James Howley, later a monsignor in the town for over forty years. Arthur's sponsor was Thomas Cotter, a neighbouring shopkeeper whose descendants still reside in the town.

That John O'Leary's boyhood years were happy is abundantly clear from the scattered glimpses of them that have been recorded. As so often happens, Arthur, then the youngest child, was the family favourite. Tall, fair-haired and with striking brown eyes, his cheerful nature and handsome appearance endeared him especially to his mother, who was of a quiet and gentle disposition. His sister Ellen remembered him as a dreamy boy who

> . . . pores o'er books while others play,
> Lying full length in a shady nook, . . .

While our picture of John as a boy is less clearly defined, it seems probable that in good looks he rivalled his younger brother and in a more masculine way. Tall also, like most of the O'Learys, he had piercing blue eyes which few of his acquaintances in later life ever forgot. Temperamentally he was high-spirited, but manly and courageous.

While the O'Leary home was obviously well-to-do, it did not deprive the children of normal outside companionship. In the little river Arra at the foot of Bridge Street, *brekeen* (the local term for young trout) were caught and prohibited paddling was enjoyed. Up beyond Uncle William's house stretched 'the Hills', a spacious and safe natural park where 125 years ago the seven young O'Learys, soon to be joined by two more, played as the children of the town still play today.

But even a normal carefree childhood is rarely wholly free from its moments of sadness. Some time in the mid-1830s, when her three children were still very young, John's mother died. The event made a lasting impression on young Ellen, the most sensitive of the three. Many years later she could recall vividly the few short years they had enjoyed together with their mother, a period that ended before Ellen was ten years old; she has left a tender picture of the four playing affectionately, with baby Arthur caressing some domestic pet.

Yet, though deprived of a mother at such an early age, the young O'Learys were by no means left without maternal love and care. Fortunately there was an old aunt to take charge, and by all accounts she made a good job of it. Who Aunt Mary was we can only guess now; she had been married to Uncle Dick for many years, but does not appear to have had any children of her own.

Clearly, however, Aunt Mary and her young charges took to one another, for she was remembered with affection long afterwards by Ellen. Apart from Arthur, we have a more distinct portrait of her than of all those who figured in John O'Leary's boyhood. Grey-haired, frail and old-fashioned in her dress, her merry disposition and her fund of lore soon made her the children's idol. She found time to teach the young O'Learys something of their country's past. Exciting tales of 'Nial, Malachy and sage old Brian Boru' she told them; and tears would fill her eyes as she recalled the stirring days of the United Irishmen. Aunt Mary, we know, lived into the late 1860s; one wonders if in her old age she felt, perhaps, that at least five of her former charges had taken their early lessons in Irish history a little too seriously.

By 1840 or so John O'Leary (senior), now moved to 23 West Main Street, was contemplating marrying for the third time. This he must have done by the spring of 1841 at the latest. On Christmas Eve 1841 his third wife, Margaret Dwyer, gave birth to a daughter, Mary, and in October 1843 to a son, Edmund. Now owner of a goodly slice of his adopted town, and one of its most prosperous merchants, John O'Leary (senior) must by the mid-1840s have been approaching old age; in fact he had only another five years or so to live. Significantly enough, it was in 1843 also that he took out, with the Sun Insurance Office of London, two policies for £500 each on the lives of his three children by his second wife, 'payable to the said John O'Leary (senior), his executors, administrators and assigns on the death of the last survivor of the said three children'.

Perhaps the need for this prudent measure was brought home to him by the realisation that some of his nine children were now past the stage of infancy. Dan, for instance, had settled abroad and

Eliza was soon to marry William King, a tanner from Clonmel.
Even young John's future now needed serious thought. Possibly
till then he had been attending one of the many private elementary
schools in the town in Catholic hands. But, as the eldest son of
a prominent local businessman in regular contact with the gentry,
Dan had received at least part of his education in a fashionable
Protestant school. To this institution John was now sent.[6]

2

AMONGST THE LANDS granted to his supporters by Cromwell after
the rising of 1641 was a lot of 48,000 acres in Munster and Connacht
which was acquired by Erasmus Smith, an English army contractor
who had supplied food for the soldiers of the Commonwealth
during their memorable Irish campaign. This grant took in a large
part of the barony of Clanwilliam, including most of the site of
the town of Tipperary. In 1662, after the restoration of Charles II,
Smith's title to these estates was questioned and he was obliged to
make over to the State Church several thousand acres for the
express purpose of endowing free grammar schools.

A royal charter of 1669 settled the form of the charity. Three
schools were to be built, in Tipperary, Drogheda and Galway, and
a board of thirty-two governors, which included the Protestant
Archbishops of Dublin and Armagh, the Lord Chancellor, the Lord
Chief Justice, the Attorney-General and the Solicitor-General, was
to administer the trust.

In Tipperary a fine riverside site, on which still stood, over a
century after its dissolution, the premises of an Augustinian priory,
was selected. The stones of the old monastery were used to build
the new school, the successor of which—now under Catholic
management—is still known locally as 'the Abbey'. In 1682 the
founder frankly admitted that his 'end in founding the three schooles
was to propagate the Protestant faith'; but over the subsequent two-
and-a-half centuries Tipperary Grammar School failed to live
wholly up to his expectations.

Soon it was patronised by Catholic boys, whose adequate education in their own country the Penal Laws would otherwise have
prevented and whose attendance, without apparent harm to their

religion, the local teaching staff—some of them also Catholics—connived at. Indeed, long before the nineteenth century, it had become fashionable for well-to-do Catholic families of the district to send their boys to 'the Abbey'. When in 1691 the town was sacked by Williamite forces the Grammar School was destroyed; but a new building was erected in 1702, to be replaced in 1820 by the handsome edifice which was destroyed by fire in 1941, three years after the passing of an Act of the Oireachtas which in effect handed over the school to the Irish Christian Brothers.

Despite various devices, such as public examinations in catechism and compulsory attendance at service, tried from time to time by the governors of the school, Catholics who could afford the fees continued to take advantage of the facilities it offered; and the teaching staff, in order to augment their incomes, relaxed the rules regarding religious instruction. The appointment to the staff in 1818 of a native of the district who had forsaken the Catholic faith and become a Protestant clergyman provoked the parish priest into prohibiting his parishioners from sending their children to the Grammar School. But by the late 1820s the dispute must have been resolved, since Daniel O'Leary and other Catholic boys were then on the rolls.

In 1830 the Reverend Denny Twiss Riordan, a Protestant clergyman from Kerry who previously had taught in the Erasmus Smith school in Drogheda and had run a successful private school in Clonmel, was appointed head of Tipperary Grammar School. By now the school was divided into two parts. Local boys and girls, numbering over 150 in some years, attended the day school, which was situated in nearby Bridge Street,[7] while boarders (boys only) continued to be taught in the recently-completed building in the grounds opposite Abbey Street. Under the new headmaster the curriculum was ambitiously expanded to include Latin, Greek, English, Arithmetic, Euclid, the Use of Globes, Geography, French, Italian and Hebrew. The annual fee for a day-pupil was four guineas and for a boarder thirty guineas.

Young O'Leary was fortunate in having such a school within a few minutes' walk of his home. In a town with so many elementary schools—by 1835 there were over a dozen in Catholic hands—there must have been a fairly high standard of teaching in at least some of them. The Grammar School started with some undoubted advantages. Possessing fine modern buildings, it enjoyed the patronage and protection of the ruling class and the State Church; it had been in operation for over a century-and-a-half and appears to have been staffed almost wholly by university graduates. Accordingly, it is no slur on its rivals, most of them of recent origin and nearly all run on the pennies of the poor, to suggest that the quality of instruction imparted at the Grammar School was probably higher than that obtaining elsewhere in the town.

The curiously loose system of management under which the Erasmus Smith schools worked until late in the nineteenth century probably meant that the success of a school depended largely on the calibre of its headmaster. Although paid a fixed salary and provided with commodious living quarters, in all other matters— fees, subjects, staff—he seems to have been given a free hand to adapt the prospectus to suit local circumstances and was not troubled by supervision by the governors.

The Reverend Riordan's first few years in Tipperary were apparently none too happy. He quarrelled with the staff and dismissed one teacher, who thereupon opened a rival school in the town to which an unknown proportion of the Grammar School's pupils changed. Yet the fewer pupils may have got even better instruction than before, and Riordan was to spend twenty-six years as head of Tipperary Grammar School before suffering dismissal himself. It needs little imagination to picture the O'Leary children making full use of the fifteen acres of riverside pasture attached to the school, or staring with amusement and curiosity as the Protestant boarders, dressed in Eton suits, deep white collars and hard hats in the latest English public-school style, and led by their masters in morning coats and silk hats, marched past the O'Leary home on Sunday mornings on their way to the Church of Ireland church in nearby John Street.[8]

Despite its ups and downs, Tipperary Grammar School had built up a fine reputation in the south, and it seems to have imparted education of a standard higher than that generally available in rural Ireland at the time. To some it may occur later on that to this early non-Catholic environment may be ascribed, at least in part, the boy's subsequent rather eccentric attitude towards religion. But it is known that during Riordan's regime Catholics still held teaching posts on the staff and that Catholic day-pupils received religious instruction outside school, in all probability from local Catholic clergy, who must have been well aware of the value of the schooling and satisfied that no real danger to the faith of their flock existed.

Although it is not now possible to say when young O'Leary left Tipperary Grammar School, it seems likely that his stay there was cut short by the unsettled state of affairs in the district. During the 1830s and 1840s intermittent violence continued in the area between landlords and tenants and their respective agents, one of the worst incidents concerning a landlord who was also the local agent of the Erasmus Smith foundation. Finally, in 1843, the commander of the British garrison for the district, General Lord Downes—also a governor of the school—sought permission to occupy the Grammar School building, which, he claimed, could accommodate 200 boys.

The school was requisitioned and, at least so far as boarders were concerned, ceased to operate. The headmaster continued for some time to give instruction to day-pupils in the building in Bridge Street. But attendances dwindled, and one cannot blame John O'Leary (senior) if he felt that the time had come for a change of school for John.

3

ONE DAY, when John O'Leary must have been well into his teens, a friend of his father entered the shop and was treated to the customary glass of punch. Observing that the lad, who was present, had not been offered anything, he asked the father:

'Why don't you give the boy a drink?'

'Oh, he's too young,' replied John O'Leary (senior).

The visitor's comment was curiously prophetic: 'You'll rue the day that you didn't make that boy's head while he was young.'[9]

Yet the apparently strict father was by no means unaware of the fact that his second son was approaching manhood. In the summer of 1845 he made arrangements for the boy to enter Carlow College, where John arrived on 18 September, a few weeks after his fifteenth birthday. Conditions in Tipperary had, as we have seen, led to the partial closure of the Grammar School, which— to borrow the jargon of a later age—could no longer be said to be a status symbol for a successful Catholic businessman. Besides, the sudden influx of a troop of English soldiery, quartered some 150 yards from the O'Leary home, hardly created the most suitable environment for an impressionable and growing boy.

John was not the first boy from the town to have his name entered on the Carlow rolls. Patrick Morrissey, a shopkeeper nearby, had sent his boy Patrick there a year or so before; Richard Bradshaw, of another neighbouring family, was also there, along with several other lads from within a radius of ten or twelve miles of Tipperary. In any event, Carlow College was then not only the oldest but also the leading Catholic boys' school in Ireland.

Here, as in Tipperary Grammar School, young O'Leary was in

the company of boys of his own class, mostly sons of well-to-do
businessmen and farmers—but with some significant differences.
First, at Carlow, John's circle of acquaintances would have been
noticeably widened by meeting for the first time many boys from
Dublin homes. Secondly, he was now amongst the majority consisting of boarders; in fact, apart from a brief period of five years
some forty years later, his departure for Carlow marked the end of
home life for John. Finally, but by no means of least significance,
he was now in an all-Catholic atmosphere; for Carlow took no non-
Catholic boys and also prepared boys for the priesthood.

A glance at the college rolls shows that the majority of O'Leary's
contemporaries in Carlow were from the nearby counties of Leinster
and from Dublin. Others, however, had come from more distant
parts of the country, especially the south; in 1847 there was even
a boy from Castletown, then the capital of the Isle of Man. Of
greater consequence to a lad leaving home for the first time was
the fact that Tipperary and the surrounding region were well
represented. In addition to the Morrissey and Bradshaw boys
from his home town—both, in all probability, also past pupils of
Tipperary Grammar School—there were Tobias Egan and John
Prendergast from Cahir, Samuel Alleyne (now Allen) from Cashel,
another O'Leary from Glin, and boys from Nenagh, Lismore and
Dungarvan.

That his stay in Carlow College, which was to prove comparatively short, helped to mould O'Leary's character, there can be
little doubt. Founded as far back as 1782, with the dual objective
of educating Catholic lay youth and providing clergy for the diocese
of Kildare and Leighlin, the college might be said to have originally
represented the putting into effect of a new policy of limited loyalty
to Dublin Castle by the Irish hierarchy. Nevertheless, right from
the year 1793, when Carlow first opened its doors to students, it
became known as a centre of nationalist thought.

Long before O'Leary arrived, Carlow had achieved a wide
reputation as an educational establishment. Although denied State
aid, the college is believed to have received financial assistance from
local wealthy Protestants.[10] In 1840 it was granted a royal charter
affiliating it with the University of London, then a unique distinction
for an Irish college and an indication of the standard of instruction
it imparted.

Through the wide gates of the college there passed boys from all
parts of Ireland; from its handsome buildings emerged laymen
such as James Fintan Lalor and clerics like Paul Cullen. The
normal total of about 110 pupils was usually more or less evenly
divided between lay boys and clerical students.[11] But, although
taught in the same building and having the same professors, lay

boys and clerical students each belonged to a separate branch of the college, though it does not appear that pupils from the two categories were prohibited from mixing.

For a lay boarder fees and expenses totalled about £50 a year, a considerable sum in those days and proof equally of the wealth amassed by better-off Catholics and the exclusiveness of the college. The curriculum, which was of a comprehensive nature, must have required fairly rigorous application to studies. Four years of classical studies were followed by a two-year period during which 'a course of study adapted to the purposes of civil life' was pursued; during this period, too, English literature was widely read. Finally, the advanced classes tackled an impressive array of subjects— general history, mathematics, natural philosophy, chemistry, political economy, and the elements of law.[12] Only one vacation was allowed each year, the period fixed being from 1 July to mid-August.

Notwithstanding this seemingly exacting régime, there is good reason to believe that most youths later appreciated the debt they owed to Carlow College and enjoyed their stay there. On exceptional occasions older boys were permitted to visit the adjoining town, and from an early period there was a ball-court for recreation, although there is no record of organised competitive games for the period when O'Leary was a student. Those who have made the early years of this college their special study maintain that the atmosphere was pleasant, even gay; there seems no reason to doubt this view.

The president of Carlow College when O'Leary arrived there was the Reverend James Ignatius Taylor, DD, a 38-year-old Dubliner who had held various posts on the staff from his ordination in 1831 until, in 1843, he became president. Although destined to remain in charge of the college for only seven years, Father Taylor was remembered long after for his teaching ability. Also on the college staff in O'Leary's time was Father Thomas W. Croke, who, almost thirty years later, was to return from New Zealand as Archbishop of Cashel and take a prominent part in national affairs, one in particular in indirect association with John O'Leary.

From the few scattered references in the college records to his stay, it is evident that John O'Leary played at least an average part in the school's activities. An account book for the period commencing 15 August 1833 contains a summary of the accounts furnished to 'John O'Leary Esq., Tipperary for his son John', together with details of how the debts were discharged. The petty book for 1835–1848, in which were recorded sundry accounts, has also survived. Under the heading 'O'Leary, John—John O'Leary Esq., Tipperary' are entered detailed matters of expenditure, mostly of a personal nature, incurred by the boy.

Taken as a whole, and read in conjunction with corresponding
entries for other boys, they give some idea of his various activities
in the college over a period of at least a year-and-a-half, ending in
mid-March 1847. In his first six months he paid an entrance fee
and a half-yearly subscription to the college library, and a fee for
Philosophy, presumably an optional subject for lay-boys. Unlike
Patrick Morrissey and Richard Bradshaw, he took no lessons in
music, piano, dancing or elocution.

Provision was also made for occupying the students' minds
during such spare time as they may have had. Between 1841 and
1848 a college magazine entitled *The Academician* was published
monthly; no copy of this has survived. *The Academician,* however,
formed only part of a wider sphere of activity which centred round
a college literary society, 'The Academy'. This group, whose
members were chosen by ballot, held public meetings in the college
once a month at which the best literary compositions, chosen by
the professors, were read aloud. In addition, there were regular
dramatic scenes, debates and musical entertainment, the college
band closing each meeting with 'God Save the Queen'. Minutes of
the proceedings have survived; but O'Leary's name nowhere
appears, whether as officer, participant or prizewinner.

CHAPTER TWO

1

AROUND THE MIDDLE OF THE 1840s Irish politics, which had been calm, even dull, since the successful conclusion some fifteen years before of the campaign for Catholic Emancipation, came to life again. The revival in 1840 by the ageing O'Connell of the repeal agitation had been followed two years later by the appearance of the *Nation* newspaper. But between them the virtual eclipse of the Liberator after the Clontarf meeting fiasco of 1843 and the sudden death in September 1845 of Thomas Davis had the effect of widening the hitherto barely latent rift between the Repeal Association and the literary clique centred round the *Nation*. In July 1846 the Young Ireland wing formally seceded and, as O'Connell's son John, with strong clerical support, launched bitter attacks on the *Nation*, the younger men of the Young Ireland group, encouraged by the inflammatory tone of John Mitchel's writings in the paper, were even talking of non-constitutional methods of achieving the national objective.

These exciting events cannot have occurred without comment in an institution with such patriotic leanings as Carlow College. Just as, a few years before, the Charitable Bequests Bill and the

Colleges Bill must have provided abundant material for debate by clerical student and professor alike, it is easy to imagine the heated discussions amongst the senior lay boys in the mid-1840s—and probably amongst the teaching staff, too, for Fr. Croke was openly to support the popular revolutionary movement in 1848.

As the spring of 1848 gave way to early summer, however, another subject replaced politics as the main topic of discussion in rural Ireland. Gradually it became evident that the potato blight of 1845 had been followed by a more disastrous failure of the next year's crop. As the price of corn rose steeply and famine became a near certainty, sporadic riots and other disturbances broke out here and there. In Carlow the college kitchen became a communal feeding-place.

In these circumstances it is not surprising that at least one of the students should have contracted one of the several dangerous illnesses then prevalent. By now young O'Leary was tall and thin and still growing ; the college records show that he wore shoes two sizes larger than most of his classmates, and that during his first half-year in Carlow he incurred comparatively large debts to the apothecary.

Whether it was before the summer holidays commenced or after his return to school in September that he became seriously ill cannot now be stated with certainty. But at all events he suffered a severe attack of what his friends later believed had been typhus,[1] and was obliged to go home, returning to the college on 26 October. The size of the remission in fees granted suggests an absence of almost three months, which in turn leads to the conclusion that it was probably relapsing fever which brought O'Leary down. This disease, which was even more prevalent in famine-stricken Ireland than epidemic typhus, usually left the patient extremely exhausted.

Chance events often alter the course of a man's life, however. During O'Leary's period of convalescence at home in the late summer of 1846 two introductions were effected which were to produce such a result. It was there and then that he first met a young civil engineer from Kilkenny who, since 1844, had been employed by the Waterford and Limerick Railway Company, and was probably lodging in Tipperary.[2] Since he was known to have been a close family friend of the O'Learys, he may well have lodged with them while working in the district. According to one of the O'Leary family, this young man, though 'a little below the middle height', was of striking appearance, with 'a remarkable head, quite Shakespearean in fact, and a fine face'. He also had 'great natural ability and a will which dominated nearly every one with whom he came into contact'.[3]

The civil engineer in his mid-twenties and the sixteen-year-old recuperating student immediately became good friends and enjoyed many a walk and talk together. According to O'Leary, they discussed mainly literature, though one finds it hard to believe that politics did not occasionally obtrude. So began an acquaintance which, despite periods of separation, was to last until the death in Dublin fifty-five years later of the older man. In July 1848 he was to stand guard beside John Blake Dillon at a barricade in the Tipperary coal-mining village of Killenaule; in March 1858 he was to found the Irish Revolutionary Brotherhood. His name was James Stephens.

Of greater importance, according to O'Leary, was the other introduction—to the writings of Thomas Davis. To the end of his life he maintained that the experience changed his whole outlook, and in an autobiographical passage penned half-a-century later vividly described the effect on him. Already he was thinking of a career as a professional man, preferably at the Bar; he had not discounted the possibility of practising in England. But after a study of the poems and essays of Davis 'everything was changed', and 'for all that is Irish in me, and, above all, for the inspiration that made me Irish, the fountain and the origin must always be sought in Davis'.

When one takes into account many of O'Leary's subsequent views on Irish politics one can more easily appreciate what parts of Davis's teachings most attracted him. Although not founded for that purpose, the *Nation* soon became all but the official organ of the revived repeal movement, which had the backing of the clergy as a whole. Yet a basic tenet of Davis's political philosophy, as expounded in the paper's columns, was that all Irishmen, irrespective of creed, could and should be nationalists.

To him politics and religion were separate matters and must be kept apart. Through the *Nation* he hoped to get away from the hitherto denominational aspect of the campaign to restore an Irish parliament, and also to win the Protestant community to that cause. Furthermore, the paper played a vital part in converting the educated classes generally, whose support the abusive haranguing methods of O'Connell would never have won. The young liberal-minded Catholics of the towns and cities came to identify themselves fully with all Davis's views, and he inevitably collided head-on with the basically Catholic foundation of the popular movement.

For O'Leary the immediate result of his conversion to nationalism was, naturally enough, that he became a regular reader of the *Nation*. By now Mitchel had taken over as its leader-writer, and it is not surprising that O'Leary, like so many others of his age, was excited by Mitchel's advocacy of unconstitutional methods. Long afterwards he admitted privately to having been strongly influenced by the writings of Davis, Mitchel and John Martin, Mitchel's brother-in-law and later editor of the *Felon*;[4] in the words of John Devoy he became 'saturated with the literature of Young Ireland'.[5]

To this movement and to his personal experiences in the exciting period from mid-1847 to the end of 1849 are traceable some ideas which O'Leary never subsequently abandoned—in particular, a contempt for agitation by Irishmen at Westminster, a dislike of clerical influence in political affairs, and a desire to convert to nationalism the wealthy Protestants. Above all, he became a lifelong believer in separatism. From then to the end of his life he regarded the political separation of Ireland from England as the only proper objective of Irish nationalists, and the usefulness of every Irish political or social movement he decided on according as it helped or hindered the attainment of this goal.

For the moment, however, it was back to school; but he was only to remain there for another six months or so. Perhaps O'Leary now felt that Carlow had little more to offer him; or possibly he may have been anxious to pursue his ambition to make a career for himself as a barrister. For in 1847—the college records suggest that it was between March and early summer—he left Carlow.

Earlier that year the seceding Young Irelanders had founded the Irish Confederation, with the *Nation* as its organ and its policy substantially the same as that of the now failing and decadent Repeal Association. Confederate clubs sprang up in many towns outside Dublin and, partly under the encouragement of the fiery, if volatile, Fr. Kenyon of Templederry, the new movement quickly became particularly strong in county Tipperary. Tipperary town had a club, at whose meetings it seems probable that young O'Leary became a frequent attender. Indeed, an event of 1848 was to suggest that O'Leary had become one of the most prominent members of this club; it may not have been a coincidence that its meetings were held in the old Butter Weigh House in Bridge Lane, of which O'Leary's father was middle landlord.

Towards the end of the year 1847 O'Leary came to Dublin and entered Trinity College with the intention of studying for the Bar. One suspects, however, that from the start his studies took second place to politics. He at once joined the Grattan Club of the Confederation, then headed by Thomas Francis Meagher, and attended not only most of its meetings but also the more important ones of the parent body. Of the leaders he soon came to know personally Fr. John Kenyon and James Fintan Lalor, and probably Charles Gavan Duffy.

Although in his old age he was critical of the standard of oratory of the movement, he readily admitted to having been intoxicated by the general revolutionary atmosphere. The end of 1847 saw what might be called the second secession, that of Mitchel, who felt that the time had come for warlike preparations. At a three-day meeting early in 1848 he was outvoted; O'Leary was apparently one of the 188 rank-and-file members, all of them young men, who voted for Mitchel.

February 1848 was the date of the revolution in France, the first of many in Europe that year. O'Leary in his memoirs, almost half-a-century later, recalled the enthusiasm with which the event was hailed in Ireland. This bloodless coup, which overthrew a government that had refused parliamentary reform, provided an analogy with this country that was all too obvious; to Mitchel and the younger men especially it proved the efficacy of armed rebellion. Within a month the fiery Newry journalist was back in the Confederation, and the ranks of the Young Irelanders re-united in preparation for the insurrection which all its leaders now considered inevitable.

From then on events moved rapidly to a climax. Indeed, it is difficult to avoid the feeling that the pace thenceforward set by the Castle authorities proved too fast for the conspirators. O'Leary himself conveys the impression of surprise—the sudden suspension of habeas corpus and then, a few days later, the news that Smith O'Brien, Dillon and Meagher had made their way to county Tipperary to start the revolt.

'This was interesting and exciting news for me,' comments O'Leary. 'I was a Tipperary man and I felt that Tipperary and not Dublin was the place for me, and so to Tipperary I went.'

The Confederates of Tipperary he found full of belligerent talk but quite unprepared for a fight. O'Leary's uncle William had been a signatory to an address sent in April 1848 from the men of Tipperary to the men of Paris; but no attempt appears to have been made by the club to enforce its own rule requiring every member to arm himself within two weeks of admission.

In the absence in America of their president the Confederates of Tipperary put young O'Leary in the chair; the next day a rumour of his impending arrest sent him into hiding with friends outside the town. Here he heard of the collapse at Ballingarry and, taking fright at the sight of a body of police near his hiding place (an understandable precaution on the part of the authorities if O'Leary's retreat was at his step-mother's home farm at Kyle, close to Limerick Junction railway station) he fled on horseback by night to the house of a namesake in Templederry, Fr. Kenyon's parish twenty miles to the north across hilly country.

The refugee presented himself to the priest and both made fruitless attempts to contact (and presumably harbour) some of the leaders then reputed also to be in hiding in the vicinity; Meagher and Leyne were in fact arrested close by, that same week. After a week or so spent largely in Fr. Kenyon's company, O'Leary returned (again by horse under cover of darkness) to his father's farm outside Tipperary. A few days later he ventured once more into the town, now denuded of armed police.

Some miles away to the northwest the villages of Killenaule and Ballingarry were quiet once more, too, and all the Young Ireland leaders were either in jail or in hiding. The rising of 1848 was over; it had passed O'Leary by in the distance.

Youthful enthusiasm, however, is hard to suppress. On 16 August Smith O'Brien was arrested on the platform of Thurles railway station and lodged in Clonmel jail with the rest of the leaders awaiting trial. Shortly afterwards O'Leary got to hear of a plot to rescue the State prisoners (as they had come to be called) and eagerly made his way from home to Clonmel, where he was present in the courtroom on 9 October when the sentences were passed. His impressions of the scene differ from those of another eye-witness, a young Cork reporter later prominent in Irish public affairs;[6] O'Leary discerned an air of unreality in the proceedings and was unmoved by the apparent emotional stress of the judges.

Nevertheless the would-be rescuers evidently took the matter seriously and went ahead with their plans, with O'Leary now an active participant. The rescue plan did not remain a secret, however. On the day after Smith O'Brien's conviction an urgent request came to Dublin Castle from Clonmel for the removal of the State prisoners because of rumours of a projected attack on the jail; ironically, the Crown law advisers reluctantly replied that there was no legal power to take the prisoners out of Clonmel jail. Three weeks later information reached the Clonmel authorities of an impending assault on the town by bodies of men from the surrounding counties, who planned to sack the town and open the jail—whose inmates numbered almost 450.

The originator of the rescue plot was Philip Gray, a 21-year-old Dubliner of Meath origin who, earlier that summer, had unsuccessfully tried to stir up insurrection in Meath, and had thrown up his job in a railway office in Drogheda to join the insurgents in Tipperary. After the collapse in July, Gray had gone into hiding in the Waterford mountains with a body of men which he had kept in readiness for just such an eventuality as this.

The idea was to collect an armed force, consisting of a group from the Clonmel area under O'Leary and another under Gray comprising his own men and a section from Carrick-on-Suir. On a specified date the two groups would meet outside Clonmel and make a surprise attack on the jail and barracks, with inside help.

Contact was duly established by O'Leary and others with some sympathetic Irish members of the garrison and, for the first time in his life, O'Leary discovered that, when confronted with a conflict of loyalties between his country and his employer, an Irishman in the British army is likely to choose that to his country—a phenomenon which O'Leary's more energetic brethren in the IRB were fully to exploit many years later. A number of pistols and a supply of cartridges were obtained from these soldiers.

But if the insurgents' plans were leaking out to the Castle, the authorities' plans were not unknown to O'Leary and his associates. Early in November they discovered that Smith O'Brien and the other State prisoners were soon to be transferred to the more tranquil town of Thurles. A conference between the Clonmel men and those from Carrick-on-Suir, held outside Clonmel on 6 November, failed to reach agreement on whether to attack the town at once or to ambush the escort on its way to Thurles. Within forty-eight hours an immediate attack on the jail was decided on.

On the night of 8 November 1848 O'Leary assembled his Clonmel contingent at a remote spot known as the Wilderness, half-a-mile out from the town on the road to Fethard. But the informer had done his job efficiently. Whilst awaiting the arrival of Gray's force from Carrick-on-Suir, O'Leary and his men found themselves surrounded by British soldiers who waited, possibly in the hope of seeing Gray and his force also walk into the trap, before arresting O'Leary and sixteen of his men and lodging them in Clonmel jail. A large pistol and sixty-five rounds of ball cartridges were later found by a loyal landowner near the Wilderness.

O'Leary years later wrote with characteristic modesty of his luckless but courageous episode. Fortunately for him, the authorities in Clonmel treated it lightly; it is clear that they did not realise that this small force had the jail as its objective. After a week in jail the would-be rescuers were released on bail, 'to appear when called upon to abide their trials at Cashel quarter sessions for having arms and ammunition in their possession'. Two days earlier, on 16 November, the State prisoners had been moved to Thurles. O'Leary's position, at the head of the return furnished to Dublin Castle, and the amount of bail in his case—£20 from himself and £10 from each of two sureties—show that he was rightly regarded as the group's leader. The magistrate responsible for this lenient decision was sharply reprimanded by the Castle authorities; he ought, they said, to have obtained further information from these young men before their discharge, in case the facts should warrant a more serious charge being preferred by the Attorney-General.

'THERE WERE SOME SPIRITS at that time whom neither defeat nor danger could subdue,' wrote Charles Kickham some fourteen years later when recalling this period.[7] Foremost among these irrepressible young men was John O'Leary. Immediately upon his release from Clonmel jail he travelled by boat to Carrick-on-Suir, where he consulted with Philip Gray. At once O'Leary set up in Clonmel and in Tipperary a small secret oath-bound society, having for its aim the simple and obvious one of liberating Ireland from British rule by force of arms. This was to be the only oath to which O'Leary was ever to subscribe.

While Gray headed for France to consult with John O'Mahony, O'Leary swore in the first members of his society in and around Clonmel. A fund was established to buy arms and powder; arrangements were made for the use of a forge in which to make pikeheads. One member, Joseph O'Grady, was sent to Dublin to make contact with some who were making similar plans there.

Thus did O'Leary come round to the view that, for the present, better results might be obtained by adopting the Wolfe Tone policy of a secret conspiracy than had hitherto been achieved through the Mitchelite principle of open defiance. At about the same time a Corkman named Joseph Brenan, also a survivor of '48, had come to the same conclusion in Dublin. In due course Gray, O'Leary and Brenan were to join forces and, under the occasionally disputed leadership of Fintan Lalor, to provide the impetus for the now undeservedly forgotten movement of 1849, itself to culminate within a year in another equally disastrous rising.

His organisation established, O'Leary went home to Tipperary, where he remained for a couple of months. The reason for his inactivity was the death of his father, who by his will left John £40 a year for six years and thereafter three blocks of house property in the town.[8] 'A moderate independence' one of O'Leary's associates of that period accurately described the bequest. This freedom from financial worries was to have a marked influence on his life for the following fifty years or so.

In the meantime Lalor had been released from prison in November for lack of evidence against him. He spent the greater part of the winter of 1848–49, as indeed he had spent most of his four-month incarceration, confined to bed with his recurring bronchial trouble. In a friend's home in Dublin he was soon visited regularly by his associates; around his sick-bed through the winter months plans for restoring the fortunes of the nationalist movement were constantly discussed.

Early in 1849 O'Leary, hearing of the progress of the new conspiracy in Dublin, left Tipperary for that city. There he soon realised that, along with Thomas Clarke Luby and Edward Keatinge, by far the most active conspirator was Joseph Brenan. Like Gray, Luby and Keatinge had both been members of the progressive Swifts Club of the Irish Confederation.

Brenan, a native of Cork city and only twenty-one, had been a journalist in that city in 1847 before moving to Dublin the following year, where he was closely associated in both journalism and politics with Mitchel, Martin and Lalor. After participating with John O'Mahony in an outbreak of violence in county Waterford after the collapse of the rising, he spent seven months in jail.[9] On his release in March 1849 he at once resumed both writing and plotting in Dublin; it seems that but for his energy there might well have been no '49 movement at all.

Some time before Brenan's release Luby had tried to set up his own secret society in Dublin; but it did not thrive. With Brenan and others he now held a meeting at which it was decided to join the secret society which Gray had previously established in the Tipperary–Waterford–Kilkenny region. Gavan Duffy, who was released from jail in April, refused to join the conspiracy, and in fact strenuously attempted to dissuade Lalor and Brenan from going ahead with their plans.

Gray, despairing of eluding the police for much longer, was obliged to seek refuge in France for the second time in a few months. In Paris he contacted the two '48 refugees, O'Mahony and Stephens; according to Kickham's account, it would appear that Gray was sent as an envoy to O'Mahony to secure his co-operation in plans for a new rising. O'Mahony is said to have first declined, but then agreed to return himself, and apparently did so during the summer. Gray also came back; Stephens did not.

By early February 1849 O'Leary was again busy building up his society. All over south Tipperary, men were sworn in. Daggers were secretly manufactured and sold to members at a shilling each. When Gray returned from France regular communications were maintained between the Tipperary and Waterford men by ferries across the Suir at night ; some of the Suir boatmen were among the earliest members of the societies.

Once again, unknown to the conspirators, their doings were reported to the authorities by informers. Within a month of its formation the existence of O'Leary's society was known to the magistrate, the mayor and the commander of the garrison in Clonmel. 'The principal person,' wrote William Ryan, a local

magistrate in a report to the Under-Secretary in March 1849, 'is
a student of Trinity College named O'Leary who was one of the
Wilderness prisoners.' On at least two other occasions that same
month conversations with O'Leary as to the progress of the insurrectionary scheme were passed on to the Castle.

As had happened in '48, the clergy also were well aware of what
was going on. On the last Sunday of February 1849 the parish
priest of Irishtown, Clonmel, publicly denounced the new secret
society and dismissed four workmen (who had been employed
erecting a new church) because they were in the society. In the
following two or three months other clergy in Clonmel, as well as
the parish priests of Carrick More, Carrick Beg and Windgap, all
condemned the work of the conspirators from the pulpit, and warned
their flocks not to heed the advice of the secret society's leaders.

The magistrates in the various towns affected by the secret
societies held varying views as to the seriousness of the threat to
peace offered by this latest movement. As a result the Castle
authorities, faced with conflicting opinions, discountenanced any
stern action against the conspirators, while at the same time instruct-
ing local officials to keep a close watch on the movements of the
leaders. The wisdom of this policy was proved by the amount of
information which was gathered during the spring and summer of
1849 on the progress of the allied movements in counties Tipperary
and Waterford.

By early summer the membership of O'Leary's and Gray's
societies had spread to a large area of Munster and south Leinster.
All along, both bodies seem to have had an almost exclusive
membership of urban residents. Tradesmen and labourers predominated in O'Leary's society, which also numbered the sons of
small farmers and of shopkeepers. The Tipperary society claimed
members as far afield as Youghal, Limerick and Dungarvan, while
Gray's society took in Portlaw and Kilkenny.

All this time regular contact was kept up with similar societies
both in Cork and Dublin, so that eventually a loose federation of
secret societies, all working towards the same end, stretched from
Dublin down through Kilkenny, Tipperary and Waterford, to Cork.
Both Gray and O'Leary visited Dublin several times; in April
Maurice Leyne, the '48 leader, visited Carrick-on-Suir and con-
ferred with local leaders there. At lower levels communications
were exchanged at fairs and markets; in Tipperary, hurling games
were specially arranged to provide 'cover' for meetings of secret
society members.

Nor, if information reaching the Government officials in Clonmel
was correct, did the men of '49 overlook the possibility of aid from
abroad. Early in May a cargo of £50 worth of arms was said to

have been secretly taken off a ship in Cork harbour; the arms were believed to have been sent by exiles in New York. Later that same month another shipload was expected; but the authorities never succeeded in finding either of these consignments. According to O'Leary, the Dublin men in May sent an envoy to New York to seek assistance from Michael Doheny; the question of a grant to pay foreign mercenaries was also mentioned.

The possibility of timing a rising to coincide with some political or military engagement of the British on the Continent also seems to have been discussed. And at a time when another revolutionary movement appeared to be still active in Britain, it would not be surprising if the artisans of Leinster and Munster in 1849 had considered the question of aid from their oppressed brethren across the Irish Sea. 'There is . . . no doubt . . . that communications are kept up continually with the Chartist leaders in England,' reported a magistrate from Clonmel in mid-May 1849 to the Under-Secretary, '. . . and that the Chartists would make a stress so that no army could be brought away from England to Ireland.'

By the start of June 1849 an executive Council of Three had been established in Clonmel, whether in charge of both societies for that part of the country or merely for O'Leary's organisation is not clear. Both the possible date and the method of a rising were now being canvassed among the leaders. At first 18 June was considered, and street-fighting was preferred, despite the known prowess of the Highlanders, then stationed in Clonmel. Members were posted on an all-day watch on the house of the magistrate in Clonmel to prevent spies bringing him information; on at least one occasion this magistrate had to arrange with an informer to meet him in the seaside village of Ardmore, some thirty miles away in county Waterford, in order to elude the watchers.

Meanwhile in Dublin, to quote O'Leary, 'various anti-English schemes and plots were taking shape in the active and fertile brain that presided over the frail body of James Fintan Lalor'. In particular, he was now directing his energies towards the formation of a new journal in which to preach his revolutionary gospel. Since such a paper, if successfully established, would have been in direct competition with the newly revived *Nation*, perhaps Duffy's opposition may not have appeared to Lalor and his friends to have been entirely disinterested. A couple of meetings were held in Dublin and the support of prominent persons canvassed without much success.

In mid-summer Lalor and Luby set off on a tour of the south to publicise the proposed new literary venture; O'Leary had returned home some time previously, but he and Lalor had kept in touch with each other by letter. The two travellers spent a fortnight

with Fr. Kenyon in Templederry and contacted other supporters
in north Tipperary before moving on to Tipperary town, where
O'Leary awaited them.

On their first night in the town the visitors from Dublin, fearing
that they might attract too much attention in the more fashionable
Dobbyn's Hotel, put up in the 'King's Arms' inn in the Main
Street; the next day O'Leary got them good board-and-lodgings,
in a private house, with a respectable widow. They were to spend
a week in the town altogether, but the irritable Lalor does not
seem to have found it either a pleasant or a rewarding stay.

He complained of the inhospitality of the inhabitants, and even
Luby had some caustic comments on the snobbishness of the town's
merchant class. But Lalor can hardly have expected a town with
a substantial Protestant community to have taken to a person with
his advanced ideas; and a story Luby later told about Lalor's meagre
tip to a waiter suggests that the lack of generosity may not have
been one-sided.

One day when out for a stroll Lalor was pleasantly surprised to
meet, in the person of a local doctor, a staunch nationalist, who
invited him to dine in his home that night. Luby, who clearly
relished congenial company and a good meal, accompanied him,
and later told of Lalor's excitement at finding two rather youthful
recruits for the secret society in the persons of the doctor's two
young sons, both still in their teens. Against Luby's advice he
insisted on swearing them in on the spot, whereupon O'Leary was
shown in and expressed even stronger disapproval of Lalor's
impetuosity.

For Luby, on the other hand, the week in Tipperary town proved
most enjoyable. It was his first meeting with O'Leary, and the
beginning of a lifelong friendship. The son of a Protestant clergyman of Tipperary origin, Luby was then twenty-seven years of
age and had just completed his studies for the Bar. In fact, he
was paying the expenses of this trip by using the money his family
had sent him for his call to the Bar, and he never subsequently
became a barrister.

As one would expect from a young graduate, he liked attending
social functions and had an eye for a pretty face or figure. Years
later he humorously recalled how he had teased O'Leary when out
for a stroll by making repeated detours in order to pass by a window
where 'a fair girl in blue' sat, and how his mild flirtations with the
milliners, the Misses Catherine and Eliza Hutchins, (sisters-in-law
of the captain of the local garrison) embarrassed O'Leary. Yet he
chivalrously declined to attend a formal social evening when he
found that the bad-tempered Lalor had not been included in the
invitation.

Luby's account of this first meeting with O'Leary provides the earliest detailed description of him that has survived. In appearance he was tall but of slight build, clean-shaven, with fine jet-black hair, and having a 'keen aquiline cast of feature'. In later life he was known to be very particular about his appearance; so it is probable that he was equally fastidious at the age of nineteen. To a stranger his piercing blue eyes seemed cold; but one soon found that they could express warmth and kindness. His whole manner suggested a scholar and a gentleman. His manner of speaking was hesitant, but this was off-set by a tendency frequently to shoot out short, sharp sentences.

Both Lalor and Luby were agreed that he gave the impression of a man lacking in energy and not disposed to exert himself unduly. Even at that early age he had become an inveterate critic. In his first conversation alone with Luby he found fault with Lalor's prospectus for the proposed newspaper; the language was tautologous, the reasoning poor and involved, there was too much alliteration, and so on.

It was evident also to Luby that O'Leary was unusually well read for his age; he obviously felt no embarrassment when discussing English literature with older men like Lalor and Fr. Kenyon. That unselfish sense of devotion to the cause which characterised his later actions was also discernible in 1849. For example, although, like Gavan Duffy, he was pessimistic as to the outcome of Lalor's movement, he admitted privately to Luby that he joined it because he felt it his duty as a patriot to do so.

Their business in Tipperary concluded, Lalor and Luby proceeded to Limerick, where Lalor made a prolonged stop and addressed two large public meetings. Meanwhile, back in Dublin, 'Joe' Brenan was apparently becoming dissatisfied with the lack of progress. In May another plot to rescue the State prisoners had been called off at the last minute on the advice of John Martin, himself one of the prisoners; the failure of this latest episode caused bitter feelings in Dublin.

Brenan, who was strongly opposed to the newspaper project, then moved quickly to bring matters to a head. The young Queen Victoria was due to visit the city shortly; he suggested that it would be an appropriate time for a symbolic insurrection. Travelling down to Cork, he held talks there with associates and persuaded a body of Corkmen to start drilling; these enthusiasts included Justin McCarthy, the Cork reporter, who had been in Clonmel courthouse and was much later to become an MP and a prominent supporter of Parnell.

Brenan's plan of action was simple but spectacular. On the night of the illuminations in Dublin, with the Queen present, barricades would go up and a retreat be made to the mountains, preferably with Her Majesty a captive; there was even mention of a possible attack on the Castle. The news from Dublin would be the signal for a number of simultaneous small risings at the same day, hour and minute in various places—Waterford, Cork, Kilkenny and Tipperary. No hope of a successful revolution was entertained; but at least the empire would know that Ireland was not yet conquered.

There is evidence that O'Leary sympathised with this extreme wing of the movement. Certainly he was in Dublin during the Queen's visit. He himself admits to having been a spectator of her procession along Sackville (now O'Connell) Street early in August, and a recent biographer of Lalor asserts that O'Leary was fully aware of 'the Queen's affair', as the August plot was referred to.[10] That such a handful should consider kidnapping Her Majesty may seem ludicrous; but in fact she was permitted to sight-see in the city with a small (and, once or twice, no) escort; with daring and a proper plan the scheme might have succeeded—at least temporarily.

However, it misfired. Although 150 men under arms gathered at James Street canal harbour on the appointed night, plans were upset by the separation of the men from their leaders on the far side of the canal upon the accidental arrival of a police patrol, with the result that no news came out from Dublin at all.

Down in Limerick, Lalor, still pushing his literary project, was apparently unaware of Brenan's doings. Now, however, learning from Luby of the Queen's affair, he became worried about the unity of his movement. Not only was Brenan undermining his influence, but the Cork section had also temporarily broken away in disgust at the failure in Dublin. A convention of delegates was hastily summoned for Clonmel for 5 September. Here, after an appraisal of the strength of the available forces, it was agreed to hold simultaneous risings in Cork, Limerick, Clare, Kilkenny, Cashel, north Tipperary, Cappoquin and Dungarvan on Sunday 16 September, the force in Carrick-on-Suir to be kept in reserve. An adequate supply of arms was believed to have been procured, and food was plentiful after a good harvest.

Cashel was O'Leary's first assignment on the night of 16 September. With his Tipperary force he was to make for that town, where Lalor intended to attack the police barracks and, if there successful, to march on Clonmel and join up with Brenan's force, which, by then—it was optimistically hoped—would have been victorious in county Waterford.

By now, however, rumours of the planned insurrection had spread like wildfire. From Thurles, Carrick-on-Suir and Clonmel came magistrates' warnings to the Castle of an imminent outbreak of violence. Public denunciations from press and clergy were followed by the drafting in of extra troops and the strengthening of police garrisons in the disaffected area, 120 extra policemen being stationed in Clonmel and 200 extra troops being moved from Kilkenny to Carrick-on-Suir. It soon transpired, too, that some of the leaders had been shadowed and their post opened.

Torrential rain fell in Waterford and south Tipperary on the night of 16 September. The signals to attack were not co-ordinated, the only serious outbreak being at Cappoquin, where 200 men under Brenan attacked the police station before being scattered. Amongst those in the Cappoquin affray was the 21-year-old son of a Dungarvan merchant, James Francis Xavier O'Brien, destined to play an important part in the Fenian movement and to become a close friend of O'Leary.[11]

O'Leary with some fifty men assembled at Garnacanty outside Tipperary but, finding his force inadequate, sent his men home and proceeded by night with two companions to Cashel, where with Lalor and another small force an all-night wait for more men was made in vain, before Lalor, too, dismissed his force. Lalor and O'Leary, finding the next morning that the local police had suspected nothing, went on to Clonmel where they heard the news from Cappoquin. A series of false alarms followed—mysterious signal-fires at night on Slievenamon, the swearing-in of 150 special constables by the mayor of Clonmel, Patrick Quinn, reports of activity by O'Mahony in the mountains. But the movement had been decisively crushed.

Of the leaders Lalor and Luby (who was arrested a week later in a farmhouse outside Cashel) spent a short spell in jail before returning to Dublin, whence Luby made for Australia. Brenan escaped to the United States, where he died tragically a few years later after a brief but promising journalistic career. Neither Gray nor O'Leary appears to have been apprehended.

In Dublin Lalor's initial mood of despondency was soon dispelled as he and his associates recommenced planning the new journal. But the arduous events of the summer were soon shown to have seriously affected his health. Shortly before Christmas O'Leary was sent for, to assist in preparing for the newspaper; on his arrival in Dublin he found that Lalor had died suddenly on 27 December.

The universal respect which he had won was manifested by the remarkable funeral a day later. This took the form of a semi-military demonstration obviously organised by 'the Secret Society men', as Gavan Duffy called them. Over 600 marched four-deep, along a specially selected route, behind the coffin carried on the leaders' shoulders. 'Some idea may be had of their numbers,' said the *Freeman's Journal* of 31 December, 'when we add that the line extended the whole length of Sackville (now O'Connell) Street.' And some idea of the prominent position which the 19-year-old revolutionary from Tipperary held may be gained from the fact that, amongst only half-a-dozen names mentioned in a report of the funeral published in the *Nation* on the following Saturday, was O'Leary's.

For the second time in two years a revolutionary movement had been crushed by the vigilance of the authorities and the inexperience of its own leaders. Although less ambitious in its immediate objective than the '48 movement, that of '49 had been more carefully planned; yet both had come to the same humiliating end. Nevertheless it can be argued that the secret society of 1849 was to have the more lasting long-term impact on Irish nationalism. For it revealed the possibilities of action through a secret society; and a decade or more later it was the ideas of Lalor, Gray, Brenan and O'Leary in 1849 that were taken up and exploited by James Stephens with far-reaching results.

It is usual to trace the origin of Fenianism to the secret mission, sent to this country in the mid-1850s by the Emmet Monument Association of New York, which resulted in Stephens's agreement to found a new nation-wide secret society if subsidised, but free from control, from the United States. Stephens's decision is frequently said to have been influenced by the success of O'Donovan Rossa's Phoenix National and Literary Society in Skibbereen. It is equally common to see emphasised the '48 associations of Stephens and O'Mahony, the leaders of the Irish and American wings of Fenianism.

But '48 was a movement of open revolution, while '49 marked the beginning (in the nineteenth century at least) of secret societies with purely political aims. And Luby and O'Leary, two of the foremost members of those societies, were also to become two of the most prominent men in the early IRB. It is possible to find evidence of even stronger links between the '49 movement and the foundation of the IRB nine years later. According to John Devoy, Lalor's society continued in existence after his death and was merged in the IRB by Stephens in 1858.[12] It was the members of Lalor's nameless '49 society, according to an old Dublin centre of the IRB in a letter to a city newspaper in 1875, who sought out Stephens on his return from France in the 1850s and encouraged him to start a new organisation.[13]

Moreover, Richard Pigott—whose memoirs, it is pertinent to point out in view of his subsequent infamous career, O'Leary regarded as the best history of Fenianism in his time—stated that Lalor's society was affiliated with an Irish-American federation of clubs, pledged to the liberation of Ireland, which later merged in a body called the Irish Military and Civil Association, of which the secret and oath-bound Emmet Monument Association was the extreme military branch.[14] If this picture is accepted, the members of the 1849 secret society must have provided the nucleus of Stephens's newly-founded society in 1858, and the Phoenix society would assume the less important position of a local group taken over by the newer nation-wide society.

Finally, the scanty information that has survived about O'Leary's society—and it is safe to assume that it differed little from the other '49 organisations—reveals several features of similarity between it and the IRB of a decade or more later. Spread by one man administering an oath in private to another, it levied a fee from members. A member who swore in a specified number of new members became an officer. By the oath he took, a new member undertook to strive to overthrow British rule in Ireland by force of arms, to establish a republic and to keep secret all the society's affairs.

3

HIS FIRST INCURSION INTO POLITICS now ended, the 19-year-old revolutionary returned to his studies—but not to law. For he had discovered, probably from Luby, that before being permitted to practise at the Bar one must first take an oath of allegiance to the Crown; this he was not prepared to do.[15] So from law he switched to medicine, and from Trinity College to the Queen's College, Cork. The new university in the south had been set up under an Act of Parliament of 1845 and the college buildings erected during the Famine years; but the first academic session did not commence until October 1849.

O'Leary, who was not in time for the opening term, successfully took a supplemental matriculation examination on 8 January 1850 and was thereupon registered in the medical faculty. He found lodgings with a Mr. John O'Brien in his boarding-house, Castlewhite, which was approved by the college as a students' residence.[16] O'Brien was a man with a known nationalist outlook, and Castlewhite (now Lapps Asylum) was a mansion in private grounds on the Western Road, a few minutes' walk from the university. Only two other students lodged in the same house, Thomas Coghlan, an engineering student from Killarney who, like O'Leary, had come from Carlow College, and John Mahony, an arts student from Cashel whose parents then resided in Tipperary town, where the boy was educated. The strenuous events of the preceding eighteen months had over-taxed O'Leary in both body and mind; now he wanted a period of quiet. In addition, he was trying to be as unobtrusive as possible, so as both to avoid notice by the police and to concentrate on his books.

He appears to have succeeded in both directions. A quiet but industrious academic year followed and, without either much effort or very regular attendance at lectures, the sessional examinations were easily passed. Weeks at a time were spent either at Castlewhite, immersed in English literature and following the course of contemporary English politics, or solely going to and from lectures.

O'Leary seems to have mixed very little with his fellow undergraduates, with two of whom at least he does not appear to have become friendly until later. One was John Pope-Hennessy, who in 1859 became a Conservative MP, was later knighted and for a quarter-of-a-century subsequently pursued an eventful career as governor of one British colony after another, before making a brief return to Irish politics in 1890.[17] The other was Theobald Mathew, from Golden near Tipperary, a nephew of Fr. Mathew and whose widowed mother, Margaret O'Leary, then managing the family milling concern, may have been related to John O'Leary. It was in Cork in 1849 that O'Leary first met Denis Holland, a young Corkman then also at the university and later to become a well-known journalist and poet.

When his year's lectures were over O'Leary decided to try for a scholarship to the Queen's College, Galway. He spent the long summer vacation at home studying, and in October succeeded in winning a second-year medical scholarship to Galway, whither he then moved. Here he was to spend three years; but they seem to have been almost as uneventful as his year in Cork. All the sessional examinations were passed and three successive annual scholarships (including a senior scholarship in Therapeutics and Pathology for 1852–3) won; much was learnt of the theory of medicine but little of the practical side of the subject. Even more so than in Cork a good deal of time was devoted to non-medical reading, particularly history, biography and literary criticism.

But it is evident that in Galway O'Leary took a more active part in the social life, after his restful year in Cork had restored his former vigour. In Galway, too, he had the companionship of his brother Arthur, who would probably have been too young to have joined him in Cork; and in Galway he would have met again James F. X. O'Brien, now a medical student but back in 1849 an insurgent, like O'Leary, in the Waterford mountains.

Moreover, the O'Learys had relatives in this part of the country, with whom visits were exchanged. These were the Kellys, of Lisdonagh near Headford, one of whom, Mary Anne, was the poetess 'Eva' of the *Nation*, whose aunt Alice had married O'Leary's uncle Jeremiah, the bank manager in Loughrea.[18] O'Leary himself referred to the more energising atmosphere of the west and compared his fellow-students in Galway, amongst whom were several with Young Ireland sympathies, favourably with those few he had met in Cork.

An important factor in increasing his popularity in Galway was the fact that his fame had preceded him there in the shape of a letter which he had written to the *Nation* on the then controversial topic of undenominational education. Since in later life O'Leary was to become an inveterate writer of letters to the press, this first venture of his into print merits at least a brief reference. Although the three Queen's Colleges in Cork, Galway and Belfast had been established as alternatives to Trinity College for Catholics, a majority of the Irish Catholic bishops was opposed to the idea, and at a synod held in Thurles earlier that year the hierarchy had condemned the project.

Nevertheless Catholics were not expressly forbidden to attend the new universities; but a scheme for setting up a distinctively Catholic university in Dublin was pushed ahead. In a leader in the *Nation* for 19 October 1850 Gavan Duffy (editor since the paper's revival thirteen months before) complained of the unrepresentative laymen on the board of the new Catholic college, mentioning specifically Charles Bianconi and Thomas Meagher, father of the '48 leader; he felt, too, that the number of lay directors should be doubled so as to balance the sixteen clerical nominees. The following number, for 26 October, contained a critical letter signed 'John O'Leary, A Catholic Student of the Colleges'; it was headed as coming from Tipperary.

Examining the position of the Queen's Colleges briefly, the correspondent mentioned as their two most objectionable features the Government appointment of professors and the absence of a Catholic chair of history. There was, however, a sting at each end of this well-composed letter. At the outset readers were reminded that Catholics were obliged to obey their Church on doctrinal points only; and it wound up by defiantly announcing that, as the writer's experience of the colleges 'has taught me that they are not dangerous to faith or morals, but are highly conducive to the well-being of my country, I shall (ecclesiastical anathemas notwithstanding) continue to afford them my best encouragement and support'.

Leaving Galway in the summer of 1853, O'Leary returned to Dublin after an absence of over three years and spent the 1853–4 session attending surgery classes in the Meath Hospital. This famous institution was then exactly a century old. Its physician was Dr. William Stokes, the internationally known heart and chest specialist, son of Dr. Whitley Stokes, the United Irishman and friend of James Clarence Mangan (who died in the hospital in 1849 under his care) and of Wolfe Tone. One of the surgeons to the hospital during O'Leary's period as a student was Sir Philip Crampton, an even closer friend of Tone, who played musical duets in his own and in Crampton's house. It was of Crampton, when he was Surgeon General to the Lord Lieutenant, that the infamous Lord Norbury remarked, upon seeing Crampton's resplendent uniform at a Castle function and on being told what post he held: 'I suppose that is a General in the Lancers.'

Autumn 1854 saw O'Leary in London, where he continued his medical studies for yet another year. In late August 1855 'Eva' married Kevin Izod O'Doherty in London; we may assume her cousin John to have attended the wedding. O'Doherty, the son of a Dublin solicitor, had been one of the State prisoners in '48; the story of his love affair is now part of Irish history. The pair had been engaged before he was arrested and put on trial in late '48. Twice the jury disagreed, but before the third trial the Castle authorities privately promised a free pardon in return for a plea of guilty to the newly-created crime of treason-felony.

'Eva's' uncompromising spirit would not permit of this course being adopted; there followed the third trial and a sentence of ten years' transportation to Van Diemen's Land. After six years there O'Doherty was released on condition that he settle elsewhere than in Ireland; he came straight to London for his wedding to the girl who had promised to remain true to him till the end of his imprisonment.

From London O'Leary crossed to Paris in the late summer of 1855. His brother Arthur, who had preceded him there, was now studying to become a teacher. The newly-wed O'Dohertys also made for the French capital, where Kevin planned to resume his medical studies. Possibly O'Leary may have felt that the experience in French medical schools would do him no harm. Indeed, according to one account he was accompanied to the French capital by James F. X. O'Brien, who is known to have studied in the École de Médecine and to have attended the hospitals of La Pitié, La Charité and Hôtel Dieu.[19] Perhaps O'Leary followed the same course.

On the boat to France he got into conversation with a 21-year-old American who had spent his boyhood partly in Russia, where his father had built railways for the Czar. After a spell in West Point military academy the lad had been allowed to pursue his own vocation; now he was on his way to Paris to study painting. This casual meeting led to a lifelong friendship, which ended only in the death, almost fifty years later, of the American, James Abbot McNeill Whistler, then a world-famous painter.[20]

In Paris O'Leary and Whistler took rooms together; their lodgings were also shared by two 19-year-old English boys. One, recently left Eton, was the son of a notable British admiral; Algernon Charles Swinburne was destined to become the last of the major Victorian poets.[21] Like O'Leary, he was to spend only a year in France just then, for in 1857 he entered Balliol College, Oxford.[22] The other English youth, John Edward Poynter, was, much later in the century, to become a famous painter, president of the Royal Academy and director of the National Gallery. Sharing a studio with Whistler and Poynter was a 22-year-old Frenchman, George du Maurier, grandfather of the twentieth-century novelist Daphne du Maurier, and himself distinguished in Britain years afterwards both as an artist and a novelist. It seems likely that O'Leary was then introduced to du Maurier, for they were friends in London only a few years later.[23]

Where exactly O'Leary, Whistler and Swinburne lodged is not known; but it is probable that they joined Arthur O'Leary, who was staying in the Latin Quarter with some other American students. What is known is that John spent much of his time in an old boarding-house in the Rue Lacepede, close to that end of the Botanical Gardens which is farthest from the river Seine, not far from the site of the modern Austerlitz railway station. Here the O'Dohertys had settled while Kevin attended the Hôpital Pitié and the Paris Anatomical School; here too lodged John Martin, another exiled Young Irelander, whom O'Leary greatly admired. This old house was immortalised by the novelist Balzac in his story *Old Goriot*; three-storied and with an attic, its front stood at right angles to the secluded, cobbled street and was covered in pale yellow stucco, while pleasant gardens at the rear were partly laid out in formal flower-beds, and vines and ivy covered the walls.

Within a short time O'Leary came to know most of the members of the small Irish colony then in Paris. From them he would have heard news of the '48 fugitives—John O'Mahony, who had left Paris in 1852 for the United States, and James Stephens, who had returned to Dublin shortly before O'Leary's arrival in France and whom O'Leary had not encountered since their first meeting ten years earlier. Another visitor to the pension at 26 Rue Lacepede just then was John O'Hagan, the barrister and Young Irelander who had defended Gavan Duffy; he was consulting eye specialists in Paris.

The undisputed leader of this exiled group was John P. Leonard, journalist, university lecturer and acquaintance of every Irish resident in Paris, with whom O'Leary became especially friendly and through whom he probably met the veteran Wexford '98 leader, General Miles Byrne, then living in retirement in Rue Ponthieu, close to where the Metro station of St. Philippe du Roule stands today. It may be assumed also that O'Leary visited the Irish college in Paris, for on its staff then was Fr. James Rice, from Kilworth near Fermoy.[24] The Rices were old family friends of the O'Learys, and Fr. Rice (later Canon Rice of Charleville) and John O'Leary were to become firm friends.

A year-and-a-half or so passed quickly in the French capital. History was being made in that country just then, and we may be certain that the significance of current events was not lost on this keen student of politics. The Second Republic, to which the Young Irelanders in early 1848 had enthusiastically sent a fraternal delegation headed by Smith O'Brien, had given way in 1852 to the Second Empire with the proclamation as the Emperor Napoleon III of the colourful and astute Louis Napoleon. The year 1858 itself has been called that empire's sunniest phase, through the French victory in the Crimean war and the birth of a male heir to the popular ruler.[25]

No doubt a voracious reader like O'Leary did not neglect his (non-medical) books; perhaps he may have even lingered a little on the quayside bookstalls, where he was to become a familiar figure later in the century. Indeed this brief experience of continental life—the Parisian atmosphere, the friendship of Leonard, the introduction to French literature—was to prove useful to him over a much longer period in later years.

Towards the end of 1856 the wandering medical student returned to London, where the 1856–7 session was partly spent in reading medical works and apparently otherwise attending either lectures or clinical demonstrations, although the prospect of his qualifying as a doctor was now growing gradually dimmer. Both Arthur and Ellen joined him here and a pleasant year—meaning, one suspects, a year largely devoted to non-medical pursuits—passed. The summer of 1857 saw John back in Dublin once more, Arthur having returned to Paris.

Shortly after his arrival in Dublin, O'Leary ran across Stephens for the first time in eleven years, and was astonished to learn that he was seriously considering a new nation-wide conspiracy. At first glance it would seem that he could have hardly chosen a more

inauspicious time for such a plot, for the 1850s had been a period
of unrelieved gloom for Irish affairs.   The mild constitutional
movement centred round the Tenant League, the Catholic Defence
Association and a group of Irish MPs in Westminster, had foundered
in 1852 with the defection to the Government side of Sadlier and
Keogh, two of the most prominent Irish MPs.   Moreover, the
Catholic hierarchy did not come out too well from its intervention
in Irish politics in this decade; even the conservative Gavan Duffy,
disgusted by what he regarded as the bishops' betrayal of a national
cause, had retired from politics and set sail for Australia.

It was at this stage that Stephens decided to sound out some
associates on the possibility of starting a new secret society. Finding O'Leary—then as always afterwards—far from hopeful of the
prospect of success, he approached, of all people, John Blake
Dillon, to whose young sons he was private tutor. Not surprisingly
his overtures were brusquely rejected.

O'Leary, now apparently losing contact with Stephens, embarked
on yet another attempt to pursue his medical studies. The session
of 1857–8 he spent in Dublin as one of forty-four students attached
to the Meath Hospital for that year. But by the summer of 1858
it was becoming clear, at least to his acquaintances, that he would
never become a doctor. The previous June, Kevin O'Doherty,
having, with John Martin and Smith O'Brien, received an unconditional pardon, had received his fellowship from the College
of Surgeons and was now in practice at 18 Hume Street, Dublin.
To this house O'Leary became a frequent visitor; here he met and
became acquainted with—but was not impressed by—the aloof
William Smith O'Brien.

From here, too, 'Eva' had written to John Martin in Paris with
news of her Tipperary cousin, for in early September in his reply
to 'Eva' Martin said: 'As to John's becoming a medical man, I
would be glad to believe that, or that he should apply himself to
any respectable work at all. But I am afraid he is going to do
nothing, and more's the pity, for he has fine faculties and qualities.'
It very soon became obvious that politics still took first place with
O'Leary.

Towards the end of 1858 Stephens again called on him; he was
now at the head of his new secret society. With a promise of
financial aid from exile groups in New York he had, on the previous
Saint Patrick's Day, founded the Irish Revolutionary Brotherhood
(later the Irish Republican Brotherhood), and had merged in it
the remnants of the secret society of 1849.

To O'Leary he unfolded his plans. Since the initial trickle of
money across the Atlantic had recently dried up, he was about to
head for the United States himself to obtain more. Would O'Leary

meet him in Boulogne, the French transatlantic port, on his return a few months later, in order to take charge of the money which he assumed he would bring back with him? O'Leary agreed; so began what he himself called his 'first direct connection with Fenianism'. To Stephens he said he believed the movement had no chance of success, but would be good for the morale of the country.

Nine months or more had elapsed since the foundation of the new movement; yet it seems unlikely that O'Leary had been entirely ignorant of affairs during that period, especially as he had in the meantime renewed his acquaintance with Luby. Now suddenly he found himself in the thick of events, chosen by the leader of the conspiracy, a personal friend, to manage its financial affairs and requested to return to France in his new role. This time Stephens was not to be disappointed; on the contrary, his second approach to O'Leary was to have far-reaching consequences for Fenianism.

About March 1859 O'Leary left Ireland for France. After a few days in Paris with Arthur he went on to Boulogne, where he and Luby had arranged to meet, and to await Stephens's arrival from America. The pair booked into the fashionable Hotel Folkestone, expecting Stephens to turn up in a few days. However, a fortnight passed before his ship docked and in the meantime Luby and O'Leary, running out of money, were obliged, in the traditional manner of impecunious young men, to pawn some of their belongings; O'Leary also wrote home for assistance.

Stephens, when at last he did arrive, quickly restored their spirits, for he had brought with him some £700 in gold for the organisation. He had news, too, of the men and the movement in the United States, at that early stage so vital to the progress of the conspiracy at home in Ireland, although in some respects he was to report that his mission had not been an unqualified success. Near the quay-side in this pleasant French port and seaside resort there was, and still is, a small public park. Here O'Leary and Luby led Stephens after he had disembarked; here, out of hearing of any eavesdropping British detectives, the three spent one fine, long spring day in discussion.[26]

One can imagine how the sharp-tongued Kilkenny man had criticised the men in America for failing to keep up the flow of funds; so unfavourable an impression did Stephens make there that only Doheny and O'Mahony of the prominent men would have anything to do with him or his society. Now at last, back in the more congenial company of loyal and admiring comrades, he bitterly railed Thomas Francis Meagher, John Mitchel and Richard O'Gorman, three of the exiled '48 leaders whose support he failed to win. Mitchel's coolness he blamed on John Dillon who, Stephens alleged, had written to Mitchel giving him such an unfavourable account of Stephens that Mitchel thenceforward was quite hostile.

The day after Stephens's arrival in Boulogne he set out with Luby and O'Leary for Paris, where the three took lodgings together in 30 Rue Montaigne, not far from the circus of the Champs Elysees. By now, it appears, Stephens's initial mood of despondency had given way to one of unwarranted optimism. He set up headquarters in the lodgings, despatched orders home to all the 'As' (i.e. the colonels) of the IRB to attend, two or three at a time, in Paris for a special course in military affairs, and appointed O'Leary as his personal envoy to the organisation in the United States. The importance of maintaining contact with the source of financial aid was not lost on the shrewd Stephens who, either on the trip back to Paris or immediately after his arrival there, overcame O'Leary's understandable misgivings over being sent 3,000 miles across the ocean to act as representative of a secret society, of which he had not even formally become a member, to a country where he was unknown.

On their first night in Paris all three sat up through the night talking and planning. Stephens wrote out voluminous detailed instructions for O'Leary's forthcoming trip to America and argued with Luby over a pet scheme of his to bring over to Ireland American officers to act as drill-masters for the IRB. Luby, unlike the other two, thought the idea ill-advised; later he was to be proved right.[27]

Shortly afterwards, in mid-April, O'Leary sailed for America, carrying with him a letter of introduction from Stephens to O'Mahony. A copy of this document survives, and it is of interest for what it reveals about both Stephens and O'Leary.[28] Running to over 4,000 words, it expresses confidence in the ultimate success of the young movement in Ireland and, in a patronising manner that must have irritated a proud man like O'Mahony, contains detailed orders regarding the work O'Leary was to undertake in New York.

It establishes that, within thirteen months of the foundation of the IRB, to O'Leary was assigned the role of financial agent of the organisation, an assignment which was to prove his undoing when later he faced a charge of treason. His visit to the United States was to be used to raise funds, which O'Mahony was to lodge with O'Leary, who would then arrange for their transfer back across the Atlantic by trusted couriers.

Stephens's letter also shows how O'Leary's political beliefs were developing. We know from Devoy that his experience of the Second French Empire made O'Leary an admirer of constitutional monarchy in preference to a rigid republican democracy,[29] though his brother Arthur exaggerated when, in a letter to a friend in

April 1858, he remarked: 'My brother John is become quite an Englishman and is a conservative in politics.'[30] Thus Stephens found it necessary to warn O'Mahony that this young envoy, although in every other respect an excellent person, was not a republican and was, indeed, averse to a republican form of government and only ready to accept it if it represented the national will.

Accordingly, added the shrewd Stephens, since O'Leary 'has neither the opinions nor the faith in the cause that could ensure the requisite results', he must be permitted neither to discuss the principles of government with 'some of our extreme friends' nor to travel through the States as a representative of the organisation. Both this leaning towards a constitutional monarchy and his lack of optimism regarding the success of the movement were to remain with O'Leary to the end of his life.

As for O'Leary's own feelings about his trip to the States, he never made any secret of the fact that neither then nor in later years could he become attached to America or its people. Perhaps this first glimpse of the country was not too promising. Before leaving France he had, according to his version, stipulated to Stephens the conditions under which he would undertake the journey. He would not travel through the States 'spreading the fame and name of the IRB'; rather would he merely go to New York and there carry out routine organisational work from O'Mahony's office—looking after correspondence, receiving daily visitors, attending regular weekend meetings, and the like. And, as befitted the envoy of a secret society, his name would not be given to the press.

But things did not work out that way for a start. O'Leary was given a public reception, serenaded by the band of the famous 69th Regiment, and prevailed upon to address a vast crowd from a window of the well-known St. Nicholas Hotel, 'not knowing in the least what to say, or why I should be asked to say anything at all, or why, in fact, I was where I was at all'. The memoirs of a man who first met O'Leary that same summer of 1859 show that the man of twenty-nine was little changed from the boy of nineteen —'very reserved, something of an aristocrat', and with that same slow, hesitant manner of speaking that he was never to lose. It is easy to see what an ordeal such a tumultuous welcome—'a queer sort of proceeding . . .' for '. . . a secret envoy' as he himself caustically called it—was to such a man; no wonder he began to regret having succumbed, against his own better judgement, to the silver tongue of James Stephens.

Fifteen years later a curious version of O'Leary's mission to New York was published in a Dublin newspaper.[31] According to this, he deliberately posed as James Stephens, with the object of confusing the police in Ireland, then said to be seeking Stephens. It was even said that O'Leary's arrival in New York was reported in the American press as that of 'Mr. Shook', a corruption of 'Seabhac', a nickname given to Stephens by the early Cork supporters of the IRB.

The available evidence is strongly against this theory. O'Leary himself promptly denied the story.[32] Admittedly, an agent of Dublin Castle, then in New York observing the doings of the emigrant Irish revolutionaries, in a note back to his employers on the St. Nicholas meeting had said: 'Shook was present and spoke. I was there.'[33] But was he, one wonders, after having seen the meagre results of his spying mission to America? Perhaps after all the agent, Sub-Inspector Thomas Doyle, merely read of the St. Nicholas meeting in Thomas Francis Meagher's paper *The Irish News*, for a hasty reading of its report might lead one to confuse 'Shook' with 'Mr. O'Leary'.[34]

Happily, however, once this initial burst of publicity was over, O'Leary found that he was able to resume the quiet life which he so obviously preferred. Taking lodgings with John O'Mahony in Brooklyn for the first month, he quickly settled down to the work in the Fenian Brotherhood's offices at 6 Centre Street. O'Mahony, whom he may already have met during the summer or autumn of 1849, he now came to know intimately and to admire; O'Leary's impressions of this aristocratic figure coincided with those of all others who came into contact with him.

One may assume that O'Leary also became friendly with O'Mahony's secretary, Michael Cavanagh, a Cappoquin man who had participated in the attack by the men of '49 on the barracks there; besides being a revolutionary, Cavanagh had literary leanings and was a good Irish scholar.[35] Amongst other notable figures he met were John Mitchel, his idol of twelve years before; Thomas Francis Meagher (Meagher of the Sword), the '48 leader from Waterford, whom he came to know intimately; and Michael Doheny, the barrister and journalist from Cashel, with whom Stephens had gone on the run in Munster after the '48 rising.

A month or so after O'Leary's arrival O'Mahony left New York on business elsewhere in the States; from then on, O'Leary and Doheny, who practised law from an office in Centre Street opposite to the Superior Court, were thrown much together. Since Doheny was the principal contributor to a new weekly paper, the *Phoenix*, it was inevitable that O'Leary should be drawn into the venture. Accordingly, for some weeks of his stay in New York he tried out his hand at journalism under the editor of this paper, one James Roche. Roche was a former policeman who had edited the *Galway Vindicator* and the *Kilkenny Journal*; although an able journalist by normal contemporary standards, he clearly lacked sufficient culture to measure up to those of O'Leary.

The few tattered copies of this, the first avowedly Fenian organ, which have survived, have done so in circumstances worth mentioning. From 1859 to 1861 one Thomas Doyle, a trusted officer of the Royal Irish Constabulary, was assigned to New York for the specific purpose of keeping the Inspector General of Police informed of the progress of the Fenian movement in America. It was a costly and unfruitful mission, for Doyle did little more than to post back regularly cuttings from the American papers, with his own comments thereon.[36] From time to time, when fired with unusual energy, he sent an entire paper, sometimes the latest issue of the *Phoenix*; these have been preserved in our State papers.

The first issue, dated 4 June 1859, was published from 44 Ann Street, New York. It showed the paper to be run by a company of 200 shareholders who had contributed twenty-five dollars each and controlled its commercial policy; but editorial control was solely in the hands of John O'Mahony with Roche as editor. The first leader was signed by O'Mahony; the second, 'The Die Is Cast', may have been O'Leary's work. The general lay-out of the eight-page production suggests that O'Leary applied his experience of the *Phoenix* when he came, four years later, to have a bigger interest in another journalistic venture in Dublin.

A couple of months previously, when Stephens on his return from America had ranted against Dillon to Luby and O'Leary in the quayside park in Boulogne, he had included in his attacks the journalist A. M. Sullivan, who had succeeded Gavan Duffy as editor of the *Nation*. During Stephens's absence in the States this paper had played a major part in provoking the arrest and prosecution of O'Donovan Rossa and other members of the extremist Phoenix National and Literary Society of Skibbereen. So, at any rate, the IRB leaders always held; the evidence supports their view, and the episode itself led to a long and bitter feud between the Sullivan brothers, with their constitutional supporters, and the Fenians.

In Boulogne, Luby and O'Leary had vainly tried to calm down Stephens and to soften him towards the Sullivans.[37] Now, by a curious coincidence, O'Leary, as a temporary member of the editorial staff of the *Phoenix* newspaper in New York, found himself drawn into a new controversy with T. D. Sullivan, who, like his brother earlier that year, appeared to the Fenians to be attempting to sabotage the new movement. In a New York Catholic weekly, the *Irish-American*, Sullivan, its Dublin correspondent, had pointedly drawn attention to the existence of a so-called Fair Trial Fund, the purported object of which was to help the Phoenix prisoners. He

1. Main Street, Tipperary, about eighty years ago, showing (on the extreme left) the house where John O'Leary was born

2. Clonmel jail, the centre of the abortive plot to rescue the 1848 leaders

3. Clonmel courthouse, where the Young Irelanders were tried in 1848

alleged that no money had reached Ireland from it. This allegation was, of course, correct, since the fund was really intended to finance the IRB; the real purpose of Sullivan's disclosure was to discredit that body.

Unfortunately, no complete file has survived of the *Phoenix*, this obscure publication in which O'Leary's first work as a journalist appeared, and which was, indeed, the first paper on either side of the Atlantic to advocate the principles of Fenianism. But it is safe to assume that he participated energetically in the controversy with the rival semi-clerical periodical.

By no means all of O'Leary's time in the United States was spent as a journalist in New York. In pursuance of the main aim of his trip across the Atlantic, the raising of funds for the IRB, he toured a wide area of the United States, particularly the mid-western states, covering several thousand miles. He visited first Massachusetts, New Hampshire and Philadelphia, and then Pittsburgh, Chicago, Milwaukee, Cleveland and Toledo. Between Camden and Pittsburgh his train was derailed, and O'Leary ended in a ditch, shaken but unhurt; in Chicago he attended a Fenian conference and met some old friends from Cork and Paris.

In the course of his trips out of New York O'Leary also organised in several places new circles of the Fenian Brotherhood. Indeed, he himself felt that in this part of his journeys he was more successful than on his fund-raising missions. 'And on no profitless mission either have I come, as I trust the seed sown will in due time bear fruit according to its kind,' he remarked in a letter to O'Mahony from Toledo. Later in the same letter comes this comment: 'May all the devils in hell lay hold of those who kept those rascally dollars from us.'[38]

Back in New York, O'Leary arranged for the immediate dispatch to Stephens of the money he had collected and for the dispatch to Ireland later of the American officers who were to act as drill-masters to the IRB. About mid-August, after having spent over three months in America, the secret envoy of the IRB sailed for Europe, arriving back in France in early September. Upon reaching the lodgings in Paris, he found that in his absence Luby had returned to Ireland; but a new lodger from his native county awaited him in the person of Denis Dowling Mulcahy. A native of Redmondstown, Clonmel, Mulcahy, who had been in O'Leary's secret society in 1849, was attending Stephens's course; he was to become a lifelong friend of O'Leary. Another recent arrival in Paris had been Mitchel, whom O'Leary ran across shortly afterwards in Martin's lodgings in Rue Lacepede; both he found to be unmistakably hostile to Stephens.

O'Leary now spent several months in Paris. Arthur had moved

into lodgings in Rue Montaigne, too, and, with so many congenial visitors from Ireland coming and going, the time passed pleasantly. The two O'Learys delighted in showing off the city's showplaces and even the normally more serious-minded Stephens, who would, of course, have known Paris better than they, was persuaded to join in some of the excursions. One of the men summoned from Dublin by Stephens later recalled visiting Versailles, the Bois de Boulogne and St. Cloud; he remembered Stephens excitedly lecturing them on the bas-relief on the Arc de Triomphe and conducting them on tours of the Luxembourg and the Palace de Cluny.

Arthur O'Leary specialised in strolls through the art studios, picture galleries and (his favourite area) the Latin Quarter, where he was known to all the students; a fine figure of a man, he rivalled Stephens as a mimic and leg-puller. His brother John, on the other hand, a quieter type except to his close friends, preferred to wander among the bookstalls scattered along the Quai d'Orsai, but was at his best at the many informal nocturnal functions held in the second-floor suite in Rue Montaigne. One wonders what the landlord, Monsieur La Cour, and his family, only recently arrived from their native city of Lyons, in the south, to the suite below, thought of these lively lodgers, most of whom looked back nostalgically years later on their stay in Paris, then, under Napoleon III's now legendary town-planner Baron Hausmann, rapidly assuming the architectural form which it retains to this day.

As the months passed, however, O'Leary became gradually a little disillusioned. Stephens he admired for his uncanny judgement in choosing the time for starting the new organisation. Stephens, too, he was chivalrously and stoutly to defend to the end of his life for some qualities which others in the IRB were too prone to overlook—his gift for leadership, his organising genius, his determination to carry on when the future looked bleak. But Stephens the man he could never warm to; 'there was a certain flabbiness of moral fibre about him which . . . always was distasteful to me'.

Perhaps unconsciously the opinions of men like Mitchel and Martin were having some effect on O'Leary, for he admits that just then neither the position of the IRB nor its prospects appealed to him. Or possibly he was merely seeking an excuse which would enable him to meet the probable and understandable criticism of his family and friends at home, by making one final attempt to concentrate on medicine. At any rate, towards the end of 1859, he abruptly left Paris for Ireland, and more than three years were to elapse before he came directly into contact with Irish revolutionary affairs again.

CHAPTER THREE

1 Stephens's Decision

2 The *Irish People*

1

FOR THREE YEARS following his departure from Paris to the late summer of 1860, John O'Leary was only occasionally in touch with the IRB. 'With some vague notion of pursuing, or rather resuming' his medical studies, he made first for London, where his concentration (if any) was interrupted shortly after Christmas by the arrival of Arthur. Arthur had, it appears, succumbed to the charm of Stephens's personality and remained on in Stephens's lodgings in Paris after his elder brother had moved to London.

Arthur had been the cause of one of the few fallings-out between O'Leary and Stephens. On his return from the United States in September 1859 John had found that, in breach of an undertaking given before he had sailed for New York in April, Stephens had (on the youth's own insistence, he alleged) sworn Arthur into the IRB and despatched him to Clonmel on a brief mission there. Subsequently, on Arthur's return to Paris, he and Stephens ran out of money; the resulting privation suffered by both was to have a literally fatal effect on young O'Leary.

Perceiving the poor state of his brother's health, O'Leary travelled with him to Tipperary, where they spent Christmas. On the way they stopped in Dublin; here John was pleasantly surprised to be able to renew his friendship with John O'Mahony, then on what was to prove his last visit to his native country.

In March 1861, three years almost to the day after the foundation of the IRB, the National Brotherhood of Saint Patrick was formed in Dublin by Denis Holland. Its primary object was 'the promotion of cordial union, based on devotion to the independence of our common country, amongst Irishmen of every creed and class'. Its first national secretary was Charles G. Doran, later a prominent IRB man; not surprisingly, one of its slogans ran: 'A member does not forego any of his social rights by knowing the use of arms.' In the next few years this constitutional body was to prove a valuable source of recruits for the IRB; indeed, it seems to have become a sort of legal 'front' for the secret society.

In Tipperary town shortly afterwards, when on another visit home—presumably to see his now gradually sinking brother—O'Leary was asked and agreed to become president of the town's branch of the newly-established Brotherhood, then in the course of formation. Amongst the more energetic members, most of whom were later sworn into the IRB by Stephens, was a teacher named Brohan, who was later to prove useful to O'Leary and the cause in a literary capacity.

O'Leary cannot have been long back in London after this before he was suddenly called home once more. On 6 June 1861, exactly a month before his twenty-eighth birthday, Arthur died of tuberculosis. To both John and Ellen the death of this vivacious young brother, though hardly unexpected, was a severe shock. Thirty-five years afterwards John still referred to it as 'the first great sorrow of my life'. When, in 1865, police ransacked his Dublin lodgings, the documents they seized included French vocabulary notes with a Paris address and in Arthur's handwriting, as well as a letter to 'Eva' from J. P. Leonard, sympathising on her young cousin's death.

The three O'Learys had been close companions since their mother's death some twenty years before, and had only recently spent a year together in London when the two brothers were studying. In Paris, Arthur had taught English, and he had shown early promise as a poet. The *Nation* published five love-poems by him in 1852; these were amongst eleven collected by John twenty-nine years later and included in the volume containing a selection of Ellen's poems.

After Arthur's funeral John remained in Tipperary for a short period before returning to London, where he spent two more years. Since his name does not appear on the rolls of any London medical school of this time, it looks as if any medical studies were confined to reading. Indeed, he himself hinted later that, as might have been expected, he did a good deal of non-medical reading then, too. He is known to have become a regular customer of Thomas Young, a London bookseller and proprietor of the Universal Reading Rooms at 76 Seymour Street, Euston Square.

From personal papers found in O'Leary's Dublin lodgings a few years later some idea of his other activities in London may be gained. He resided at 4 Thames Parade, Pimlico, and seems to have teamed up with several other Irish medical students then in London. The names Tom Cahill, Michael Hanly and P. J. Kelly are mentioned in correspondence: like O'Leary, the last two were customers of a wine merchant in Bristol, who appears to have received substantial orders for Burgundy and claret from all three.

With the aid of a loan from the generous O'Leary, Kelly emigrated to Jamaica, where he built up such a good practice that he wrote to O'Leary in Pimlico urging him to join him. But O'Leary had run across Whistler, the American art student of his Paris days, and not surprisingly preferred London. In vain did his uncle Jeremiah, the bank manager in Loughrea, whom John had recently visited, write to London urging his nephew to adopt more regular habits and to 'shake off his indolence'. Jeremiah would probably have been shocked could he have guessed what was to rouse his nephew into action two years later.

Meanwhile, with regular cheques arriving from his brother-in-law William King, who was managing O'Leary's house property (now grown to twenty premises) in Tipperary, London was clearly preferable to either Ireland or the West Indies. That he took at least some slight interest in English political affairs is evident from the fact that he went to the trouble of looking up his former fellow undergraduate from the Queen's College, Cork, John Pope Hennessy, then an MP. From Hennessy he obtained an introduction to the House of Commons, which he visited at least once. As if realising that this was a curious excursion for one who professed such contempt for parliamentary agitation (if only, perhaps, for Irishmen), O'Leary later said that he had been little edified by what he saw and heard at Westminster.

The three-year period ending in the summer of 1863 was one of intermittent growth for the IRB. Stephens, now a full-time revolutionary, travelled the length and breadth of the country, mostly on foot, setting up new centres, meeting the heads of existing centres, addressing and encouraging officers of the organisation everywhere —all without once attracting undue publicity. Branches were established in England, Scotland and Wales; envoys were sent on missions abroad—Luby spent almost six months in the United States in 1863 —and the society penetrated all the lower ranks of the British army.

At an opportune moment early in 1861 the Brotherhood received a fresh injection of blood by the recruiting in Dublin of a new and better type of member. To the Dublin artisan with republican and separatist leanings was added the steadier young man (often a non-Dubliner) in secure employment like that of the city's main business houses. Most important of all, however, were the historic McManus funeral demonstrations in November 1861, culminating in a remarkable show of strength by some 50,000 men marching through the capital, unarmed but in military formation, to Glasnevin cemetery, watched by 200,000 people who lined the city streets.

All this time money continued to be the organisation's main weakness. From across the Atlantic funds came infrequently and in small amounts. In those early years, recalled O'Donovan Rossa near the end of the century, the men at home spent more money than ever came from the United States. 'The receipts of the house yonder,' said Stephens in a letter to Luby in mid-1863, written in the commercial jargon frequently used in such IRB communications, 'have not reached £250 a year.' According to another IRB man the amount sent by O'Mahony between 1858 and 1863 totalled only £1,500.[1]

Since not one of the leaders of the IRB at that time was a man of means, one can only wonder how a nation-wide conspiracy managed to survive at all on such insecure financial foundations. By March 1861 all the American drill-masters had returned home, most of them destitute and having achieved nothing in Ireland. From time to time it appears that some criticisms of Stephens's dictatorial leadership arose; it looks as if he failed to make as much use of the triumph of the McManus funeral in strengthening the organisation as he might have done if really energetic.

But none of his critics could deny the personal sacrifices he made at this critical period; as had happened when Arthur O'Leary had been lodging with him in Paris, he endured actual privation. Fortunately Hugh Brophy, one of the earliest and most prominent Dublin members of the IRB, came to Stephens's rescue and provided him with a tiny cottage at Harold's Cross on the southern outskirts of Dublin, where he was able to survive—and to indulge in his favourite hobby of cultivating flowers. Here, according to his critics, Stephens devoted excessive attention to 'Jane and his hollyhocks'; for the man who had ruled that conspirators should not marry was now in love with the sister of one of his Dublin associates in the movement.

By the spring of 1863 it was clear that the financial plight of the IRB had become almost desperate; by May Stephens himself was destitute and now totally dependent on the generosity of Brophy.[2] By the end of July he became so despondent that he even considered throwing up revolutionary work altogether. But the resource-fulness of the Kilkenny man had not yet been over-taxed. A new idea gradually took shape in Stephens's mind; and what matter if, like his own love affair, it broke one of his oft-quoted rules?

Hitherto he had always been contemptuous of newspapers in general, asserting that he could mould Irish public opinion without the aid of any paper; moreover, he held that a conspiracy should not have an organ. Now suddenly to his inner circle of confidants he announced that, since the American wing (or, as he and Luby both regarded it, subsidiary branch) of the organisation had failed to keep up the promised supply of money, and since they at home had failed to persuade their members to part with sufficient money directly to the movement, the necessary funds would be raised by publishing a newspaper.

This would, he asserted, preach the IRB creed and would at the same time have an assured sale amongst the now impressive membership. '. . . The paper shall be called the *Irish People*. . . . The people are in sore need of a paper at once reliable and capable of supplying the knowledge they require so much—a knowledge of their rights and duties—of the dignity and power of labour—of what they are and might and shall become. . . . The paper is the only source of revenue we can now rely on.' And writing to O'Mahony shortly before Christmas 1864, Stephens said: '. . . the establishment of the paper has become a *necessity—a matter of life and death to the organisation.*'

That even most of his loyal lieutenants doubted the wisdom of this project cannot occasion surprise. The idea of a secret revolutionary society openly publishing an official organ seems a little incongruous. Yet, whatever opinion he may have formed at the time, no less prominent an IRB man than John Devoy later approved of the plan, and his reasons may strike one as sound in both theory and practice.[3]

That the paper when it ultimately appeared needlessly exposed the IRB leaders to government action cannot be denied; Luby admitted later that the members of the editorial staff were con-stantly watched and followed by detectives.[4] Yet to criticise the leaders for using the newspaper office as the headquarters of the organisation is not to say that it was wrong to start the newspaper itself. As Devoy pointed out, by mid-1863 the IRB, with some 80,000 members in these islands (exclusive of a further 15,000 in British military uniform), was no longer in any sense a secret conspiracy. Now by far the most powerful political force in the land, its next aim was to convert the remainder of the people to its views. For this a public propaganda campaign was essential, and all the existing Irish newspapers were hostile to the aims and methods of the IRB. Secrecy at the top was still not merely desirable but possible; but secrecy alone would not win over the uncommitted.

Curiously enough, Stephens did not at this stage consult the now distant O'Leary, of whose literary leanings he had known as far back as 1846, about his latest idea. Had he done so, he would have found immediate and unqualified support for his project. Then, as later, O'Leary was strongly of the view that a national movement must have a public voice.[5]

And it would doubtless have occurred to O'Leary also that, because of both his long acquaintance with Stephens and his literary knowledge, he himself would probably have stronger claims to edit the new paper than anyone else but Luby, whose journalistic experience in Dublin since 1850 should have made him the first choice for editor. When the call came O'Leary was to respond at once.

On 8 August Stephens set off on another tour, this time of the southern counties where the IRB was particularly strong, his main purpose being to sell the idea of an IRB paper to the centres of the area. Behind him in Dublin he left a special committee, headed by Luby, to plan the details of the new project. In his customary elaborate manner Stephens travelled armed with copies of a private circular or prospectus, setting out the details of the scheme; these he distributed to the officers in each town. He also called for subscriptions in advance totalling £1,000 to start the paper; less than a quarter of this sum was ultimately collected.

At the start of the tour Stephens had written to O'Leary in London, bringing to an end the aimless life which O'Leary had been leading there, out of touch with the movement at home. This letter made two announcements of particular interest to O'Leary; the writer was soon to get married and wished O'Leary to be his best man, and he was also soon to publish a newspaper in which he wished O'Leary to take a leading part—not as editor, but as nominal proprietor and permanent writer, starting at £150 a year.

O'Leary returned to Ireland at once. Travelling by Bristol to Cork, he joined Stephens there at 77 Grand Parade, the home of the Cork Fenian John Lynch, and spent several pleasant days in and around that city in the convivial company of its leading IRB men. Several of these, such as Brian Dillon and John Kenealy, he was to meet again within a few short years, when all were inside the walls of a British convict prison. On his return to Dublin in the second half of September, Stephens found that discontent had grown in his absence over his alleged inactivity generally since the McManus funeral. At a meeting with the Dublin centres, however, he was skilfully able to stifle the opposition, partly by showing that the rest of the country was solidly behind him.

Plans for the forthcoming publication were now vigorously pushed ahead. Almost the entire of the spacious premises at 12 Parliament Street was rented from a Mr. Samuelson, and carpenters were soon busy fitting out offices for the editorial and commercial staffs and a caseroom for the printers. After securing the consent of each man to his appointment to a particular post, Stephens announced the staff of the new journal.

Luby, Charles Kickham and O'Leary were to be joint editors and permanent leader-writers, 'a plan arguing considerable ignorance of the practical working of a newspaper office', as O'Leary caustically commented—and, one might add, a plan quickly altered by those concerned with the practical working of this particular newspaper office. Denis D. Mulcahy was to be the paper's sole sub-editor—it was unusual in those days to have more than one—and Jeremiah O'Donovan Rossa would manage the commercial end of the concern, while John Haltigan of Kilkenny would be in charge of printing.

When Stephens returned early in September 1863 from his tour of the south, O'Leary left Cork for Tipperary, where he remained for a short while before going on to Dublin. Here he took lodgings in the same house as Stephens, now preparing for his wedding. His fiancée was Jane Hopper, the daughter of a Dublin tailor, at least two of her brothers being in the IRB.

Their leader's proposed marriage was strongly opposed by some of Stephens's lieutenants, who snobbishly alleged that he was marrying beneath his class; their real objection to the union was a natural fear that matrimony would further divert Stephens from revolutionary pursuits. O'Leary felt these fears to be groundless; he seems to have been correct in his later assertion that at no time was there any evidence that Mrs. Stephens in any way deflected her husband from the path of a revolutionary.

The marriage took place privately in the parish church of Saints Michael and John in Lower Exchange Street, on the south bank of the Liffey adjoining Wood Quay, on Sunday evening, 24 January 1864, the best man being O'Leary, the bridesmaid Mary Hopper, and the officiating priest Father John O'Hanlon, later a well-known writer and historian, who subsequently refused a letter of freedom to O'Donovan Rossa.[6] By now the new newspaper was almost two months in existence.

ON SATURDAY 28 NOVEMBER 1863 the first issue of a new weekly paper, the *Irish People*, appeared in Dublin and the provinces. Somewhat smaller than the *Nation*—what today would be called tabloid-size—it ran to sixteen pages of three wide columns each, and was well supported by reputable advertisers. The curious and unsuspecting Dubliner—if any there still were—who purchased a copy (price twopence unstamped, threepence stamped), in order to ascertain who or what body was behind this new journal, cannot have long remained in any doubt that its sponsors were those who were then politically referred to as the extreme nationalists.

Its registered proprietor was Thomas Clarke Luby and its publisher and manager Jeremiah O'Donovan Rossa. Both had been known to the public for some years as leading advocates of this so-called extreme nationalism. In accordance with the practice of Victorian journalism, the name of the editor was not revealed.

A full page of advertisements at both front and back, together with several pages of foreign news near the front and some more pages of miscellaneous items (such as theatrical and cultural matters, literary and art gossip) near the back—all this, indeed, made innocent and harmless reading. But two columns of intelligence from the American civil war, followed by detailed reports of the progress of the Fenian Brotherhood in the United States, may have startled our unsuspecting reader.

Even a glance at the centre pages would have sufficed to end his doubts. Four editorials, all well written, were clearly of a more aggressive, not to say warlike, character than one was accustomed to from the editorial pen of either A. M. Sullivan in the *Nation* or Richard Pigott in the *Irishman*, the new paper's two chief rivals if it was to succeed. 'True national independence never was and never will be anywhere achieved save by the sword'; thus ran a provocative sentence in the third leader of this new journal.

Further on was a whole page of original poetry, perhaps mediocre in quality but entirely patriotic in sentiment. And on page eleven there were two letters to the editor, one from Skibbereen on the controversial topic of felon-setting, the name given by James Stephens to the fashionable, if shabby, practice of pointing out (whether overtly or otherwise) members of the physical force party to the police authorities.

Here at last was the new organ of the extreme non-constitutional group; this was the oft-rumoured and much discussed paper of the so-called Fenians, the popular, but incorrect, name for the members of that secret society whose spectacular growth had been a cause of concern to both Church and State in the previous few years. On the whole this *Irish People*, while undoubtedly daring in its views, so far seemed otherwise surprisingly conventional, perhaps even a little dull. But no paper can be judged on its first issue alone, nor on the first half-a-dozen for that matter.

Before long form and style and content were to improve, and the *Irish People*, under its able and energetic editor, John O'Leary, was, despite its brief existence of less than twenty-two months, destined to play an important part in influencing the trend of Irish affairs for the remainder of the century—and even beyond. For it was the message of the IRB, of which this paper was the main—almost the sole—propaganda machine, rather than the message of the repealer, the tenant leaguer or any other non-violent agitator of the years yet to come, that was to prove the decisive factor in the settlement (such as it was) arrived at between Britain and Ireland some sixty years later.

That the *Irish People* took three or four weeks to settle down to what was to prove its characteristic style can be accounted for as much by the normal initial troubles of any new journal as by the fact that Stephens had a hand in these early issues. 'He had,' says O'Leary, 'the most magnificent literary projects, which were mostly intended to be carried out by himself, a history of political institutions, if I remember aright, certainly a history of socialistic theories, and many other vast schemes, ranging over whole realms of criticism, poetry and the like, which have now gone clean out of my head, in which they never probably made any very serious lodgement.'

Stephens wrote the first editorial in each of the first three numbers, and nothing more. While well planned and cogently argued, they are, on the whole, fulsome, wordy compositions even for that period and hardly of a type likely to appeal to the class of reader the paper was principally aimed at. The effort, however, proved too much for Stephens, and he wisely seems to have realised that he had no flair for writing. Thereafter he was content to leave editorial control in the capable hands of O'Leary and Luby. Luby willingly consented to O'Leary's becoming editor while he himself and Kickham, who had returned from a visit to the United States in December, became the principal writers for the paper.

Rossa, in order to leave himself free to travel round the country canvassing support for the paper, took on as his assistant manager and book-keeper James O'Connor, a Wicklow man who was one of the three Cork city centres. Later a prominent IRB figure and Dublin journalist, O'Connor was for many years before his death

in 1910 a Nationalist MP for Wicklow. Michael Moynihan, a
brother of Mortimer Moynihan, one of the Phoenix Society men
from Skibbereen and a friend of Rossa, was assistant book-keeper.

John Haltigan, a printer on the *Kilkenny Journal* and one of
the two Kilkenny centres, brought up a small staff of IRB men from
Kilkenny, including his son James as foreman printer, Edward
Martin and John Neville (nicknamed 'Fireball') as printers, and
Jeremiah O'Farrell—one of whose hobbies was cultivating shamrocks in flower-pots with which he patriotically adorned the sills
of the windows looking on to Parliament Street—as resident caretaker. Another resident of the office was the eccentric 'Pagan'
O'Leary, specialist in swearing into the IRB Irishmen in the British
army; by night he assiduously cast home-made bullets in his room.

A young brother of James O'Connor, John, then a mere boy,
acted as office messenger. This lad was to devote his entire adult
life to secret work for the IRB, holding for many years the post
of secretary of the Supreme Council and operating from Paris,
where he led a lonely life. Thomas Irwin, a notable contemporary
poet and probably a friend of O'Leary, was appointed to the
regular editorial staff when O'Leary took over.

Others who appear to have joined soon after were George
Sigerson, who had graduated in medicine from the Queen's College,
Cork, four years earlier at the age of twenty-three; George
McMahon, a Limerick man who had been in the Queen's College,
Galway, with O'Leary and was a barrister and minor poet; Daniel
Downing of Skibbereen, another Phoenix Society man and one of
three notable brothers in the movement on both sides of the
Atlantic; Cornelius O'Mahony, William F. Roantree, the energetic
centre for Leixlip; and Cornelius Dwyer Keane, the centre for
Skibbereen. The paper's first London correspondent was Denis
Holland, whom O'Leary had first met in the Queen's College,
Cork, fourteen years earlier.

Some six weeks after his marriage, Stephens, although his paper
was still anything but firmly established, left again on a fund-
raising tour of the United States. He was to be away over five
months and to return not merely amply provided with American
cash, but also with promises—to be kept this time—of greater
financial aid than ever before. His visit followed closely on the
much publicised Fenian Fair in Chicago, which, despite episcopal
censure, proved a resounding success from both the organisational
and financial points of view.

Stephens's departure at this juncture benefited the *Irish People*.
Ably and enthusiastically assisted by Luby and Kickham, O'Leary,
now in sole control, moulded the paper to his own ideals. Previously
hampered by Stephens's dictatorial tendencies and unrealistic

schemes, it now improved rapidly in both appearance and style, and through the energetic work of Rossa soon penetrated to every one of the thirty-two counties.

Like most newspapers then and today, the format of the *Irish People* soon assumed a similar pattern each week. The cover-pages (that is, pages one, two, fifteen and sixteen) were almost invariably filled with the usual advertising matter and paid notices, while foreign news items, mostly from continental countries, occupied the few pages subsequent to page two. Then came a page or two of assorted news, including some from Irish provincial and British sources, but also containing always lengthy reports of the doings of the Fenian Brotherhood across the Atlantic.

The central pages contained from three to six leading articles of varying length, preceded every week by a column or two (in minute type) of answers to correspondents, a regular feature of contemporary periodicals. The remainder of the paper was normally filled with an assortment ranging from gossip items to births, marriages and deaths notices, but invariably preceded by a page or so of original poetry (most of it patriotic in character) and by from one to four pages of letters, from readers or correspondents in various parts of Ireland and Britain and even from the United States.

As might have been expected from a journal published on slender resources, the miscellaneous news items and other non-original matter were largely 'lifted' from other papers, but never in such a case without acknowledgement. Amongst Irish papers regularly 'milked' were the *Freeman's Journal,* the *Cork Herald,* the *Northern Whig* and the *Galway Express.* Cross-Channel papers quoted included the *Times,* the *Morning Star* and the *Economist,* while the *Boston Pilot,* the *Chicago Sentinel* and the New York *Freeman's Journal and Catholic Register* were used to provide material from the United States.

As one would expect from the organ of a movement seeking the overthrow of British rule in Ireland, the whole tone of the *Irish People* was uncompromising. In every issue of the paper, whether in calm and logical argument or in fiery bursts of invective, readers were reminded that the source of all Irish ills lay in British misgovernment through Dublin Castle. The utter futility of reliance on constitutional agitation to secure justice for Ireland was constantly emphasised, and every form of mild nationalism past and present was mercilessly lashed, the editorials being particularly severe on contemporary parliamentary agitation and its foremost exponents.

Inevitably and incessantly the all too obvious moral from these two premisses was bluntly drawn. Irishmen would never secure control of their own destinies save by preparing for the day when they would throw off the foreign yoke—not with the pen or through talk at Westminster, but by the sword, the only weapon which had ever succeeded in wringing concessions out of England.

Preparation, quiet but careful preparation, was the main theme of the editorial advice given to its readers by the *Irish People*. For a journal backed by a physical force movement based on a secret military society, the editorial columns of the paper were comparatively free from provocation. Not a line of its leaders could be regarded as direct incitement to immediate military measures; on the contrary, they went to considerable trouble to create the impression that the day for action was still distant, since it must be preceded by a prolonged period of planning so as to ensure ultimate success.

The possibility of any link between the paper and any existing secret society was strenuously and frequently denied. The attitude adopted was the strictly correct one that all criticism in Ireland of the Fenians was pointless, since the Fenians were a body that flourished in America only, and the *Irish People* was not their spokesman in any sense. As the activities of the IRB were wholly clandestine, not a single occasion arose during the life of the paper for mentioning in its pages the name of Stephens, Luby, O'Leary, Kickham, Rossa or any other leading member of the organisation.

This clearly preconceived practice was rigidly adhered to up to the late summer of 1865, when it was relaxed slightly—once or twice obviously inadvertently, but more often in order to offer serious advice to over-enthusiastic members. Not a single well-informed member of the IRB would be ignorant of the fact that, notwithstanding the editorial protestations to the contrary, the paper he read every Saturday was in everything but in name the organ of his Brotherhood. On the other hand, the public generally, by now heartily sick of parliamentary movements, would gradually come around to the view that perhaps the policy of stealth advocated by this lively new journal (surely unconnected with the Fenians since it was allowed to continue publication) might be a worthwhile alternative for patriotic Irishmen.

This deliberate discounting of the inevitability of revolutionary action in the near future may be partly traceable to the views of the editor of the *Irish People*. It is difficult to picture the scholarly O'Leary, now approaching his mid-thirties, and known to be of a gentle and chivalrous nature, as one of the leaders of a force that contemplated violent and unavoidable action on a large scale.

It is true that he firmly believed that political freedom for Ireland presupposed complete separation from England, and that he was convinced that England would yield only when force of some sort was used. It is equally true that, as a youth of eighteen and nineteen, he was unhesitatingly prepared to fight, with whatever weapons were at hand and whatever small force of men he could muster, the army of an alien occupying power. But the headstrong lad of eighteen was now a deeply read and widely travelled man of thirty-three, and it is evident, both from an analysis of his editorial pronouncements and from statements he made in later life, that force had for him a somewhat different meaning from that attached to it by men like Stephens and Rossa.

O'Leary's approach to the new movement was by no means that of a man who believed in violence as an essential step in achieving its aims. Rather to him was the principal motivating idea behind the IRB the need to create a powerful force which would convince the authorities of the coercive strength behind demands for independence, keeping the threat of violence as a sort of last resort. It appears that his study of European history had persuaded O'Leary that political independence could be attained once a united and strong public opinion was formed, supported if necessary by a body like the IRB which threatened to resort to military action if all else had failed.

Writing long afterwards of Gladstone's conversion to a policy of remedying Irish grievances, he asked sarcastically: 'Is it talking and walking that have altogether converted Mr. Gladstone, or rather something that he feels or fancies to be behind the talkers and walkers?' And, referring to events of a still later period, he commented: 'Ballot boxes, with their outcome in the shape of members, speeches, and votes, are surely of small avail save for the forces, physical and moral, that lie behind them. . . . Without that spirit which would lead men to the hill-side, either in hope or in desperation, little, if any, good can come to this or any country.' It is not without significance that (as will be seen later) it was early in 1864, with the IRB approaching its period of greatest strength, Stephens away in the United States, and Luby, O'Leary and Kickham in charge of both the organisation and the paper, that an attempt was made to get some of the most prominent constitutionalists into the movement.

To some it may appear that the *Irish People* lacked any positive policy for Irish affairs. Certainly, if by a negative attitude is meant clear and unequivocal encouragement to organise and plan for the day when British rule in Ireland would end, and to benefit from the lessons of recent Irish history and steer clear of agitations centred on Westminster or movements seeking redress for minor Irish grievances only, then admittedly the policy of the *Irish People* was frankly destructive rather than constructive.

Considering the circumstances which brought this paper into

being, it can be argued that its attitude generally could not be otherwise than negative. This was the organ of a secret society which advocated the ultimate use of force to overthrow the existing system of government. This was a journal which, in the hands of its editorial triumvirate, became a vehicle of propaganda, a means both of publicising the secret society which backed it and of converting non-members to its views.

As in the case of many a revolutionary body before and since, the main and immediate concern of its leaders was to prepare for the revolution, be it violent or peaceful; what would happen in the event of its succeeding had scarcely been considered by any of the IRB leaders. To expect a paper launched against such a background to produce many constructive ideas or to formulate plans for the future is both to credit the sponsors of the *Irish People* with foresight with which revolutionaries have rarely been endowed and to risk their being considered idealists and dreamers by supporters and potential allies alike.

All this is not to say that the *Irish People* was completely devoid of ideas. It deplored emigration and suggested that Irish men and women would be better advised to remain in Ireland and play their part in making the country more prosperous. It warned readers of the need to avoid all types of sham patriotism, whether in reading, writing or talking. It urged them to take pride in their country's past, to study contemporary politics and to form opinions without either being led by public figures who had achieved nothing or being dictated to by priests or bishops who, in the view of the *Irish People*, were unqualified to advise their flocks on political matters.

More important still is the fact that the *Irish People* paved the way for the coming struggle between landlord and tenant in rural Ireland. By the insistence in its editorial columns on the right of the people to own the land they inhabited and worked, it anticipated the ideals of the Land League by a decade-and-a-half, and prepared its readers for the campaign against the landlords and the government which would be necessary for the establishment of a tenant-farmer class in Ireland.

Notwithstanding the apathy of the one and the opposition of the other to the objectives of the Land League in their later lives, it seems clear that both Luby and O'Leary had become infected with Fintan Lalor's schemes for undoing the English conquest in Ireland through an agrarian revolution. Kickham, too, who was responsible for most of the editorials on the land question, was intensely interested in the lot of the poor Irish peasant all his life, and Stephens had returned from his continental exile frankly impressed and influenced by some of the theories of the French

A Return of the Different Persons Baild & amount
of their Several Bails accordy to the circumstances in the
Clonmel, T.R. Novr 18 1848

Names	Occupation	Amt of Bails
John OLeary	Student, J.C. &	Himself in 20 & two Sureties in 10
John Mullea	Son of a Shopkeeper	Same Rule
James England	Mason	Himself in 10 & two Sureties in 5 each
John Noonan	Gardener	Same Rule
John Walsh	Son of a Corn Buyer	Same Rule
Wm Dunne	Farmer	Same Rule to appear at Nenagh & Thurles
Maurice Walsh	Labourer	Do	Do
Patk Burke	Farmer	Himself in 10 & two Sureties in 5 each
Danl Ryan	No Trade	Same Rule
James Gan (Vespomyny)	Shoe Maker	Himself in 5 & two Sureties in 2/10 each
John Gan	Do	Shoe Maker	Same Rule
Robt McNulty	Brush Maker	Same Rule
Edwd Kinnane	Painters	Same Rule
James Sempsy (spooy)	Labourer	Same Rule
Condy Lonergan	Labourer	Same Rule
James Cunningham	Mason	Same Rule
James Brennan	Smith	Same Rule

Wm Ryan
Mor
Clonmel

4. The magistrate's list of prisoners captured
in the Wilderness affair, Clonmel, November 1848

5. Cappoquin police barracks, scene of the 1849 rising

socialists. 'The abolition of landlordism was part and parcel of the original Fenian doctrine.'[7]

Examination of the *Irish People*, especially in its first year before it really warmed up to its campaign against the parliamentary agitators and Archbishop Cullen, strongly suggests that this emphasis on the need for reform of the land tenure system was the result of a deliberate act of editorial policy. Several articles early in 1864 explained to the small farmers of Ireland how the position of the small landowner in continental countries had recently undergone substantial improvements; even the lot of the poor Russian peasant-farmer was now far better than hitherto.

A translation (which had appeared in a London paper) of a French essay on land tenure in France, where a method was in operation whereby tenants could become proprietors by a purchase instalment-system of from twenty-five to forty years, was also published. The conclusion to be drawn by Irish readers from such articles was too obvious to need stating.

At regular intervals readers were reminded that what the landlords of Ireland had was theirs only by conquest, and that a conquest backed by British rule in Ireland. The issue of 16 July 1864 contained a leader on the land system which, after remarking that 'modern landlordism . . . is not a native product of these islands', went on to tell how southern England had been parcelled out by the Norman invaders, after which the system had spread 'to every part of the three kingdoms of Ireland, Scotland and England'. Two weeks later, the issue for 30 July contained two editorials on the land system; one was entitled 'The Land for the People' and the other dealt in detail with 'that enormous evil called territorial landlordism'.

Nor was the practical revolutionary side of the matter lost sight of. Occasionally land reform was mentioned in a context suggesting that, to the editor of the *Irish People*, it equalled in importance political independence. Thus the opening sentence of the first leader in the issue for 6 February 1864 ran: 'We have insisted, over and over again, that there is but one way in which Irishmen can benefit themselves fundamentally, and that is by regaining their lost independence and at the same time reconquering the land for the people.'

An editorial for 25 June of the same year boldly advocated that 'to save herself and her people, Ireland should make herself independent, and establish a peasant proprietary. This is the sole remedial measure for Ireland.' Less frequently a leader dealing principally with land reform would close with the obvious moral being drawn. The landlords, said one such article in mid-1864, would wipe out the Irish peasantry if allowed; but would they be allowed?

On a few occasions the subject even crept into a book review or was treated in the course of an answer to a correspondent. On the whole it can be said that, while John Devoy's claim that the Land League would not have been possible without the *Irish People* seems a little exaggerated, the paper played an important part in creating the atmosphere needed for ensuring public support for the later campaign for reform of the land system.

The essence of the *Irish People* was contained in three of its features—the editorials, the answers to correspondents and the letters to the editor. Of all three, O'Leary, as both editor and one of the paper's three permanent writers, was in charge; with the first two at least he had a special personal connection. Each of the three features fulfilled a particular function to which neither of the other two was suited; in furthering the objects of the paper all three were connected and must have produced a combined impact on the reader's mind. It was no coincidence that these three features were grouped together in the principal central pages of the paper.

It is by its editorials that the *Irish People* will be best remembered. To them the student of a century later must go to ascertain what sort of a paper this was, what views it held and how it expressed them, what were its guiding principles and what it opposed. At the outset it can be said that neither before nor since the *Irish People* was published has the Irish separatist creed been so ably and so forthrightly stated as it was between 1863 and 1865 by O'Leary, Luby and Kickham.

All three proved to be talented, courageous writers, each with his own individual style of stating the case for Ireland's total separation from Britain. After Stephens's initial effort at composing editorials, hardly any appeared that were not from the pen of one of this trio; O'Leary himself said later that about ninety per cent of the paper's editorials were by the three.[8] As far as can now be judged by a comparison of their respective styles, the opening leader was in most cases the work of either Luby or Kickham, and more frequently Luby.

Luby, though inclined to be verbose by modern standards, wrote attractively and forcefully, usually drawing on Irish history for his examples and giving the impression that what he wrote came with effortless spontaneity. Often the tone of his editorial was jubilant and optimistic; when occasion required, he could also be bitingly sarcastic—as he was from time to time, for example, when dealing with the Sullivans.

Kickham, by way of strong contrast, wrote a much simpler style, often emotional in content and always directed straight at the heart of the reader. Of the three he, because of his family background, had by far the deepest insight into the mind of the typical Irishman. In particular, he understood his Irish countryman with a sympathy and intimacy that O'Leary, the son of an urban shop-keeper, and Luby, with his undeniably ascendancy origin, could never hope to equal. How close to the Irish rural dweller Kickham could come with his pen can perhaps best be judged from the steady sale, a century after its appearance, of his most popular novel, *Knocknagow*. Admirers of Kickham know also how varied were his literary talents; along with his racy, if discursive, stories he was the author of some short stirring patriotic ballads that may yet outlive his novels in popularity.

In the editorial columns of the *Irish People* the novelist and poet was also the author of some examples of political invective that are as powerful and brilliant as anything written in English in his time. In particular, his literary gifts were reserved for dealing with the onslaughts, on both the paper and the organisation behind it, by the hierarchy and the clergy; for to Kickham, as the only devout Catholic of the editorial triumvirate, was shrewdly allotted the task of writing editorials in any way critical of priest or bishop.[9]

To anyone familiar with Kickham's better known writings, these leading articles may come as a shock initially. Indeed, it is at times difficult to realise that this bold forthright language, setting out in unmistakably frank terms its writer's belief in the right of the Irish people to form their own political opinions without clerical dictation, is from the same pen that painted the tender portraits of the simple folk that peopled the Tipperary hamlet of Knocknagow. A closer look reveals the same qualities—the flair for the pungent saying, the precision of thought, the rejection of any but the simplest words to express even a lofty idea. And no-where is there a trace of scurrility.

To say that O'Leary as a leader-writer was far different from either of his colleagues is not to suggest that he was much inferior to either. The truth is that his approach to the difficult specialised task of leader-writing was totally different from theirs; so, too, was the result. As in real life so in print he was at this period a man of few words, and those words came out hesitantly and only after careful deliberate thought. Accordingly, his editorials were far shorter than those of Luby or Kickham. Moreover, they contained neither the rhetorical eloquence of Luby's nor the incisive simplicity of language of Kickham's.

What they lacked in quantity they compensated for in qualities of a different kind. Each leader by O'Leary—and it is easy to pick them out even today—is a model, self-contained sermon in political doctrine. Containing as few as half-a-dozen sentences, it is care-fully planned, carefully written and carefully revised; each sentence is deliberately formed in regard to number and choice of words.

The result is quite often a striking economy of both language and thought, with an impact as deep and lasting as that of many an editorial four times as long and twice as elaborate from Luby or Kickham.

At the same time, just as Luby's verbosity must have been the despair of many a reader, and as Kickham's verbal battles with mitred dignitaries probably shocked many a pious reader, so O'Leary's editorials on occasion suffered from similarly serious defects. Above all, he over-emphasised style at the expense of subject-matter and effect.

He was too high-brow for Irish readers of newspapers of those days; to them his literary and historical allusions were meaningless, so that the required moral was probably rarely drawn from the brief piece of abstract writing. Nevertheless, it is easy to see that O'Leary's polished leaders must have appealed to the well-educated reader and, as the paper continued to flourish, especially in Dublin and the other cities of Ireland and western and northern England, his show of learning undoubtedly helped the paper's prestige value outside the ranks of the IRB.

O'Leary, curiously enough for one with such select tastes generally, produced a more effective humorous editorial than either Luby or Kickham. Kickham rarely tried to be funny; Luby's attempts were inclined to be overdone. O'Leary, on the other hand, seemed better able to take a detached view of his opponents which permitted humour that was at the same time obvious and biting.

'Our thundering friend the *Times* comes it occasionally rather strong in the comic line,' began an editorial (clearly O'Leary's work) in the issue for 2 April 1864, 'but of course its fun is of a rather elephantine kind. . . . The Irish exodus is, perhaps of all subjects, the one most steadily regarded by the *Times* from a comic point of view. A Poland in the agonies is something found rather amusing, and the American civil war is very good fun indeed, but for a roaring laugh commend us to an article on the clearing out of the Celts.'

'You might roughly distinguish between our articles in this way,' wrote O'Leary to a friend some thirty years later, in a letter which showed that he believed his own editorials to be the best of the lot in the paper. 'All articles of two columns or so are by L; all of half a column or less are by me, while K's are nearly all of the regulation standard of about a column.' His half-brother Edmund used a somewhat different method to differentiate between the three leader-writers. According to him, one distinguished between Luby and O'Leary by assigning any leader containing 'certainly', 'indubitably' and the like to Luby, whereas a leader with 'perhaps', 'possibly' and the like came from O'Leary's pen.[10] All others presumably were Kickham's.

Of almost equal importance to the editorials for propaganda purposes were the correspondence columns of the *Irish People*. Because of their frequent local appeal they were probably more widely read, especially by the less-well-educated class of reader, and formed one of the most attractive features of the paper.

From the start this section was fully exploited by O'Leary. Topics not of nation-wide significance, and hence unsuitable for treatment in editorials, were discussed here; local controversies were publicised and the strength of the new movement in a particular part of the country was evident to every other part from the correspondence columns. Correspondents were not only freely permitted but also actively encouraged to discuss public affairs and public men; not even IRB policy, its leaders or its paper were immune from criticism in the pages of the *Irish People* reserved for letters from its eventually far-flung readership.

It is clear, too, that information from letters the general public sent in enabled the IRB leaders and the editor to gauge the impact of the organisation's policy and to act accordingly. O'Leary also put the correspondence columns to shrewd use in advancing the circulation of the paper. A careful balance was maintained in regard to the town or county of origin of each week's batch of published letters, with the obvious result that the arrival of the paper was eagerly awaited in many a town and village every Friday night.

All through the 22-month life of the *Irish People* the progress of the movement was mirrored with remarkable faithfulness by both the subject-matter and the general tone of the published letters to the editor. As the year 1865 progressed, for example, the correspondence columns filled up with views and counter-views regarding the opposition of the hierarchy to the 'Fenians' and the indignant reaction of the secret society to what its leaders and the rank-and-file felt was unwarranted condemnation of their actions and motives.

The heat and bitterness of the feelings on both sides are evident even to the reader of a century later, who may be shocked by the attacks on bishop and priest if he is unaware of the part played by the hierarchy in the discredited constitutional movements of the previous decade. That some supporters of the IRB were also perturbed by the apparent anti-clerical feelings expressed in the paper must be admitted; in fact the *Irish People* was frank enough —and strong enough—to print letters expressing such concern. On the whole, however, it seems equally clear that, as in the case of the McManus funeral and the several cases of deliberate IRB wrecking of public meetings of constitutional agitators, the bold

attitude of the organisation towards Archbishop Cullen and its
other clerical opponents convinced the public and its own supporters
of the strength of the new movement and gained for it far more
support than the society lost through the same boldness.

The premeditated use of the paper's correspondence columns is
evidenced by the fact that in many areas the most regular letter-
writer to the *Irish People* was also a leading IRB man, who invariably concealed his identity behind a pen-name. As examples of
this tendency may be mentioned three correspondents who were
by far the ablest and most effective to correspond with the editor
for the entire life of the paper. 'De L'Abbaye' and 'Hugo del Monte'
wrote from widely separated parts of Ireland; but their letters were
quite similar in approach and, to a lesser extent, in style. 'De
L'Abbaye' was James Francis Xavier O'Brien, who had studied
medicine with O'Leary, had travelled extensively abroad and was
now a prominent Cork IRB man; he was in later life to become
a well-known journalist and Nationalist MP.[11]

O'Brien had a forceful and, at times, aggressive style which held
the attention of the reader no matter what the topic. By mid-1865
O'Brien, then residing at 6 North Abbey Square, Cork, had become
the most uncompromising, not to say vicious, anti-clerical correspondent of the *Irish People*. Even O'Leary himself felt obliged on
at least one occasion to append a footnote disagreeing with a far-
fetched opinion advanced by O'Brien and stemming directly from
his strong feelings against the clergy.

'Hugo del Monte' was the appropriate nom-de-plume of one
Hugh Byrne from the village of Tinahely in county Wicklow.[12]
Trained as a teacher in Dublin, he taught for some time in a
national school in Dun Laoghaire before securing an appointment
in Singleton's Academy in Dawson Street, Dublin. A clever writer
who was more down-to-earth in his approach than O'Brien, he
occasionally used the Irish variant of his pen-name, 'Aodh an
tSleibhe', and was less inclined than O'Brien to dwell on the clerical
opposition to the movement.

A favourite device of the *Irish People* letter-writers was to relate
incidents, whether true or fictional, with a local and topical flavour,
leaving the reader to draw the obvious moral. Byrne elaborated on
this idea by inventing a so-called Laconic Club, the proceedings
of which he described in his weekly letter. The most prominent
members of this club were the leading personalities of the IRB
disguised; Stephens's period of alleged inactivity was caustically
referred to at least once.

Easily the most talented, and probably by far the most effective
of these epistolary propagandists, was 'Harvey Birch'. This
pseudonym, borrowed from a character in Fenimore Cooper's

novel *The Spy*, was used by a teacher named Thomas Dougherty Brohan (or Broughan) in O'Leary's native Tipperary town, who was next in rank in the IRB in that county to the centre, Michael O'Neill Fogarty of Kilfeacle.[13] 'Harvey Birch's' first letter appeared early in 1864 in the eighth issue of the paper; from then to the end of the paper's career he missed hardly a week without at least one brief contribution.

Brevity was one of his principal merits; but it was by no means his only one. In a deceptively simple style reminiscent of Kickham's, he contributed countless anecdotes of Irish rural life, allegedly collected by himself in the course of his travels as a pedlar through the county Tipperary, accompanied invariably by his little dog Dan, which knew a felon-setter by his unpleasant smell. Sometimes 'Harvey' confined himself to a single incident of fifteen or twenty lines; but rarely was it necessary for him to explain the moral to his readers.

A brilliant satirist, he also employed sarcasm with devastating effect. Thus in the issue for 2 April 1864 he recalled a game he used to play as a schoolboy, when he and his companions invented new words, the winner being he whose word contained most letters. In a pastoral just issued, went on the letter, Archbishop Cullen said: 'I shall now merely add one word of caution against secret societies.' But, remarked 'Harvey', that one word occupied more than a column of print in the *Morning News*.

Unpolished and trivial many of Brohan's letters may appear at first glance; but a more careful look reveals the work of a remarkably shrewd and skilful propagandist, whose frequently brief contributions must have made a more lasting impact than many a letter three times their length and erudition. It is probable, too, that Brohan used more than one pen-name. For instance, the style and approach of letters which appeared a few times under the names 'Tipperary Boy' and 'Davy Druhan' (also from Tipperary) are so similar to Brohan's that it is difficult to avoid concluding that these too are the work of 'Harvey Birch'. Or perhaps it may have been a decision of O'Leary to change the name deliberately.

Other prominent letter-writers whose identities have survived include Dr. John T. Campion (who called himself—accurately— 'The Kilkenny Man') and Arthur Forrester (who wrote under 'William Tell' and 'Angus'), both of whom will be mentioned later amongst the poets of the *Irish People*, as well as Thomas O'Donnell O'Callaghan ('Libertas' of Kilmallock), a cousin of the literary brothers Robert Dwyer Joyce and Patrick Weston Joyce; and John Devoy, who sent some letters from Naas under a pen-name that cannot be identified.

The weekly column headed 'Answers to Correspondents' had a

somewhat different and more long-term objective. Here there was little scope for comments of a political nature, though when opportunities for such views did present themselves they were capably used. A couple of readers who asked for reading-matter on military treatises and books on warlike weapons naturally got full answers. Another who innocently asked about the hostility towards A. M. and T. D. Sullivan provoked a typical IRB account of the feud. Female readers were urged to plan for, rather than to dream about, the national cause. Occasional queries calling for comments on priests who had opposed the movement were not disappointed either, though on a few occasions O'Leary declined either to enter into private quarrels or to comment on inadequately proved statements.

This column also served other miscellaneous purposes. For example, it appears to have been used occasionally to send disguised messages to IRB men outside Dublin. And in the issue for 15 July 1865 the decision of a well-known Dublin publisher to refuse to supply review copies of books was scathingly criticised. Assuming that the reason was because 'a notice of Banim's recent novel was not eulogistic enough', O'Leary asked: 'Has he (i.e. the publisher) been in the habit of buying praise from other papers by gifts of books?'—and ended scornfully by saying that 'all the books in Mr. Duffy's shop would not buy one line of undeserved praise from us'.

To O'Leary the 'Answers to Correspondents' was primarily a section of the literary department, to which also belonged the pages containing original poetry and articles. As one who had stumbled on Irish nationalism through the writings of Davis, it was only natural that he should hold strong views on the type of reading and writing fit for patriotic Irish people. Sentimental poetry like that of Moore, for example, to which (in O'Leary's opinion) patriotism was merely incidental, he had little time for.

Poems on abstract topics which tended to infuse genuine national feeling into their readers, and poems of stirring events which preached action or encouraged defiance—these above all he advocated. To get them for his paper he was ruthlessly blunt in the answers he gave to correspondents sending in contributions. He told them what authors to read, and what subjects to avoid; he criticised with brutal frankness poor writing, but encouraged any signs of talent, often picking out a single verse and emphasising its special merits. At one stage in 1864, he appealed for old local ballads of '98 and several good examples were sent in, which he duly published.

Examination of this column shows clearly that O'Leary considered each poetic contribution individually; it is also evident that

many contributors took the advice proferred and submitted more
and better writing later. On a few occasions the column was
honoured—inadvertently, one suspects—by having poems published
there by one of the better-known authors normally appearing on
the literary page. Although the result of his work was unconven-
tionally refreshing, for a busy editor to undertake single-handed
this task of cultivating the literary powers of his readers, many of
them obviously not well educated, was a thankless task.

There are indications that it tried the editor's patience at times.
'Nine-tenths of these effusions are patriotic,' he wrote in the issue
for 3 February 1864. 'They usually commence by addressing "green
Erin", or "dear Erin", or "poor Erin"; and after fifteen or sixteen
stanzas—in which "tore" always rhymes to "gore", and "crag" to
"flag" and "sheen" to "green"—we find the poets asking her . . .
to succour her woe-stricken mother, a very odd thing to expect
Erin to do . . . "Liberty" does not rhyme with "nativity", and
when one line has thirteen short syllables, and the next fifteen long
ones, they usually won't scan.'

Some few weeks of more sympathetic advice followed, until in
the issue for 16 April the harassed editor again gave vent to his
feelings. To 'R. O'C.' he replied: 'Your verses must wait till you
can put some sense as well as sound into them. If "A brooklet 'mid
the copsewood shone with adamantine gloss" it did a very high-
sounding thing indeed, but what that thing was the Lord only
knows.'

For its literary reputation the *Irish People* could—though it need
not—rely almost entirely on its poetry. 'It contained literature of
a very high character,' said that very unrevolutionary Irish nationalist, Isaac Butt.[14] Unfortunately the achievement of the paper in
this direction has been wholly forgotten, the poetic output of its
more distinguished predecessor the *Nation* having completely overshadowed the work of O'Leary in this field.

One serious disadvantage from which the *Irish People* has suffered
is the absence of any collection of poems which first appeared in its
pages; one cannot point to any single volume of poetry and say:
'The *Irish People* gave us that.' In the famous *Spirit of the Nation*
on the other hand Davis's paper has built up a solid but partly
unjustified reputation for its poetry, for some of the poetry associated
with the Young Ireland movement never appeared in the *Nation*,
which published a good deal of poor and immature verse.

Considering the much shorter life of the *Irish People*, and bearing in mind that it was principally a propaganda machine and was
not built around any established literary circle, its achievement in
the field of poetry is remarkable. From the start it attracted a
number of talented poets, some of whose work is justly popular

a century later. In its almost total failure to attract any new poetesses of merit it fell short of the *Nation's* achievement. On the whole, however, its poetical columns were far more exclusive than those of the *Nation*, and issue for issue its poetry was of a much higher standard than that in Davis's paper.

As for its contemporaries, both the quality and quantity of poetry published in either Sullivan's *Nation* or Pigott's *Irishman* were negligible in comparison. Amongst its contemporaries in Britain, all of which must have abhorred its political views, no less distinguished a journal than the *Pall Mall Gazette* openly praised the poetic content of the *Irish People*. For all this most of the credit goes to O'Leary, whose high standards and contacts with literary men made the poetry page of his paper a really high-class section of the paper.

Foremost amongst the poets of the *Irish People* ranks Robert Dwyer Joyce, some of whose ballads, such as 'The Boys of Wexford' and 'Fineen the Rover', are still widely sung or recited in rural Ireland. A Limerick man, he was a teacher in early life, graduated in medicine in the Queen's College, Cork, in 1862, became Professor of English Literature in the Catholic University in 1865, and emigrated to Boston in 1866, where he practised medicine until shortly before his death in Dublin in 1883. A brother of the prolific historical writer P. W. Joyce, Robert Dwyer Joyce was always on the fringe of the extreme nationalist movement, though not apparently a member of the IRB.

His co-operation with O'Leary was itself a striking tribute to the paper. From being 'Feardana' of the *Nation* he transferred his allegiance overnight to the *Irish People*, where he became 'Merulan'. O'Leary received from him a large manuscript of unpublished poems of varying quality, at least a dozen of which appeared in the first volume of the paper. Later, when residing in the United States, Joyce attained a remarkable popularity, one of his books selling 10,000 copies in a week. O'Leary, always a keen judge of literary style, once remarked of him that he was the most objective of poets writing in English since Scott.

Easily the most frequently recurring pen-name in the poetry page of the *Irish People* is 'Spes', which concealed the identity of a man who provided a living link between the *Irish People* and the first issue of the *Nation* twenty-one years previously. Dr. John T. Campion of Kilkenny was one of the earliest of the *Nation* poets; later his poems appeared in other nationalist organs of different hues. At least thirty hitherto unpublished poems of his appeared in the *Irish People*, some of them clearly hurriedly composed and consequently unpolished in style. In addition Campion contributed a long serialised biography of Michael Dwyer, the '98 hero of Wicklow.

Probably the next most prolific poets of the *Irish People* were 'T I' and 'Kilmartin'. The first was Thomas Caulfield Irwin, one of the most widely acclaimed Irish poets of his time and in the 1880s considered second only to the young Yeats as a writer of so-called fairy poetry. A doctor's son from Warrenpoint, Irwin had travelled extensively abroad as a youth and then joined the *Irish People* staff. Like Sigerson he was never an IRB man.

The second was John Walsh, a Cappoquin man who taught for most of his life in the town of Cashel and is buried on the Rock of Cashel. A brother-in-law of Michael Cavanagh of the Fenian Brotherhood, whom O'Leary had met in New York in 1859, Walsh was for many years the most popular poet in the south of Ireland, some of his verses fully justifying his reputation. Like Joyce he, too, changed his patronage from the *Nation*.

'Conaciensis' concealed the identity of a gifted Dublin tailor, Mathew F. Hughes, another *Nation* contributor. John Francis O'Donnell, a former editor of the *Tipperary Examiner* and a journalist in London in the 1880s, wrote poems which bore the pen-name 'Monckton West' and 'P. Monks'. O'Donnell, who contributed poetry to the *Kilkenny Journal* at the age of fourteen, died in 1874 aged only forty-seven, and was so highly thought of by his contemporaries in London that they erected a monument over his grave in Kensal Green cemetery and had a collection of his poems published posthumously.

Amongst four poetesses of the *Irish People*, O'Leary's own sister Ellen was undoubtedly the best. Some of her output is of a higher standard than that of many of the poets contributing to the paper. A year younger than John, she had previously (like their brother Arthur) contributed to the *Nation* when Gavan Duffy was its editor; shortly after her death much later in the century John arranged for the publication of a selection of her poems. In the *Irish People* she usually used the pen-name 'Eily', changing to 'Lenel' (an anagram of her own Christian name) on a couple of occasions.

'Mary' of the *Irish People* was 'Mary' of the *Nation* and of Mitchel's *United Irishman*, Ellen Mary Patrick Downing.[15] Born in Cork city in 1828, she contributed over forty poems to Davis's paper, and was engaged to Joseph Brenan, the '48 revolutionary with whom O'Leary had plotted. Later she was in turn a nun and a nurse in her native city before dying there in 1869. Like Ellen O'Leary she was a devout Catholic, and religious themes figured prominently in many of their poems.

Religion formed no part of the subject-matter of the poems of two more poetesses of the *Irish People*. At infrequent intervals a well-dressed American lady, quite unlike an IRB supporter, visited

the paper's offices in Parliament Street, accompanied by her young
daughter, not much more than ten years old, and a son somewhat
older. At correspondingly infrequent intervals a poem would
appear in the paper under the name 'Aleria'. 'Aleria' concealed
the identity of this talented young girl; she was none other than
Fanny Parnell, the founder seventeen years later of the Central
Land League of the Ladies of Ireland, her mother about the same
time having become president of the Ladies Land League of New
York. The older brother who went with their mother to deliver
their sister's manuscripts was not, it has to be admitted, Charles
Stewart Parnell. 'Cliodhna', who had at least nine poems published
in the second volume of the paper, was O'Donovan Rossa's third
wife, Mary Jane; since her maiden name was Irwin, she occasionally signed poems 'M.J.I.'

Several other poetic contributors to O'Leary's paper deserve
mention, not so much for the quality of their contributions to that
paper as for their later reputations either as poets elsewhere or in
other walks of life. A solitary poem signed 'Patrick Henry' was
by Dr. George Sigerson, who at his death in 1925 must have been
the last survivor of the staff of the *Irish People*. Charles Kickham
wrote a few poems for the paper also under the initial 'C'; one
was a clever and effective Fenian version of the 'Soggarth Aroon',
in which the clergy are castigated for their recent desertion of the
national cause.

O'Leary's cousin Mary Anne Kelly ('Eva' of the *Nation*) wrote
only one poem for the paper; it was in the issue for 26 August 1865.
Joseph I. C. Clarke, then a civil servant in London but later editor,
in turn, of two famous New York newspapers, had his first poem
published in the *Irish People*; another poet of the *Irish People* to
succeed in American journalism was Arthur Forrester, a Monaghan
man then an IRB arms agent in Manchester—a position in which
he was succeeded by a young Mayo emigrant named Michael
Davitt.

John Locke of Callan, the popular Kilkenny poet, and O'Donovan
Rossa himself also had poems published in the IRB paper, Locke
under 'The Southern Gael' and Rossa under the easily identifiable
pen-name 'Jer'. Locke also contributed letters under the pseudonym
'Vi et Armis'. 'The Galtee Boy' was John Sarsfield Casey of
Mitchelstown, a popular patriotic writer. At the age of seventeen
or eighteen Michael Davitt had poems published in the *Irish
People* under a pen-name not now known.[16]

To O'Leary his period as editor of the *Irish People* was by far
the biggest event of his life, 'summing up, in a sense', as he remarked
thirty years later, 'all that has gone before and directly leading to
nearly everything that has come after'. His discovery and study

of Davis's writings convinced him of the need for a literary side
to any future national movement; his experience of the collapse
of the '49 movement converted him for life to the idea of a secret
revolutionary society.

Given these two basic assumptions, it was inevitable that he
should enter enthusiastically into the running of the IRB paper.
His education, his mature judgement and his critical capacity all
combined to make him an ideal editor. Although, unlike Luby,
lacking any practical journalistic experience save for that gained
during his brief period on the New York *Phoenix* in 1859, his wide
reading of literature, his long study of the contemporary press and
his views on the power and use of the printed word all ensured
that he approached his task in the *Irish People* with carefully thought
out and clearly defined ideas of what such a paper should be like.

In the result the paper in its essential features bore his unmistakable stamp. To some it doubtless over-emphasised matters
literary at the expense of things revolutionary; to more it probably
affected too many of the features of the press of a nation from
which the society backing the paper was so anxious to sever all
connections. But the *Irish People* served its purpose well as a vehicle
of propaganda. It strengthened an already strong national movement, impressed all its opponents and weakened some; and these,
after all, were what counted no less to O'Leary than to Stephens
and his lieutenants.

John Devoy, who himself spent a large part of a long life editing
papers which preached Fenianism, said in 1907 that 'O'Leary
possessed to a high degree the peculiar faculties of judgement and
decision which an editor requires'.[17] This view, from one who did
not lavishly bestow praise, is confirmed by a study of the files of
the *Irish People*. Kickham, when recalling his *Irish People* days
some years later, called O'Leary 'the Bayard of journalism'—
though it might be remarked that O'Leary at times lacked one of
the characteristics of the chivalrous knight of mediaeval France,
his uncanny knowledge of his opponents' weaknesses.[18]

Of O'Leary's private life while editor little is known. He barely
mentioned the subject in his memoirs; none of his principal
colleagues in the venture is more informative. Clearly, apart from
the carefree days of his childhood, this must have been the happiest
period of a long life that was not to be without its periods of hard-
ship, disappointment and loneliness. After years of aimless travel
and unmethodical study he had now found an ideal outlet for his
talents; unexpectedly his long period of reading of literature and
history was to be put to good use advocating the independence of
his country.

Subsequent to 1849 he had, it appears, taken a conscientious objection to all forms of oath and, on the formation of the IRB, had insisted on being absolved from both taking and administering its oath. Notwithstanding this stipulation, his lack of faith in the movement's success and his anti-republican leanings, here he was in his early thirties occupying a trusted position in the inner councils of the IRB, and editor of a paper that was, in fact if not in name, the society's organ.

His longstanding acquaintance with Luby he now renewed, while with Mulcahy (whom he had known since '49 in Tipperary) and Kickham, he strengthened the foundations of what were to prove lifelong friendships. Despite a diversity of both family background and religious belief, the fact that all four had connections with the same part of the country must have helped to strengthen the team-spirit among these permanent members of the new paper's editorial staff. More important was the complete identity of political opinions amongst all four.

Despite the hard work which the weekly production of a paper of such size and quality must have entailed, it is evident that O'Leary found time for a pleasant social life. Every Thursday night, after the paper had gone to press, the literary staff all repaired to O'Leary's lodgings at 16 Palmerston Place, off Middle Mountjoy Street. Here in his two-roomed first-floor bachelor lodgings many convivial hours passed in discussion of the week's events, of literature and, above all, of the progress of the paper itself. Kickham, Luby and Mulcahy were regular attenders at these nocturnal sessions which often lasted well into the middle of the night; George Sigerson came, too, and so did Stephens himself on some occasions.

O'Leary's sister Ellen and his half-sister Mary, who frequently visited Dublin at this period, often joined the group; so did his half-brother and fellow-lodger Edmund, then a medical student in the city. Some of O'Leary's cousins, the Kellys from Headford, were also in town, and O'Leary even took to theatre-going, a practice he abandoned altogether in later life. When General F. F. Millen of the Fenian Brotherhood visited Ireland in the summer of 1865 O'Leary joined in outings to the Wicklow mountains; and an amusing account has survived of a convivial party held by the IRB leaders when admirers of Rossa sent some wild fowl from Cape Clear.

Nor was he apparently averse to entertaining visitors to the city; for example, J. F. X. O'Brien thanked him by letter for showing round Dublin, early in 1864, some of his family. He even managed to get in a holiday in London in the summer of 1864, when he did the social round for another brief period. He renewed his friendship with Whistler, Poynter and du Maurier, the last of whom was now on the staff of *Punch*. In Whistler's rooms he made a new friend in Alfred Stevens, a leading artist in metal, who had won the competition for the monument over Wellington's tomb in St. Paul's Cathedral.

Two letters to O'Leary from Whistler during this vacation have survived. One briefly but effectively gives the atmosphere of O'Leary's visit. From 7 Lindsey Row, Old Battersea Bridge, Chelsea, on 21 August 1864, came this invitation: 'Dear John— Just got back. *Do* come to-night—tea and coffee and smoke and lots to tell you. Jim Whistler.' The 'lots to tell' included news of new paintings of the Thames and other scenes done in Holland.

Moreover, although he took almost no part in the military work of the IRB, O'Leary is known to have attended some of its meetings, and, since the *Irish People* office became a regular port of call for country members, he must also have got to know at least a cross-section of the membership. As might have been expected, he did not neglect his reading; Devoy later recalled that he had never seen O'Leary either going into or coming out of the *Irish People* office without a book in his hand.

A copy of a photograph of Luby, Mulcahy and O'Leary taken at this period, and preserved for many years in New York by Joseph Denieffe, one of the earliest IRB men, has survived. O'Leary is easily the most striking of the three, a tall, lean, handsome man, with long black hair and a thick, short black beard, unusually slender hands and fingers, somewhat better dressed than either of his colleagues, in a more conservative style of coat, and looking directly at the camera with a steady penetrating stare.

As a commercial venture it is clear that the *Irish People* was not a success; '. . . we could barely, and by almost incredible efforts,' wrote Stephens to O'Mahony in December 1864, 'succeed in bringing out the paper from week to week.' To begin with, despite a steady flow of advertisements all during its career, the paper was constantly short of money in all its other departments. Then, as today, any Irish newspaper needed a good circulation if it was to survive economically.

In the case of the *Irish People*, while no really reliable figures have been recorded, it does not seem that its weekly circulation ever exceeded 10,000, and a later estimate of 30,000 cannot be regarded as reliable. Even this was a fairly creditable achievement for the period, although one critical member of the staff said ten years after its demise that, given an efficient organisation, it should have sold 20,000 copies a week; that, in fact, was the figure Stephens himself had predicted in his letter to O'Leary back in August 1863.

The commercial end of the venture was handicapped in several respects, not least by the probable inefficiency of the critic just mentioned. Rossa, it is true, seems to have taken his job as manager very seriously. He travelled all over Ireland canvassing orders, using the organisation which Stephens had built up in the preceding five years. Agencies were established in all the major towns and cities, not only in Ireland but in England and Scotland; London, Leeds and Chesterfield all had agents, and Liverpool alone had no fewer than eighteen, while subscribers paid from as distant a place as the Channel Islands.

After some initial lapse the paper was registered for foreign transmission, and a scrutiny of lists of subscribers which appeared intermittently in the paper's early period shows that it had a respectable circulation in the United States and Canada. As might have been expected, the Fenian Brotherhood supported the paper in the United States; a circular has survived in which John O'Mahony urged support for 'our Irish organ' and suggested the formation of 'clubs of subscribers . . . wherever possible'.

It was on Dublin and rural Ireland, of course, that the paper had to depend for the bulk of its circulation; and in this respect the evidence suggests that the results varied widely as between the capital and the rest of Ireland. A glance at the commercial advertisements shows that in Dublin the *Irish People* at once took on and was soon widely read each week by all classes of the population. Amongst regular advertisers who could hardly be suspected of having IRB sympathies were the Dublin Gas Company, the Sick and Indigent Roomkeepers Society, the Royal Bank of Ireland, and Arnotts' drapery store.

It is not surprising to learn that the paper's subscribers' lists were later found to contain names like Parnell and Butt.[19] What is astonishing is that it was not apparently considered *infra dig.* for either bodies patronised by Archbishop Cullen himself or for high officials of Dublin Castle to insert advertisements and similar notices in this allegedly seditious, anti-religious and socialistic production.

Down the country the position appears to have been different. It is true that even there clergymen, and others not then noted for a nationalist outlook, were known to be regular readers of the *Irish People*; but what was disastrous from the paper's point of view was the extent to which a single copy of the paper was passed round. The arrival of the train from Dublin on Friday nights was eagerly awaited in many a town or village as the progress of a particular local controversy was being followed; but the rate of literacy was still such that it was necessary for one man to read aloud for the benefit of a dozen or more.

During Rossa's prolonged absences from Dublin the commercial department was in the hands of James O'Connor, who appears to have been anything but businesslike. He admitted in 1874,

when writing anonymously for a Dublin paper, that great care-
lessness was evident in the conduct of the business affairs of the
office—for which he was responsible for long periods.

Moreover, it seems certain that in a large number of cases no
real effort was made to ensure that subscribers to the paper paid up.
John Devoy, who was the *Irish People* agent in Naas, got twenty-
five copies of the paper for a start, all of which he gave away free;
later his quota went up to fifty, but still he was never asked to
pay.[20] This casual practice may have been partly justifiable,
since the paper was principally published for propaganda
purposes; but it hardly helped to put it on a sound financial
basis.

Undoubtedly the most serious check to the success of the *Irish
People* in the commercial sphere was the combined opposition of
Church and State. The Church has been mentioned first, for it is
probably from that quarter that the most effective opposition came.
The paper was only a few weeks old when clearly co-ordinated
action against it began by clergy in all parts of the country and in
Britain. Men were first urged, and then warned, not to read the
paper, both from the pulpit and also in private conversation.

They were questioned on the matter in the confessional, where
the answer to the question obviously entered into the decision of
the confessor on whether his parishioner was or was not a 'Fenian';
a penance frequently imposed in Kilkenny was that the penitent
should refrain in future from reading the *Irish People*. They were
preached at, on the topic, by distinguished visiting clergy during
retreats and missions; in September 1864, for example, an English
clergyman told a congregation in Dublin that it was a mortal sin
to read the *Irish People*!

The occasional stout-hearted supporter of the IRB or the loyal
officer of the Brotherhood who dared either to argue or to refuse
to sever his odious connection was warned of the consequences,
culminating in eternal damnation. If a man showed no fear of his
prospects in the next world, then his livelihood was threatened.
The local *Irish People* agent was in many places approached by his
priest and pressed to cease selling the paper; in such a case the
consequences of a refusal to comply must have been obvious to
every shopkeeper.

On visitations to private houses and in conversations in the
street the sinful implications of association with the paper were
constantly emphasised. Rossa, by then married for the third time,
mentions a priest in county Antrim who assured his flock that the
manager of this dreadful paper was now living with his ninth wife.
And all the time these tactics were powerfully supported and given
implicit approval by the utterances of high ecclesiastics, and

especially by the frequent pastoral statements of Archbishop Cullen of Dublin.

From the civil authorities, too, as was only to be expected in all the circumstances, attempts were continually made to prevent the paper from being a success. The IRB, to give one example referred to by Devoy in his memoirs, was not slow to appreciate the advantage of having the teaching profession on its side; so teachers regularly received free copies of the *Irish People*. The government, however, retaliated by warning teachers not to have anything to do with the paper, and when met with wholesale refusals threatened dismissals. In fact, many such dismissals took place of both male and female teachers who insisted on patronising the *Irish People*.

Apart from teachers, others in official positions who dared to read the paper also had pressure put on them. All over the country agents of the *Irish People* were specially singled out for intimidation by the authorities, which at times produced the opposite effect from that desired.

Nor were the clergy and the civil authorities averse to co-operating with each other in trying to prevent the spread of the paper. Rossa gives one example of a priest in county Waterford who successfully objected before the local magistrate to certain publicans obtaining renewals of their licences—on the ground that they sold not only liquor but also the *Irish People* on the premises. In the circumstances it seems obvious that the paper would not have succeeded at all but for the strength of the local branches of the IRB in most areas. Stephens had done his work well.

With the progress, if not the existence, of the *Irish People* hampered in these various ways it is not surprising that the going was hard for the editorial and commercial staff at times. O'Leary never received one penny of a salary, being satisfied to rely on his modest private income from house property in Tipperary. No doubt he lived frugally then as he certainly did years later even when his income was considerably higher.

Presumably the other members of the editorial staff received some sort of payment, however small and irregular; how much is not now known. John Haltigan's salary as printer was £150 a year and Rossa's as manager £112; in addition, both got expenses for IRB work entailing travel out of Dublin. 'We have established the *People* for a purpose independent of money making,' wrote Rossa to a friend, 'and connection with it is not a labour of love or profit to any of the staff.'

O'Leary, unbusinesslike all his life, confined his activities to the editorial section and left the commercial department to itself. In retrospect this may have been a pity; for, since he was always a shrewd judge of human character, it is possible that he might have had doubts about a certain over-pious paper-folder named Nagle who, though his duties required his attendance only one day a week, seems to have been given the run of the office—with what were to prove disastrous consequences for the entire IRB. It also looks as if O'Leary had for some months to undertake more than his share of the work, for he once accused Luby of having neglected his editorial duties for six months.

Stephens, it will be recalled, had started the *Irish People* for the purpose of putting his secret society in funds. Every circle, every member, it was argued, would buy a paper which he knew came from the top ranks of the IRB. Moreover, the wide emotional support which the Brotherhood undoubtedly had would also ensure a good sale among the general public. Money would flow into the secret coffers of the IRB, which would use it to spread the organisation still further.

But things worked out far differently. Instead of the *Irish People* supplying the IRB with money, the IRB had constantly to supply the *Irish People* with cash to prevent its disappearance overnight, and from a financial viewpoint the paper became a drag on the society's resources. There was always a shortage of money from the start; from the first week of the paper to its last a heavy loss was incurred, and every week the deficit (or so much of it as had then to be met) was made up from the general funds of the IRB itself.

During the first six months or so there was a continuous struggle to keep the paper alive, and by far the biggest burden fell on O'Leary as editor and Rossa as manager. Rossa was obliged to pay the current expenses for the first month or so out of his own pocket, until the initial payments for advertisements began to arrive.

But if the editorial staff was short of money, such a state of affairs was not tolerated by the printers. Christmas 1863 was a critical period; the scarcity of money was unusually acute and panic seized the printers. On Christmas Eve they downed tools and informed the management that no more work would be done till their wages were met. It was time now for panic to seize the management; Stephens pawned his own and his wife's clothes and his colleagues made similar sacrifices.

These same printers, it might be added, had a shorter working week than most Dublin printers of their day; and for this they received—perhaps inclusive of some element of danger-money for working for revolutionaries—half-a-crown a week more than any Irish printing house at the time gave to its employees. Moreover, they did not have to do all stages of the printing, for the office was not fully equipped. Every Thursday night when the type had been set it was locked in formes and carried to the printing premises, in Essex Street, of Mr. Pattison Jolly, a loyal (but enterprising) subject of Her Majesty, who completed the printing processes of this avowedly revolutionary organ. As the papers rolled off the presses they were taken, 500 at a time, back to Parliament Street for parcelling.

After this last crisis Kickham (not Stephens, be it noted, presumably because of the strained feelings still persisting between himself and O'Mahony) penned a desperate plea to New York for funds. The Fenian Brotherhood rose generously to the occasion, and sufficient cash for several months was speedily despatched across the Atlantic and safely into 12 Parliament Street. But by January 1865 the organisation's assets totalled only £112, according to Stephens.

After the authorities in Dublin Castle, the principal opponents of the IRB in its early days were the Church and the constitutionalist nationalists. Since the power of the nationalists had declined considerably by the late 1850s, and as the secret operations of the IRB made it difficult for the government to counteract the Brotherhood's activities by positive measures, the Church quickly became the most formidable obstacle the secret society had to contend with.

As early as the first half of 1862 strong statements had been made on the so-called Fenians by several Irish bishops. At a three-day conference of the archbishops and bishops of Ireland held in Dublin in May 1862 the resolutions passed included one warning Catholics against all combinations, whether oath-bound or otherwise, 'and especially those that have for their object to (*sic*) spread a spirit of revolution'. At its August meeting in the same year the Hierarchy condemned even the milder and non-secret Brotherhood of Saint Patrick for tendencies similar to those of the IRB.

The teaching of the Catholic Church on secret societies is clear and simple; its attack on such bodies has been two-pronged. First, it prohibits Catholics absolutely from membership of the Freemasons and other societies of the same kind which plot against Church or State, breach of this rule involving automatic excommunication. In the case of the IRB and the Fenian Brotherhood this ban was not expressly imposed until 1870.

Secondly, a less serious prohibition is applied by the Church to societies whose secrecy about their affairs prevents the Church from exercising what it regards as its right to be informed about such matters in the interests of Catholics, or to societies which, though not secret, are seditious in character because their methods are subversive or disruptive of public order. The popular misconception that an oath of secrecy is necessary to incur the censure of Rome appears to have been as widely held a century ago as it is today, for Stephens and Luby wasted some considerable time and ingenuity between 1858 and 1861 modifying the IRB oath for the misguided purpose of transforming the society into a military body having what they claimed was merely a simple pledge of obedience—all to no avail, as the various episcopal utterances of 1862 clearly showed.

In these circumstances a clash was inevitable between the *Irish People*, as the *de facto* organ of the seditious society against which Irish Catholics had been warned, and Archbishop Cullen of Dublin, from whose diocese the paper was published and who had constituted himself the spokesman of the Hierarchy in its campaign to render ineffective Stephens and his followers. That the controversy when it broke raged with some ferocity on both sides need not occasion much surprise. What is curious is the length of time it took for the battle of words to develop; not until late in 1864, when episcopal critics themselves entered the field of parliamentary agitation, did the *Irish People* train all its editorial guns on Archbishop Cullen, the power behind the new movement.

Although the greater part of a year elapsed before his name appeared frequently in the paper's editorial and correspondence columns, the enigmatic figure of Paul Cullen stands in the background of every issue of this paper. Born in 1802, Ireland's first cardinal came of prosperous Kildare farming stock who—John Devoy's contrary assertions notwithstanding—had been staunchly nationalist for generations; an uncle of Cullen had been hanged as a rebel in '98. Educated in the same Quaker-run rural non-denominational school which produced Edmund Burke, and in the same Catholic boys' college, Carlow, as his future antagonist John O'Leary, Cullen was sent to Rome as a boy of eighteen to study for the priesthood.

Here he was to remain for almost thirty years, becoming first a professor and then Rector of the College of Propaganda, and finally Rector of the Irish College. In 1849 he returned to Ireland as Archbishop of Armagh, whence he was transferred to the archdiocese of Dublin in 1852 on the death of Archbishop Murray.

Always recognised as a leading figure in the Church of his period, Cullen's stature as a churchman has grown as study of the Vatican Council of 1870, in which he played a leading part, has intensified. Equally, however, as research into Irish history of Cullen's period progresses, his various incursions into Irish political affairs become the more difficult to understand and almost impossible to defend. But it is clear that his Roman training and his experience of Italian politics coloured his outlook on political matters for the rest of his life.

He was in Rome during the revolution of 1848, when the Pope was forced to flee his capital for several months. In February 1849 the Papal government was abolished and a republic set up, which ended only the following July with the surrender of the city to the French army and the restoration of the Papal State. Cullen at this time was a supporter of Daniel O'Connell and, since these events in Italy coincided with the rise in Ireland of the Young Ireland group, he seems to have regarded the latter as the Irish counterpart of the Young Italy movement under Mazzini. The distrust between Cullen and Gavan Duffy proved lifelong, and an Irish bishop had only to express mild nationalist or agrarian views for Cullen to class him as a Young Irelander on the spot.

Towards secret societies he showed a particular hatred. Whilst his admittedly unfavourable experience of their work in Italy may have caused this, he blindly, and on insufficient evidence, assumed that the aims of Irish secret societies were the same as those on the continent. Only after the Fenian trials of 1865 and 1866 did he relent, somewhat belatedly, and admit (but only in private) that the IRB leaders were not as evil as their continental counterparts.

He was obsessed with the idea that secrecy bred informers; on several occasions he stated incorrectly that the movements of both '98 and '48 had been ruined by traitors. He was convinced that success for either Young Ireland or the IRB would have greatly harmed the Catholic faith in his country. He delighted in pointing out to his clergy and flock that the IRB leadership was composed partly of Unitarians and Presbyterians; he repeatedly—again without any evidence—alleged that its proceedings were attended by drunkenness and dissipation. Cullen's enmity of the IRB was indeed deep and bitter and unthinking, and it forced him to words and deeds that are otherwise inexplicable.

On the other hand, the IRB leaders cannot have expected the Archbishop to view their new journal with anything approaching approval. This, they must have reflected, was the man who had strenuously backed the constitutional movement of the 1850s, the man who, in the view of both Gavan Duffy and Archbishop McHale, was largely to blame for the treachery of Sadlier and Keogh. This, too, was the man who had closed the doors of his churches on the remains of the '48 survivor, McManus, and who subsequently led the episcopal offensive against their new national movement.

It is not surprising to find that, almost from its first issue, the *Irish People* was ready to cope with this formidable opponent. Its editorial strategy was simple but effective. The Hierarchy and the clergy, while to be respected as clerical leaders, would be resisted in any attempt to influence—much less participate in—political affairs. Two months after the paper had come to an abrupt end Luby, in a speech from the dock of Green Street courthouse, said:

'The *Irish People* said (they should) . . . reverence the priests as long as they confined themselves to sacerdotal functions . . . the priest from the altar is deserving of all reverence, but when he descends into the political arena he becomes no more than any other man. . . . The *Irish People* taught the people that they should not give up their consciences in secular matters to the clergy.'

In retrospect it seems a naive approach, but it was not merely obviously successful but also was adopted by, and appealed to, more than the IRB and its supporters. Perhaps the paper's success in warding off the onslaughts of Archbishop Cullen may be largely attributed to the fact that the actual implementation of the editorial policy on clerical interference in politics was left by the editorial triumvirate in the capable hands of the only one of them who was a practising Catholic.

Luby, the child of what a later age calls a mixed marriage, was a non-churchgoing but broadminded Protestant who leaned sharply towards Rome for long periods of his life. O'Leary, whose incipient anti-clerical feelings of 1848 had grown in intensity ever since, appears by 1864 to have ceased practising his religion. Indeed, his appearance at Stephens's wedding was to prove his last unequivocal act of adherence to Rome for over forty years; his eccentric views on religion seem to have been widely known in contemporary literary Dublin. There remained the devout but courageous Kickham to handle this delicate problem, and if his treatment of Cullen was firm it totally lacked bitterness—something that cannot be said of all Cullen's own statements on the IRB.

To anyone expecting an immediate and open clash between Archbishop Cullen and the *Irish People* the first ten months or so of the newspaper proved something of an anti-climax. It is true that mild anti-clerical views are to be found here and there. An early issue contained an unnecessarily harsh comment by O'Leary on a 'harmony of feeling between Catholic priest and Orange scribbler' in a Carlow controversy referred to by a correspondent; a defiant letter from a well-known Cork IRB man to his bishop was given considerable prominence; and a stern pastoral of Cullen in May 1864, clearly aimed at the IRB, was sarcastically dealt with in the paper's editorial columns.

Perhaps most pertinent of all, the paper from the close of 1863 organised public gifts and cash subscriptions on a national scale for the great forthcoming Irish National Fair due to be held in Chicago in March. Popularly referred to as the Fenian Fair, this gigantic fund-raising event was openly sponsored by the Fenian Brotherhood and had incurred the censure of Bishop Duggan of that city.

This did not deter the *Irish People* from publishing weekly lists of donors and donations, often running to several columns—lists which give a revealing idea of the volume of public support for the IRB and form a mine of information about the early members in many parts of Ireland. This appeal by the paper, incidentally, was a great success; Henry C. McCarthy, joint secretary of the Fenian Brotherhood, came over specially to supervise the dispatch of the donations, and a special parcel-packer had to be employed for over a month in the *Irish People* office.

But there was as yet no direct attack on the Archbishop of Dublin, who in turn, apart from the pastoral mentioned above, was strangely silent since the *Irish People* had commenced publication. But if the archbishop was silent he was not idle. Apparently convinced that the IRB was leading his flock to its doom, and probably impressed, too, by the growing public support for the secret organisation, he decided that some political alternative to the IRB must be found.

Accordingly, after at least one false start, the formation of the National Association of Ireland was announced at a meeting in the Rotunda, Dublin, late in December 1864, attended by the Archbishops of Dublin and Cashel, five other bishops and—alone of prominent lay figures—John Blake Dillon. Dillon's presence indicated how desperately Cullen felt the need to supplant the IRB in the public mind; for here he was now on the same platform as a '48 man—albeit one whose revolutionary ardour had noticeably cooled in the intervening seventeen years. Dillon, like A. M. Sullivan, was as convinced as Cullen of the danger and futility which he felt were inherent in the IRB conspiracy.

About the principal objectives of the NAI the IRB leaders could justifiably feel as they did about the policies of the *Nation* under Sullivan's editorship; they confined themselves to minor, if genuine, Irish grievances, without ever getting to the root of all Irish ills. The new Association aimed at persuading the Government to pass three new Bills—one dealing with land reform, another to disendow the Established Church in Ireland, and a third to secure for all denominations free and equal educational rights. Exactly how all this was to be achieved is not clear; the by then discredited method of petitioning the authorities was not apparently ruled out, although direct participation in parliamentary elections does not seem to have been contemplated.

Almost from the start the NAI ran into trouble, and from an unexpected quarter. A. M. Sullivan and the IRB might differ fundamentally on many topics, but on the dangers inherent in a new and makeshift parliamentary agitation, and on the ineptitude of Archbishop Cullen as a politician, they were in full agreement. The *Nation* for 7 January 1865 set out its reasons for declining

6. Denis Dowling Mulcahy, Thomas Clarke Luby
and John O'Leary in 1865, when on the *Irish People*

Paris
8 Rue Geoffroy-Marie
Feb 16th 1865

My Dear Colonel

Here Mr Cooney arrived, and
[illegible] me he will tell you himself. It will
also tell you how he found my idea was
ting, and how a second messenger, who
Offerman Roza, arrived last evening.

I was very sorry I could not
myself convey to your letter
for I could not leave Paris, but I did
the next best thing—I read? it over
carefully to my sister and told her in
the strongest possible manner not to let
Mr Cooney leave the country without
a despatch.

He left Paris on Tuesday week
carrying £600 in Bank notes. Wm O'Donovan
left on Tuesday evening and [illegible]
[illegible] to give to the Papers the arrest

arrived with a fellow [illegible] but with no
despatch for you. Here he had left O'Donovan?
here on Sunday [illegible] with £615. From that
time up to the last Sunday the 12th [illegible]?
neither messenger nor letter. On Monday as
we were reading at [illegible] we saw about the arrest of Stephens. And on Monday night the £5.
was back again but without a letter. [illegible]
He brought us good news however. She
[illegible] as not in the least [illegible], knowing
that they claim can get [illegible] the prisoners out
absolutely whenever they like. There was a meeting
of the Dublin centre, to take place that night and
the result of that meeting I have just heard from
another messenger—that you [illegible] has been appointed [illegible] in Stephens place—but I am
very to say that this is all absolutely unofficial
[illegible] not sending the despatches. I
can only absolute to the want of I. and my
not having been able to send a letter. I need not
say how much I am disgusted at it—for
[illegible] from everything that I know how badly you
have been treated in this respect and am of
said you will consider this my [illegible] in stating
of it. I am sorry indeed I have nothing more
to tell you than that I shall never forget your
kindness to me when I was in America, and
but I hope that even at the last moment the new
despatch may come. I [illegible]

Paris
8 Rue Geoffroy-Marie
Nov 16th 1865

My dear Colonel,

How Mr. Cooney arrived, and found me he will tell you himself. He will also tell you how he found my sister waiting and how a second messenger, Mrs. O'Donovan Rossa, arrived that evening.

I was very sorry indeed that I could not *myself* convey the meaning of your letter for I could not leave Paris, but I did the next best thing —I read it over carefully to my sister and told her in the strongest possible manner not to let Mr. Cooney leave the country without a despatch.

She left Paris on Tuesday week carrying £600 in Bank notes. Mrs. O'Donovan left on Tuesday evening with £500 and the following Friday Capt. Smith arrived with a letter (quite short and ambiguously worded) for me but with no despatch for you.

When he had left Dublin, my sister had not arrived. Capt. Smith left Paris on Sunday Nov. 5th with £425. From that time up to last Monday—the 13th—I had neither messenger nor letter. On Monday as we were reading at Galignani's we saw about the arrest of Stephens. And on Monday night Mrs. O'D. was back again but without a letter. She brought us good news however. The men are not in the least discouraged, knowing that they can get all the prisoners out *absolutely* whenever they like. There was a meeting of the Dublin centres to take place that night and the result of that meeting I have just learned from another messenger—that Gen. Millen has been appointed pro tem in Stephens place—but I am sorry to say that this is all absolutely unofficial. Their not sending the despatches I can only attribute to the arrest of S. and to my not having been able to send a letter. I need not say how much I am disgusted at it—for apart from everything else I know how badly you have been treated in this respect and I am afraid you will consider this only another instance of it.

I am sorry indeed I have nothing more to tell you than that I shall never forget your kindness to me when I was in America, but I hope that even at the last moment the despatch may come.

Yours faithfully,
Edmund O'Leary.

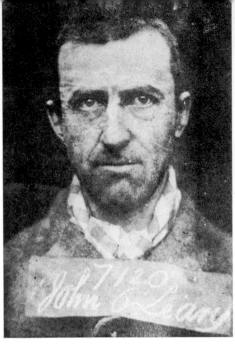

8. John O'Leary

9. John Haltigan

10. Thomas Clarke Luby

11. Denis Dowling Mulcahy

Reproductions of four unpublished photographs taken in Mountjoy jail, Dublin,

to support the new venture. It was unrepresentative and must be remodelled; it was dominated by Cullen, whose judgement in political affairs had led him to conclusions 'not in accord with those of the immense majority of the Irish people'; finally, without an explicit declaration on 'place-traffic', so as to avoid another Sadlier-and-Keogh type of desertion, 'the Association cannot and ought not to have the confidence of the public'. Neither a widening of its committee membership nor any pledge to refuse Government posts would satisfy the IRB, however.

To the *Irish People* the very formation of the NAI was a mistake and readers were promptly and bluntly advised not to support it at all. The '50s, they were reminded, had entirely discredited parliamentary agitation and petitionary methods; the time had come to try more forceful action to redress Irish grievances, especially the major one—the country's enforced political union with Britain. So ran the editorial thoughts of the *Irish People* on the new organisation; no doubt, too, the IRB leaders saw in the NAI a thinly-disguised attempt by Archbishop Cullen to supplant the IRB as the most powerful political force in the country.

Even before the body was officially formed the *Irish People* had attacked. The editorials of the last few issues for 1864 assumed a gradually more uncompromising line, both on Cullen himself and on the general topic of the priest in politics. As the year 1865 opened, the intensity of the attack on Cullen and the NAI steadily increased. The issue for 7 January, for example, referred to the new body in two editorials. 'Here at home the year has opened . . . with a mischievous attempt to revive the outworn system of agitation; but we may confidently pronounce that there is not the slightest symptom that Doctor Cullen . . . can materially influence the public mind.'

So ran the leading article; a sub-leader, dealing specifically with the Rotunda meeting, sneered at the Catholic Lord Mayor McSwiney (a leading supporter of Cullen) for his rushing from the conference to greet the Lord Lieutenant at a Mansion House function, and ended: 'But Doctor Cullen and the pseudo-Nationalists will find that the people are not the idiots that they take them for.'

The following week a further editorial commentary, before dealing with 'the dreary talk of Doctor Cullen and his co-plotters against the cause of Ireland', remarked that 'we believe it (the NAI) has been got up somewhat on the principle of the celebrated razors that were made, not to shave, but merely to sell . . . it has been called into existence . . . to draw the people aside from the only path to freedom'. A fortnight later, the fears of the *Nation* that NAI members might not be able to resist offers of Government positions having been confirmed by the elevation to the Bench of Thomas

O'Hagan, QC, the *Irish People* remarked that 'the new Association has been afforded the opportunity of doing its first stroke of business'.

Thereafter, while the IRB organ never ceased to oppose the entry of clergy into the political field, the pace of the *Irish People* attacks on Cullen and the NAI slackened somewhat. The *Nation* maintained its editorial campaign against the new body. During the first six months of 1865 A. M. Sullivan continued to snipe at the ineffectiveness and shortcomings of the NAI, the climax coming in a remarkable two-leader outburst on 1 July which rivalled the *Irish People* itself for invective. Traitors and knaves (said the *Nation* of this date) were entrusted with the favours of Archbishop Cullen, while honest men, resisting them, found themselves in conflict with, and visited with only hostility from, him; 'as a politician his grace is a disastrous mistake, and his retirement from politics would be a national advantage'.

Moreover, the NAI was beset by internal differences which it was unable to keep private. Cullen's action early in the year in issuing a pastoral urging his clergy to support, and even participate, in the new organisation confirms other evidence that there was antipathy, and even some opposition, amongst priests to the NAI. Sullivan's demand for a pledge by members not to take official posts found wide support and led to some changes in the rules. The lack of support from provincial clergy had to be seen to, and resulted in a meeting in Dublin in May between a provincial delegation and the NAI governing committee.

Even Cullen himself proved critical of some of the Association's proceedings, and John Blake Dillon found himself voluntarily acting the role of mediator, drawing from the *Nation* the comment that 'Mr. Dillon . . . by his strenuous efforts to save the Association . . . is not a spectacle to cheer the country'. Several prominent public figures also noticeably declined to support the NAI. Archbishop McHale came out in February in hostile criticism; George Henry Moore, a leading MP of the Independent Opposition of the 1850s, commented publicly on the venture in terms remarkably similar to those of the *Irish People* and showed that, unlike Dillon, he had not forgotten the role the bishops had played in Irish politics in the previous decade. Even the exiled Gavan Duffy, home on a prolonged visit in June, for long remained studiously aloof from the new movement. In short, apart from the apparent public antipathy to the body, the work of the *Irish People* in opposing the NAI was taken over by others of whom Cullen, who had recently called the paper 'the organ of the friends of violence', was likely to take far more notice.

Second on the list of favourite targets for the editorial attacks of the *Irish People* came the constitutionalists of the period. In this case the attack, though sustained for longer than that against Cullen, was much less bitter. There was an obvious reason for this. The abysmal failure of the constitutional agitations of the 1850s had completely discredited this hitherto accepted method of attempting to remedy Irish grievances. With the defection of Sadlier and Keogh, the retirement and emigration of Gavan Duffy, and the premature death of Lucas, 'parliamentary representation', to quote O'Leary himself, 'had reached that state in Ireland from which no honest man, not a fool or a prophet, could well see anything but the most disastrous outlook'.

It is recognised today that the IRB movement owed much to the general disgust at the collapse of the movements of the 1850s. It is signficant that even that ardent supporter of petitions to Westminster, Archbishop Cullen, does not appear to have contemplated direct intervention in parliamentary elections by the NAI.

With the reputations of the parliamentarians fallen so low, the task of the *Irish People* in this direction was not difficult. There was no need for trenchant writing to ensure that the cause of constitutionalism remain discredited; instead, the main weapon used was sarcasm. The principal figures supporting parliamentary agitation were mercilessly lampooned, and the press reports of the proceedings of their various organisations were analysed with a pitiless sense of humour that makes entertaining reading even a century later.

The National League of John Martin, the '48 leader and journalist who had been converted to more peaceful methods, was the subject of some quite hilarious leading articles from the pens of O'Leary and Luby. O'Connell's nephew, The O'Donoghue, MP, Peter Paul McSwiney the Lord Mayor, John F. Maguire the Cork MP ('one of the most egregious of Irish political humbugs'), John Blake Dillon (never, one suspects, forgiven his initial refusal to support Stephens in 1858), and even the respected Gavan Duffy, home from Australia in 1865, were all sneered at in turn by the IRB paper.

Of John Martin, an editorial by O'Leary in the issue of 17 September 1864 ended thus: 'At present he seems to us to be labouring under a most serious form of cerebral disease which we may call League of the brain.' Of Gavan Duffy, after he had appeared at a meeting in support of parliamentary agitation, another leading article—in all probability by O'Leary, too—commented: 'There was a time—in the days of the Tenant League, for example—when a certain parliamentary patriot is said to have been accustomed to drink the Queen's health sitting, and in a single small teaspoonful of whiskey punch. But to be an "ex-Minister of the Crown" with a pension of £1,000 a year, makes a wonderful difference.'

Of Dillon, the paper pointed out that he was now being eulogised from the same altars from which he had been condemned in '48. And all the time parliamentary agitation was held up to readers as a useless device, a method which had failed in the recent past and would never achieve the basic Irish aim, political independence. 'However ably and honestly conducted, (it) is a delusion and a snare.'

Although established primarily as a vehicle of propaganda and for fund-raising purposes, the *Irish People* quickly became the ablest advocate of Irish separatism of the nineteenth century. Of an astonishingly high literary quality, it was soon widely read by all classes of the population from Castle official to country curate, from city tradesman to rural labourer. In its editorial and correspondence columns could be gauged the steady growth of the extreme nationalists. While its racy creed of nationalism stirred the blood of countless thousands, its relentless attacks on mild nationalists and place-hunters must have earned it hatred in upper-class Castle-Catholic Dublin.

In what on the whole, despite the naturally prejudiced views of its brilliant editor, was less eloquent language than that of Davis and his colleagues, it revived the spirit created by the *Nation* of the 1840s. It paved the way for the later struggle with Irish landlordism, and carried the teachings of Young Ireland to a later generation. That it was allowed to continue for so long to preach what under British law was clearly sedition, and to advocate what was equally obviously treason, is one of the minor mysteries of the period. Admittedly, in a legal opinion given early in 1864, the Solicitor-General advised that it would be impolitic to move against the *Irish People* for sedition while the *Irishman* and the *Nation* were also seditious in tone. But this view does not appear to have weighed with the Castle authorities a year-and-a-half later.

CHAPTER FOUR

1 Arrest

2 Trial

3 Imprisonment

1

THE *Irish People* so overshadowed all other events in the IRB movement in the two years beginning in the autumn of 1863 that, having told the story of the paper, one has to a large extent at the same time described the progress of the secret society itself. 'Its appearance,' claimed Stephens a year after the paper first appeared, 'gave a new life and colour to the organisation.' A few important events, however, remain to be recorded. In November 1863 the first annual convention of the Fenian Brotherhood was held in Chicago; the attendance included Charles Kickham as delegate from the IRB. Kickham on his return home published his impressions of this visit anonymously under the title 'Leaves from a Journal' in the early issues of the *Irish People*.

In mid-March 1864 James Stephens, having by a formal document dated 9 March appointed Luby, O'Leary and Kickham as an executive committee in his absence, with the same powers as he himself had in the IRB, left for the United States as 'J. Daly'. He was away until late August on what proved to be his most successful tour of the United States. Visiting every state in which the Fenian Brotherhood flourished, he met all its principal officers, addressed meetings (at which he created a favourable impression), reported on the strength of the IRB and satisfactorily settled his differences with the head of the Brotherhood, John O'Mahony.

Most important of all for the movement in Ireland, Stephens appears to have at last impressed on the Brotherhood the vital necessity of regular and substantial financial aid to the IRB. That some such agreement was reached seems an inescapable conclusion to draw from the known fact that, from shortly after Stephens's return to Ireland in August 1864, large sums of money began to arrive at more or less regular intervals for a period of over twelve months. According to the Fenian centre for London at this time, Stephens brought back the greater part of £12,000 from this American tour.[1]

Two attempts were made between 1863 and 1865 to end the dictatorial position which Stephens occupied in the IRB. Some time early in 1864 negotiations were opened with the moderate nationalists, including The O'Donoghue, MP and the Sullivan brothers, A. M. and T. D. When touring the west, Rossa and Edward Duffy, who organised the IRB in Connacht, had a meeting towards the same end with George Henry Moore, probably the outstanding survivor of the parliamentary movement of the 1850s.

A conference between Moore and Stephens was arranged and later held in Dublin; according to Devoy, no agreement was reached because Moore refused to accept a suggestion of Stephens that he tour the United States lecturing on behalf of the IRB. Any such broadening of the upper councils of the IRB would naturally have necessitated Stephens's sharing control, and while Moore was subsequently treated with great respect by the IRB and its paper, it looks as if Stephens was not prepared to loosen his hold over the organisation.

The same implications were present in a proposal from the Fenian Brotherhood itself in 1865 that the form of government of the IRB should be altered. As in the case of the approach to the moderates in 1864, the picture is far from clear. But a formal 32-page document embodying the suggested necessary changes seems to have given rise to acrimonious discussion.

At this time some leading members of the Fenian Brotherhood, including Generals Kerwin and Millen and Colonel Thomas F. Bourke, had arrived in Ireland. According to Devoy, the leading IRB figures in Dublin were solidly behind Stephens on this occasion; a meeting of centres, presided over by the deaf Kickham with the aid of an ear trumpet, established this. Denieffe says that Luby and O'Leary repeatedly urged Stephens not to yield to anyone wishing to displace him. Denieffe's own high-class tailoring establishment at 32 South Anne Street, Dublin, was the scene of several important conferences between Stephens with his lieutenants and the American delegates. O'Leary and Luby attended all of these and both strenuously supported Stephens.

In the work of the IRB for these two years O'Leary played an important part. In addition to being the full-time editor of the organisation's paper, he was also, to borrow a phrase used by Crown counsel at the subsequent State trials, Chancellor of the Exchequer to the revolutionary movement. It will be recalled that his first connection with the IRB was in the capacity of treasurer or financial manager when, early in 1859, he travelled to the French transatlantic port of Boulogne with Luby to take charge of the money which Stephens then brought back from his first trip to the United States, and that later that same year O'Leary, too, toured parts of the United States collecting funds for the IRB.

Upon his return to Dublin from London in August 1863 it appears that O'Leary at once resumed this position. With what now looks like a grim sense of humour, the shadow Minister for Finance of the underground republican movement opened an account in the head office of the Royal Bank of Ireland. Here he lodged each draft as it arrived from New York; from this fund were paid the various expenses of the IRB.

Naturally the subsidy to the *Irish People* came first in priority. After that came a variety of items of expenditure, ranging from Rossa's trips for the paper or rent for halls used for secret indoor drilling by night, to John Haltigan's recruiting trips to his native Kilkenny and Michael Moore's pay as a blacksmith, sent home specially from New York by O'Mahony, to devote his whole time to forging pikes in the heart of Dublin city.

From the large sums of money which passed through O'Leary's hands, especially in the year or so following Stephens's American tour of mid-1864, it looks as if this must have been by far the most prosperous period of the IRB, looked at from a purely financial point of view. The normal type of monetary transaction between the Fenian Brotherhood and the IRB was effected by way of bill of exchange drawn by the New York bankers Auguste Belmont & Co. on Rothschild's of London in favour of O'Leary and payable at three days' sight.

Between 9 August 1864 and 12 September 1865 fourteen such bills crossed the Atlantic; they were for a total of approximately £8,000, a very substantial sum by the standards of a century ago. Of these fourteen drafts, twelve were paid into O'Leary's account in the Royal Bank, all twelve having been endorsed by him, save one which arrived while he was in London in August 1864 and was signed by his sister Ellen. The remaining two failed to reach him for a reason soon to be explained.

Nor was this all the money that reached the IRB from the United States during the 1863–5 period. On 21 February 1863 a draft for £205 had come; and Stephens brought back with him from the United States in August 1864 a sum of money variously estimated at between £1,000 and £12,000. Furthermore, from time to time drafts, mostly for somewhat smaller amounts, were made payable by the Fenian Brotherhood to George Hopper, suggesting that Stephens's brother-in-law was the assistant financial manager of the Irish movement. Three such unlodged cheques totalling £150 were found in O'Leary's room by the police in 1865, and when Edward Duffy was arrested some weeks later he was found to possess a cheque for £1,525 in favour of Hopper.

That these large sums of money, often £500 or more, arriving at more or less regular monthly intervals, played a big part in the success of the movement between 1863 and 1865 there can be little doubt. So, of course, did the weekly issues of the *Irish People*, so that it can be said that O'Leary had a hand in what may be claimed to have been the two principal factors in the growth of the IRB at this time.

By the summer of 1865 the strength of the revolutionary movement had reached alarming proportions, from the viewpoint of Dublin Castle. It had survived the severe censures of the Catholic Church and had obviously succeeded in rendering almost impotent the moderate nationalist bodies such as the National League and the National Association. Its weekly organ continued to prosper and kept the insurrectionary spirit alive in all parts of the country.

From the start this paper had promised that at the right time Irish-American military aid would be forthcoming for the extreme nationalists; Castle officials had smiled at this seemingly preposterous claim, and the other nationalist organs had sneered at it. Yet now quite suddenly American officers of Irish descent or origin had begun to arrive in the country and were establishing themselves with apparently abundant funds in many areas. Gradually the editorial tone of the *Irish People* became bolder and more provocative.

Then a rash of open drilling and marching broke out all over the country; nocturnal Fenian manoeuvres were reported even in the Phoenix Park within sight of the Lord Lieutenant's drawing-room. Down in Cork, where the IRB was known to be particularly strong, a meeting of 150 magistrates was held to discuss measures necessary for public order, in circumstances suggesting that an insurrection was imminent.

But in the midst of all these rumours and preparations Dublin Castle had no tangible evidence on which it could proceed against

the IRB leaders. For two years its leading detectives had been
shadowing the leading IRB figures—eavesdropping on conversations
in public-houses and following them to and from their residences,
meeting-places and the office in Parliament Street.

For eighteen months a paid informer, intimate with every one of
the leaders of the IRB and having the run of the *Irish People* office,
had been at work for the Government; yet he appears to have
turned up nothing that many an intelligent and observant member
of the public could not also have ascertained. Admittedly, early in
September 1865 the Post Office intercepted and detained two drafts
for £1,000 each from O'Mahony's secretary in New York to
O'Leary; but who was to prove that they were to be spent other
than in a perfectly legal manner?

Then suddenly, on 14 September, the informer just mentioned
handed to his employers a letter stolen from a drunken IRB man
and clearly in Stephens's handwriting. 'There is no time to be lost.
This year—and let there be no mistake about it—must be the year
of action. I speak with a knowledge and authority to which no
other man could pretend; and I repeat, the flag of Ireland—of the
Irish Republic—must this year be raised.'

To many an IRB officer in Dublin, and elsewhere, there was
nothing new in this boast; Stephens had been saying this for many
months past. But coming in an atmosphere of American officers,
public marching, magistrates' meetings, and £1,000 drafts, it was
apparently enough to panic the Lord Lieutenant and his officials
down to the lower ranks of the Dublin police.

A meeting of the Privy Council was summoned, so hastily that
not all members were notified to attend. It sat late into the night,
considering what it obviously regarded as the sudden serious turn
of events and how an insurrection might be forestalled or crushed.
Somebody doubtless remembered that it was Thursday night, the
evening the *Irish People* went to press; what better place to catch
all the Fenian leaders together?

Against the advice of the Lord Lieutenant, Lord Wodehouse—
so it was rumoured later—but on strong pressure from the lawyers
on the Council, it was decided to seize the newspaper office and
arrest the top IRB men. The plan was kept secret although a
warrant was—reluctantly, so it was also said—obtained from Mr.
John Calvert Stronge, chief magistrate for the Dublin metropolitan
magistrates courts. Both the police and the military were ordered
to prepare for an emergency.

At 8 p.m. on Friday 15 September 1865 the *Irish People* office
was closed to the public by 'Jerry' O'Farrell the caretaker, and the
editor went off to the theatre. Though he did not know it then,
O'Leary had edited the last issue of his paper. It was No. 43 in

Volume 2, the ninety-fifth issue of the *Irish People*, making in all some 1,500 pages in almost twenty-two months.

The leading article of this last issue was as defiant as ever. 'We saw clearly that the people should be taught to distinguish between the priest as a minister of religion and the priest as a politician, before they could be got to advance one step on the road to independence. The people for whom God created it must get this island into their own hands. . . . Our only hope is in revolution.'

Meanwhile, up in the Castle yard some 200 yards away, the entire G division, the detective force of the city police, prepared to show that when it came to illegal action Dublin Castle could outdo the so-called Fenians. Shortly after 9 p.m. the G-men went to work swiftly and efficiently. Taking up positions at each end of Parliament Street, they closed the thoroughfare. 'So interested was the government in the prompt execution of their order,' said the *Nation* of the following Saturday, 'that Mr. J. L. O'Ferrall, Commissioner of Police, and Colonel Wood, Inspector-General of Constabulary, personally superintended the proceedings in Parliament Street.'

A large crowd gathered and watched in silence as Superintendent Daniel Ryan broke into, entered and took over the *Irish People* office, arresting several IRB men who were still on the premises. Every scrap of paper—stationery, account books, proofs, correspondence, manuscripts, even obviously personal letters—was seized; the very floorboards were ripped up lest anything might be overlooked.

A police float was summoned from the Castle and the entire type-setting machinery was loaded on to it, removed to the Castle yard and there unceremoniously dumped in an irreparable condition. At the same time in various parts of the city the ordinary police force was busy arresting previously watched and carefully selected leading IRB men. The Under-Secretary remained in his office in the Castle until 1 a.m. directing operations.

It was after midnight before O'Leary returned to his lodgings, having seen home after the theatre a cousin of his, a sister of 'Eva'. As he opened the front door of 16 Palmerston Place at 12.20 a.m. he found himself confronted by two detectives, Dawson and Magee; at the same time two more G-men, Smollen and King, appeared from behind and pushed him into the hall. They said they had a warrant for his arrest; he told them to read it out to him; they did so.

Commenting, 'a lawyer will be the best judge of that', O'Leary calmly seated himself in an arm-chair and proceeded to smoke his pipe 'flavoured with a glass of whiskey and water'. This brief comic interlude over, O'Leary was escorted to Chancery Lane police station where, after the usual police formalities, he was put into a bedless cell with two other minor IRB men—without so far having been charged with any breach of the law. When searched some American drafts had been found on him.

The following afternoon, Saturday 16 September, O'Leary along with twenty-two other IRB men was conveyed by prison van to the Lower Castle Yard, Dublin Castle, and from there to the nearby office of the Commissioner of Police. Here, rather than in the normal police court of the city because of the fear of disturbance or even an attempted rescue, Chief Magistrate Stronge—whose conduct of the proceedings against the IRB men in the subsequent two months led even the *Freeman's Journal* to circulate a rumour that he was to be knighted—sat with a colleague named McDermott. A formal charge of treason was preferred against the prisoners; they were remanded in custody for a week and conveyed to Richmond jail, now Griffith barracks. Another meeting of the Privy Council was held later that day.

There then followed one of those supposedly spontaneous, but clearly officially-inspired, press campaigns which, even today, a British government is capable of conducting for the purpose of influencing the course of political affairs. Although top IRB men had been apprehended up and down the country on the night of O'Leary's arrest, there still remained at liberty Stephens, Kickham, Brophy, Duffy and Mulcahy—not to mention the unknown number of adherents in every county.

The extent of the penetration by the IRB of the army, police, coastguard and fire brigades was unknown to the authorities. A series of wild rumours swept the country, and details of them were published daily in the loyalist press, both metropolitan and provincial. Not even the mildly nationalist and staunchly Catholic *Freeman's Journal* was able to resist the temptation of adding to the stories.

On several occasions so-called Fenian warships were reported cruising off the coast—from Liverpool, Queenstown and elsewhere. Arms and ammunition were said to have been landed on the Donegal coast. Seemingly indefatigable but invisible companies of Fenians were alleged to be marching here, there and everywhere. A large part of the province of Munster, including the whole of Cork city and county, was proclaimed, that is, declared to be in a state of emergency. In towns and villages all over the country copies of the last issue of the *Irish People* were seized and confiscated by the police; a constable in Loughrea was astonished to find one with the manager of the National Bank—until he discovered that he was an uncle of the editor of the paper.[2]

A special supplement to the official *Gazette* offered a reward of £200 for the capture of Stephens, 'alias Power, alias Butler, alias

Kelly, alias Shook'. Detachments of British troops raced from one part of Dublin to the other—from this jail to that barracks, from Pigeon House Fort to Dublin Castle, manoeuvring here and reinforcing there. A body of police took possession of the *Irish People* office, which was thenceforward occupied night and day.

At the same time this deliberate campaign of terrorism (to which, to his credit, A. M. Sullivan in the *Nation* took strong exception) was backed by a more vicious press campaign against the IRB and its leaders, inflaming the mind of the public (including prospective jurors) against the arrested men, and ensuring that in due course they would not obtain even the semblance of a fair trial. And in this campaign not only the pro-Castle *Irish Times, Daily Express* and *Saunders News Letter* co-operated with enthusiasm, but also the *Freeman's Journal*, the *Nation* and even Archbishop Cullen himself—until effectively silenced by legal process.

Exaggerated stories about the suppressed secret society, its policies and plans were printed; almost daily in leading articles the arrested leaders and the still free Stephens were convicted of treason, murder and less serious crimes. The Fenian Brotherhood in the United States was pictured as a powerful organisation with a mighty force poised for an invasion of Ireland. In fact, it was on the verge of a serious split in its highest councils, which finally came in December with the deposition of John O'Mahony from the position of Head Centre.

Meanwhile, in Richmond prison O'Leary and his companions were kept in solitary confinement day and night, with only one hour's exercise every twenty-four. Because Rossa and, following his example, Luby and O'Leary refused to permit themselves to be described in the records as Roman Catholics—they humorously protested that they were Irish Catholics—all three were prohibited from using the jail chapel. Rossa, whose cell was adjacent to O'Leary's, demanded proper food but was told that his request could not be acceded to because he was not obliged to work. On being informed that the quality of food would improve if he agreed to pay for his maintenance, Rossa (in spite of a ban on communications between prisoners) got in touch with O'Leary and persuaded him to join him in this arrangement.

After two remands the lawyer who had been acting for the principal prisoners, a Dublin solicitor named E. A. Ennis, expressed fears for the future of his practice if he continued in association with the disreputable Fenians. The prisoners considerately dismissed him, and O'Leary and Rossa—apparently the only two able to communicate with each other—decided to ask P. J. Smyth MP to represent them. However, the Castle authorities vetoed this plan by refusing to allow Smyth to visit the jail on the grounds that he,

too, was a suspected Fenian; Smyth then recommended that John
Lawless, a well-known Dublin solicitor, be approached. This was
done and Lawless, a '48 man who had been in Newgate prison
with Fintan Lalor, at once undertook to arrange for their defence.[3]

Accordingly, when the prisoners appeared once more, on 30
September in the emergency courtoom in the Castle, both Crown
and accused had Queen's Counsel. The small room was packed to
capacity, largely by armed police and Castle officials; the attendance also included the private secretary to the Lord Lieutenant,
two high-ranking military officers and the Commissioner of Police.
The public were not allowed in, the magistrate, Stronge, specifically
refusing admission to Rossa's wife and O'Leary's sister.

On this occasion at last the Crown was ready to go into evidence.
According to press reports the charge against the more important
prisoners, including O'Leary, was now treasonable conspiracy,
although Governor Marquis of Richmond jail had told them at
parade one morning that they would be charged with high treason.
Charles R. Barry QC, Law Adviser to the Castle, began the two-
day proceedings with a long and detailed opening statement that
made a travesty of justice of the proceedings of the subsequent two
months. From start to finish his speech was an inflammatory
political address, interspersed with facts which were to be proven
by doubtful evidence, and full of allegations of a scandalous nature
in support of which not a scrap of evidence was produced either
then or later in Green Street courthouse.

After some initial laudatory remarks on the British Constitution,
Barry began to describe the Fenian conspiracy in language that must
have made it well-nigh impossible for tens of thousands of rank-
and-file IRB men to recognise this as the IRB. The Fenians were
socialists, catering principally for the lower classes; their design was
not merely revolutionary but socialist 'in its most pernicious and
most wicked phase'; they had promised a redistribution of property
to the lower orders. Their revolution was to have begun with an
indiscriminate massacre of all above the lower classes, starting with
the Catholic clergy; here O'Leary and Rossa were observed to smile
at each other incredulously.

To manage this revolution American officers had been poured
into Ireland; thousands of pikes had been found, as well as breast-
plates for belts and revolvers; in two recent weeks some £3,500
had come in from America for the Fenians. The Fenian chief James
Stephens had been plotting secretly for twenty years; his force was
divided into mysterious ranks known as As, Bs and Cs, and details
of membership were recorded on cryptic muster-rolls in the form
of squared sheets of paper on which O represented an unarmed
man, V a pikeman and A a man with fire-arms. And so on.

On the following day, after hours of detailed evidence, mostly that of a spy named Pettit and the informer Nagle, the accused were committed for trial—but not before some of them had succeeded in getting in a few words. On the first day the bench listened in silence to a brief but caustic speech by O'Leary, in which he criticised the Government for its fear of the nationalists. On both days Rossa, who spurned the aid of lawyers, continually interrupted with sarcastic comments on the proceedings; on one occasion when he lost his temper he was forcibly restrained by O'Leary.

But he managed to make a protest against the prison conditions and to read aloud a copy of a letter signed by himself, O'Leary, Luby, James O'Connor and Hopper demanding facilities of the governor for consultation between the prisoners. Most effective of all, he succeeded in reading out in court also a biting satire on the illegal seizure of the *Irish People* office, in the form of an allegorical dispatch from the Polish correspondent of the *Times* (the Polish insurrectionaries having aroused great admiration in Britain recently) describing the seizure by the despotic Russian authorities of the office of the *Polish People*.

The accusations levelled in the magistrates court against the IRB created a national sensation. The pro-Government papers naturally cried out in horror in their editorial columns and gave thanks to the Castle for its timely intervention. The *Freeman's Journal* and the *Nation* both began by doubting the accuracy of the theory of the massacre plot, but then went on to discuss the matter in terms which clearly implied belief in those accusations.

Archbishop Cullen was for some days silent. On 9 October he issued a letter to his clergy warning of the cholera and other evils. On 18 October he attended a committee meeting of the National Association, where he confined himself to his customary praise of parliamentary agitation and criticism of violent methods.

But it was only the calm before the storm. On 20 October he issued a trenchant pastoral on Orangeism and Feniansim. The IRB leaders were attacked for their irreligion, their insobriety and their lack of business acumen. He repeated the Castle theories of a massacre and of IRB links with socialism; he thanked the authorities for the suppression of the *Irish People*.

Then, remarking that he would leave the courts to deal with the legal merits of Fenianism, he returned to his old topic of secret societies in general. Mazzini, Garibaldi and the French revolutionaries were cited as typical examples of men who fomented revolutions that ended in 'massacres, anarchy and despotism'. Finally, displaying his prowess as a political prophet, he announced to his flock with an inelegant variety of metaphor: 'Fenianism indeed now seems to be at an end; a few policemen demolished the structure; not a hand was raised in its defence; probably after a short time we shall hear no more about it.'

This remarkable document, appearing a bare week before the opening of the State trials in Green Street, could not go unchallenged. An action for damages for libel was at once instituted against the *Freeman's Journal* in the names of Luby, O'Leary, Rossa and Mulcahy for publishing the pastoral, and a preliminary motion in the High Court succeeded in so far as the portion of the archbishop's letter and the paper's editorial consisted of comment. Thereafter Doctor Cullen remained decently silent.

Nor was this the only lawsuit arising out of the seizure and arrests. No less distinguished a trio than the Lord Lieutenant, the Under-Secretary and the Chief Magistrate for Dublin were named as defendants in an action by Luby, as proprietor of the *Irish People,* seeking damages for illegal entry into the paper's premises. This suit was later set aside.

Finally, O'Leary was plaintiff in the shortest and most successful case, an action against the Royal Bank for refusing to meet a cheque of his, drawn on his account there. The bank had done so in pursuance of a direction (bereft of any legal authority) from the Attorney-General to freeze what he believed to be the IRB treasury. Within twenty-four hours of the matter being publicised in the High Court the bank agreed to honour the cheque, with the result that thenceforward the fund was used to pay the costs of defending not merely O'Leary but also all the other prisoners.

On 12 October the number of political inmates in Richmond jail rose by four with the arrival of Stephens, Kickham, Brophy and Duffy, who had been arrested the previous day at the house in Sandymount where Stephens—who had eluded the police on the night of the *Irish People* seizure by hobbling away from the vicinity on a stick, disguised as a cripple—had been quietly residing for some weeks as the Rev. Mr. Herbert of Killarney.

Stephens's stay in jail was to end with dramatic suddenness. At his sole appearance in court on 15 October, when he was honoured by the appearance on the bench alongside the magistrate of no less a personage than the Under-Secretary, Sir Thomas Aiskew Larcom, he gave a hint of an impending escape which the authorities chose to ignore. On the evening of 24 October, at a consultation in jail when the prisoners were preparing their defence with Lawless in the hearing of the warders (some of them also IRB men), Duffy whispered to O'Leary and Rossa that Stephens planned to leave that night. And so he did.

Meanwhile, a rumour in the press was duly confirmed by the announcement of the setting up of a Special Commission, presided over jointly by Judge Keogh and Judge Fitzgerald, to try all the IRB prisoners. The opening of the Commission was fixed for 27 November in Dublin, and an application made on 23 November by counsel for the prisoners for trials elsewhere than in Dublin, because of the press campaign against the accused, was rejected.

2

ON 27 NOVEMBER 1865 the Special Commission set up to try the prisoners charged with complicity in the Fenian conspiracy opened at Green Street courthouse in Dublin. The scene in the city that morning was strongly suggestive of a government that, despite its two-month campaign of intimidation, still feared that it might be overthrown. Great crowds filled the streets, the vicinity of the court itself being jammed with people. Mounted police patrolled the area and detachments of soldiers stood at specially selected spots nearby. Elaborate precautions had been taken to forestall any attempt to rescue the IRB leaders as they were conveyed to the courthouse, although there is no evidence that the police knew of a plot by some Dublin IRB centres to rescue the prisoners while they were being conveyed from the courthouse to the jail.[4]

As ten o'clock approached, the throngs in Green Street surged forward and it was only with difficulty that the various dignitaries —the judges, Lord Mayor and High Sheriff—gained access to the court building. Finally came the prison-van preceded and followed (as had been the case at all the earlier proceedings at the Castle) by detachments from British regiments and escorts of mounted constabulary. A great cheer rose from the crowd as the prisoners were quickly hustled inside. Fifteen men of the 8th Regiment and twenty-five members of the city police force took up positions outside.

Inside the historic courtroom itself the scene was much more subdued—and for a good reason. The attendance of the general public, said the *Freeman's Journal* timidly, was 'rather limited'; according to the *Nation*, 'four-fifths of the Green Street "public" were police either in or out of uniform'. In the gallery special seats had been reserved for Mrs. Luby, Mrs. O'Donovan Rossa and Miss Ellen O'Leary, and were now occupied by them.

The whole setting was significant and ominous. Dublin Castle meant to get its men this time. The replacement of the ordinary courts of the land had long been recognised as the safest and surest way of obtaining a conviction in a political trial.[5] Members of the judiciary were specially chosen by the Government to sit on a Special Commission and only carefully selected cases, in which a conviction was a near certainty, were sent for trial. Not since 1848 had there been a Special Commission in Ireland; then it had tried the Young Ireland leaders in Clonmel after the failure of their rising in Tipperary. Not for sixty years had Dublin seen a Special Commission; then the prisoner had been Robert Emmet.

The selection of the judges in 1865 showed how carefully the Castle had laid its plan to thwart the course of justice. The Honourable Mr. Justice William Nicholas Keogh, second judge of the Court of Common Pleas, was one of the most remarkable political adventurers Ireland produced in the nineteenth century. In Parliament he had been in turn Catholic independent conservative, Tenant Leaguer and Catholic nationalist before, in 1852, with the equally infamous John Sadlier MP, he had accepted office from the Whigs.

Notorious for his intemperate and spending habits, Keogh had recently become anti-Catholic and was later to turn anti-Irish.[6] In 1878 he died by cutting his throat with a razor; 'one of the few decent acts of his whole career' John Devoy called it. Quite unfit for judicial office, Keogh should have been the last to try the IRB leaders, since he had been regularly attacked by their paper for nearly two years.

For slightly less discreditable reasons it was equally improper for Mr. Justice John David Fitzgerald to sit on the Commission. Like Keogh, a Castle Catholic and former MP, he was also personally acquainted with Stephens, who had been tutor to the Fitzgerald boys until their father discovered the tutor's political views and promptly dismissed him.

As a member of the Privy Council not only had Fitzgerald attended both meetings on 14 and 16 September; he was also said to have been instrumental in forcing the decision to arrest the leaders. Now he was about to sit in judgement on the men of whose guilt he had presumably satisfied himself two months before on hearing the evidence against them in the privacy of the Council. Little wonder that a reputable London journal, in a commentary by a lawyer, suggested that trial by commission was unconstitutional, that the two judges were biased and that one was combining the office of prosecution and judge. O'Leary later contemptuously referred to his two judges as 'the renegade ruffian Keogh and the mere time-server Fitzgerald'.

The Crown was represented by four Queen's Counsel and the

prisoners by three. For the prosecution there appeared James A. Lawson MP, Attorney-General for Ireland, a Chancery lawyer who was not at ease in this type of case; Edward (later Sir Edward) Sullivan MP, who was the father of the saintly Jesuit, Fr. John Sullivan, and was in 1883 to become Lord Chancellor; Charles R. Barry, and J. E. Walsh, destined to become Master of the Rolls in 1869.

Leading for the prisoners was the great Isaac Butt, then by far the ablest lawyer in Ireland and known to Irish history as the father of Home Rule. Now just fifty years of age, he had represented most of the '48 leaders and had the previous year been in a notable case involving Sir William Wilde, father of Oscar. With Butt were Richard Dowse, an able northern Protestant, former Young Irelander and noted legal wit who was to be elevated to the bench in 1872, and William J. Sidney, later disbarred.

At this first sitting of the Commission, which lasted eighteen days, five IRB men—Luby, O'Leary, Michael Moore the pike-maker, John Haltigan the printer and Rossa—were tried before the Commission moved on to Cork in mid-December. The proceedings began with the swearing of the Grand Jury. In an editorial two days earlier the *Nation*, commenting on the escape from Richmond jail the previous night of James Stephens, had remarked: 'The solemn Commission on Monday next will look rather farcical now.' And, ironically enough, the first man called to serve on the Grand Jury asked to be excused because he was involved in 'an investigation of great importance respecting the Richmond prison'; he became foreman.

The Grand Jury having found true bills against the first batch of accused, Mr. Justice Keogh proceeded to deliver an opening address which for untruths, half-truths and bias generally against the prisoners almost equalled the now famous 'massacre speech' of Mr. Barry QC some two months earlier. It was common knowledge, Keogh told the jurors before any evidence had been heard, that for some two or three years a widespread conspiracy of a treasonable nature had existed in the country, extending to all classes and spreading even to the United States, having for its aim the separation of Ireland from the United Kingdom. Arms and money had been collected for the purpose of establishing some form of democratic or military despotism and a general division of property.

Although originally charged with high treason, the prisoners were now to be tried for treason-felony, a crime specially manufactured by Act of Parliament to humiliate the '48 leaders. Accordingly Keogh went on to discuss the Treason Felony Act of 1848, pointing out that, for the Crown to succeed, it must prove overt acts of treason-felony—such as, he solemnly added, meetings, purchases of arms, the collection of money, the preparation of weapons, and the administering of oaths. Finally, he reminded the jurymen that 'the object of British law is not retaliation—is not mere vengeance'.

This address by Keogh was to set the pattern for his conduct of these trials generally. He was to allow in evidence what was clearly inadmissible; he was to argue continually with counsel for the defence and to interrupt their addresses. His charges to the juries were to be manifestly biased against the prisoners and occasionally inaccurate, and to roam over a wide field of political matters quite irrelevant to the charges in the indictments.

The reduction of the charges from high treason to treason-felony was no act of clemency by the Castle. It was merely the result of an unexpected difficulty which the Crown had encountered in proving its case. Only one informer could give certain vital evidence for which at least two witnesses were needed by statute to sustain a charge of treason. Admittedly a conviction for treason-felony did not carry the death penalty, but (as Rossa was to discover in a few short weeks) it could lead to imprisonment for any term up to life. And in later cases where the evidence warranted such a course the Crown did not hesitate to prefer a charge of high treason.

After Keogh's address the clerk read out details of the charges, which occupied thirty-two printed pages, almost unprecedented even for such an important trial. Not only the decision to reduce the charges but also the actual indictments were withheld from the prisoners and their legal representatives until the Commission sat, a shabby course which drew vehement protests from Butt, who vainly demanded an adjournment. Summarised, the charges amounted to plotting the deposition of the Queen, levying war against her and inducing foreigners to invade her realm.

The first prisoner to be tried was Thomas Clarke Luby. His trial took four days, the assembling of the jury alone occupying three hours because of the systematic challenging of jurors by Butt. The evidence closely followed that of the preliminary hearings in the Castle, perhaps the most damaging revelations being the amount of documentary material most of the IRB leaders left for the police to find, only Stephens and Rossa showing some caution in this respect.

The Crown repeated the allegation of the plan for a general massacre, but in noticeably milder tones. Indeed, editorials from the *Irish People* had to be strained both for this purpose and to suggest IRB designs on the Catholic Church. 'Dick' Dowse QC found only one opportunity to display his wit. When Schofield, the spy who proved O'Mahony's handwriting, said he had been in

the perfumery business in New York, Dowse commented that he
must have been a 'head scenter'.

When found guilty, Luby made a short speech, strenuously
denying the anti-clerical accusations against the paper, but curiously
admitting that he had had a fair trial. Keogh sentenced him to
twenty years' penal servitude.

On Friday 1 December 1865, while the first jury was still out
considering a verdict in Luby's case, the trial of John O'Leary
began. Destined to be by far the longest of the five trials at this
first sitting in Dublin, it fills close on 300 pages of the official report.
After four days of pleasant conversation with his solicitor and
Rossa 'in the subterranean regions of the Green Street courthouse',
the accused, apparently quite unconcerned about his fate, was
brought up to the dock.

Still almost entirely unknown to the public, he was referred to
by one Dublin paper as 'Doctor O'Leary' through confusion with
his half-brother Edmund. Another city journal described him as
having 'an intellectual head, pale thin face, Roman nose, and a fine
close black beard far down onto his breast'; he was 'handsome, of
gentlemanlike appearance, and had a piercing eye'. Alone of public
figures John Martin had claimed O'Leary as a friend; he had known
him in Paris, he told a meeting of the National League, and regarded
him as an honourable, virtuous and sincerely patriotic man, utterly
above any mean or sordid motive.

Butt, as he had done in Luby's case and in the trials of 1848,
challenged the credentials of nearly every juror called and succeeded
in proving non-residence for about one-third of them. In all, nearly
eighty had to be called before twelve were sworn; the foreman was
David McBirney of Aston's Quay.

The trial began with a minor but startling outburst by the prisoner
himself. When put the formal question by the clerk 'Are you
ready?', O'Leary acidly remarked: 'As the Crown are, I must be.'
Immediately after this, when asked the equally formal question 'Are
you guilty?', he answered contemptuously: 'It is the Barrys, and
the Nagles and the Government of this country that are guilty and
not I.' When the question was repeated the reply came in a loud
tone: 'I am not guilty.'

The Attorney-General opened for the Crown. His statement
followed the corresponding speech in Luby's case, save for the
obvious changes. He emphasised that O'Leary was being prosecuted
not merely as the editor of the paper, but chiefly as a leading member
of the treasonable conspiracy. Yet even the opening statement
showed that this side of the case was somewhat thin against O'Leary
—until Mr. Lawson came to the damning evidence of O'Leary's
position as financial manager of the movement, the man through

whose hands some £8,000 had passed from the other side of the Atlantic in the previous two years.

The following day, 2 September, the evidence began; it was to take a day-and-a-half. On the first day eleven witnesses were called. Joseph Seymour, a clerk in the Foster Place branch of the Royal Bank of Ireland, gave evidence of O'Leary's bank account there and proved O'Leary's signature and handwriting. Some jurors questioned Seymour about the words, 'Editor *IP*' on some papers. Charles Chabot, a handwriting expert, proved both O'Leary's and O'Mahony's handwriting. A smug witness, he was to be put some searching questions by the foreman, McBirney, when recalled the next day.

Nagle, the informer, covered much the same ground as in the Luby trial, with some natural emphasis on O'Leary's doings. A native of county Tipperary, he had been a national teacher at Powerstown near Clonmel, had lost his job in curious circumstances, spent a short period in America and returned to Dublin, where he became a clerk in a city church by day and a folder of papers in the *Irish People* office at night. Since April 1864 he had been supplying the Castle with information about the IRB for small weekly payments, an offer to turn informer in 1862 having been turned down.

A searching cross-examination of Nagle by Dowse erupted into a sharp clash between Butt and Judge Fitzgerald, which terminated only when his Lordship declined to answer a sarcastic invitation by Butt to come down and act as counsel for the prisoner. Five members of the G division of the Dublin police force also gave evidence that day. Detectives John Smollen and Patrick King told of the midnight arrest of O'Leary at his lodgings and of searching his papers, while Detective Edward Hughes described his search and discoveries in the newspaper office earlier, and Detective Richard Woulfe proved more papers which a second search of the lodgings revealed.

On 3 December the proceedings resumed with yet another minor and characteristic diversion by O'Leary. Through his lawyers he protested against being brought to court without collar, tie or breakfast; Butt obtained a brief adjournment to remedy the nutritional deficiency. Nineteen more witnesses were called for the Crown that day, but none was as important or as sensational as those of the previous day.

First came the story of the finding of the lost American drafts at Kingstown railway station some months earlier, one of the events that had started the panic in the Castle. The telegraph boy, two female postal officials and a police superintendent involved in the find all told their stories. Six other police witnesses that day included the well-known G-man Launcelot Dawson, and a constable from Queenstown who identified Rossa as the man who had travelled to the United States the previous June under an assumed name.

Two Post Office officials proved other drafts from New York which, on instructions from the Castle, had been intercepted in the post; an employee of Rothschilds, the London banking concern, testified to the cashing of all the non-intercepted bills. Other minor witnesses included O'Leary's landlady, Mrs. Teresa Putt (to whom, incidentally, he owed almost five weeks rent at 11/6d. a week), and her maid, Eliza Walsh. Detective Dawson had told the jury of a night in the previous August when, with a colleague, he spent several uncomfortable hours lying full-length in the cabbage-garden outside O'Leary's front window and was rewarded by a conversation in the course of which a voice, later identified as Luby's, loudly claimed that with £5,000 he could land 8,000 troops from America at Galway.

The jury, naturally anxious for some corroboration of this belligerent discussion, took the opportunity of questioning Mrs. Putt as to the possibility of sound travelling far enough to reach the incumbent sleuth's receptive ears. It remained for Butt to poke fun at the unlikely story in cross-examination; and the student of Fenianism a century later, with access to the confidential report Dawson made to his superiors, cannot avoid doubting that any such statement was ever made from inside that room.

When the Crown case closed Isaac Butt rose to make the opening address for the prisoner. It was to prove a masterly speech, one of the greatest in a distinguished career at the Irish and English Bars, and easily the outstanding event of all the trials of the Special Commission. Spread over part of two days, it was to last five hours, and to occupy forty-one pages of the official report, totalling some 20,000 words. Marking a significant point in the gradual conversion to nationalism of the future Home Rule agitator, it was a provocative and controversial indictment of the Castle for its clumsy handling of the whole IRB conspiracy. On at least eight occasions Butt was interrupted—four times by the Attorney-General, three times by Judge Fitzgerald and (oddly enough) only once by Keogh.

Beginning with a sharp reminder to the jury that, in view of all the evidence they had heard of O'Leary's associates, it was he and not O'Mahony or Stephens or Rossa who was being tried, Butt went on to explain two points of vital importance in the Crown's case. The jury must find O'Leary guilty of the specific charges in the indictment only; and they must find him guilty not on inference, conjecture or speculation but on clear, distinct and coercive evidence. With the whole of the British Empire turned into a detective machine furnishing proofs against O'Leary, Butt continued, this was surely a case in which to expect such evidence. Yet of all the witnesses, Nagle alone had referred to O'Leary as the editor of the *Irish People*.

As Butt proceeded to analyse the informer's evidence O'Leary himself interrupted from the dock—the sole occasion on which he did so during the whole case—to object strongly to what he thought was the implication in Butt's previous remarks that it was discreditable to have been connected with the paper; he for one disagreed. The momentary interruption appears to have upset Butt, who soon afterwards complained of exhaustion, and on the suggestion of the foreman, Mr. McBirney, the hearing was adjourned to the next day.

On 5 December Butt resumed his address, clearly back at the top of his form. He first directed the jury's attention to the so-called Executive Document, the paper signed by Stephens before his departure to America in March 1864, appointing Luby, O'Leary and Kickham to act in his absence at the head of the society. Did O'Leary consent to be named in this obviously incriminating document, or did he subsequently adopt the act of appointment in it? These, Butt forcibly argued, were what should determine the value of this document as it affected the man now in the dock.

From the Executive Document Butt moved on to deal with the bills of exchange from New York addressed to O'Leary. Here he was on weak ground. His strongest criticism of this evidence was that these drafts should not be held against O'Leary until the jury was satisfied what use the money had been put to. He suggested that the Crown should have been able to trace the cash notes exchanged for the drafts, an unconvincing line of argument.

All the evidence dealt with, Butt finally made a powerful emotional appeal to the jury.

Let none of us mistake our position—we are acting history to-day. The verdict you record will be another entry in the annals of this country. . . . There is in the evidence here abundance, if you approach it in the spirit of detectives, to lead you to the moral probability that this man is guilty; but there is not that legal evidence which alone can coerce your minds. . . . The day may come to all of us, when we will ask . . . to have the best construction put upon our acts; and I call upon you to judge John O'Leary as you would be judged if that day should come.

Deal mercifully in the disposal of your brother's life. I use the word advisedly; for conviction will be worse than death to a man of the prisoner's habits and tastes; and it was his literary tastes that led to his connexion with this journal. If he had not been able to write, he would not be standing in that dock, to be subject to the indignities of prison dress, discipline and convict labour; to be hurried from this court in the prison van; to have the prison door closed upon him; to be put amongst felons and pardoned murderers; to be obliged to work as a beast of burden.

To such a man all this is worse than death; it is a long, a living torture, inflicting the agony of death, from which at last the victim may find relief in death itself. . . . If you pronounce a verdict of not guilty, be sure that when you return home to domestic endearments, to the wife, child or the sister that you have left, you will appreciate them the more, when you feel that you have sent a fellow-countryman back to fond and affectionate hearts; and when prejudices and passions shall have passed away, you will look back on the verdict and feel that you have done your duty to the prisoner at the bar, to the liberties of your country, and, above all, to that law which sustains those liberties.

As Butt sat down at the close of this stirring speech history repeated itself. For from the public galleries, from which the Castle authorities had done their best to exclude the ordinary citizen, there burst forth a great and prolonged round of applause—just as, in 1848, Butt's speech for Smith O'Brien and Meagher of the Sword had drawn cheers. Neither judge made any effort to stop the demonstration.

Although it was to continue for another day-and-a-half, O'Leary's trial was now all but over. Only two witnesses were called for the defence. First came John Joseph Meehan, a building contractor, who proved measurements he had made outside O'Leary's lodgings, to strengthen the defence suggestion that it was impossible for Detective Dawson to have heard any conversation in the first-floor room when hidden in the garden underneath.

Father John O'Hanlon, then a curate in the city church of Saints Michael and John, next went into the witness-box to prove his officiating at and recording of the marriage of James Stephens, and O'Leary's acting as best man. Butt had understood the Crown to have alleged that a reference, in a letter from Stephens, to O'Leary as his 'best man' should be construed in the sense of O'Leary's occupying second place in the treasonable organisation. Upon the Crown's denying this allegation the priest was directed to stand down before completing his evidence.

Dowse then closed for the prisoner in a comparatively brief, wholly unemotional but entirely efficient speech which, curiously, impressed his client more than Butt's magnificent address. He was followed by the Solicitor-General for the Crown in a speech lasting several hours and occupying the remainder of that day, the main feature of which was a spirited interruption by Butt himself, in which he found surprising support from an unidentified juror.

The following morning Judge Fitzgerald, in a speech lasting just over two-and-a-half hours, charged the jury in a scandalously biased and occasionally inaccurate address, which clearly demonstrated that the Crown had wisely chosen him as Keogh's partner on the bench. Opening in a political vein, he referred to the alleged aim of the Fenians to secure a redistribution of property; not a scrap of evidence had been offered in support of this claim. Turning to the evidence of the informer Nagle, he issued the customary warning about accepting the word of such a man, but gave it as his opinion that Nagle's testimony was amply corroborated.

Analysing the rest of the Crown case, he sneered at O'Mahony, interpreted the Executive Document in a manner that even Crown counsel had not dared to do, and read out wholly incorrectly a document in O'Leary's handwriting containing numerals, to each of which Fitzgerald added the word 'pound' despite the prudent omission by the writer of the monetary symbol. After having been checked by a juror when giving incorrectly the total of the seized drafts, Fitzgerald went on to advance the view that the financial documents showed decisively that O'Leary was the real leader of the whole conspiracy.

Finally, he reversed the old maxim of English justice that every man is presumed innocent until the contrary is proved. It had been said, he remarked, that the Crown should have proved where the money sent to O'Leary had gone; on the contrary, it was up to O'Leary to prove that it had been innocently applied. If the jury put an innocent explanation on this evidence, they should do so; otherwise, said Fitzgerald, 'it leads directly to the conclusion that the prisoner is guilty'.

At 12.35 p.m. the jury retired. After deliberating for an hour and forty-five minutes they returned at 2.10 p.m. and announced a verdict of guilty. This news was received quite calmly by O'Leary. When asked the customary question as to whether he wished to advance any reason why sentence should not be passed on him, he looked round the courtroom defiantly and, scowling at the judges, began to speak in his usual hesitating and now barely audible tone: 'My lord, I was not wholly unprepared for this. I felt that the Government which had so successfully packed the bench could not fail to make sure of its juries.'

Here Judge Fitzgerald stopped him momentarily, but raising his voice O'Leary continued: '. . . It is only by the most forcible interpretation of that highly elastic instrument, English law, that these men dare to make out a case against me.'

Then, in pointed reference to Fitzgerald's now silent but fuming colleague on the bench, he remarked: 'No doubt men will always be ready for money or some other motive to place themselves at the disposal of the Government.' Halted once more in his tracks by Fitzgerald, O'Leary insisted on spitting out a contemptuous refutation of the allegation of a massacre plot levelled against himself and his fellow prisoners by 'that miserable man Barry'.

Finally, in an immortal passage that has taken its place amongst the great speeches from the dock in Irish history, he concluded:

I will say only one word more, and I shall have done. I have been found guilty of treason—or treason-felony. Treason is a foul crime. The poet Dante places traitors in the ninth circle of his hell—I believe, the lowest circle. But what kind of traitors are these? Traitors against kin, country, friends and benefactors. England is not my country; I have betrayed no friend, no benefactor. Sidney was a legal traitor, a traitor according to the law, and so was Emmet; Jeffreys and Norbury were loyal men. I leave the matter there.

This time there was no applause. No doubt everyone present realised what such a speech would bring to its speaker. Few could have anticipated the brief scene which was to follow, and angry exchange between judge and prisoner, now convict, that hardly bore out Keogh's assurance some days earlier that the object of British law was not mere vengeance. After a ten-minute retirement Fitzgerald and Keogh returned, and Fitzgerald addressed O'Leary directly. In a brief speech containing the conventional remarks about the painful duty he had now to carry out, he remarked that O'Leary ought to have known that the game he had entered upon was hopeless. The official report continues:

O'LEARY: Not hopeless.
JUDGE: You knew that insurrection or revolution meant a war of extermination.
O'LEARY: It meant no such thing.
JUDGE: You have lost.
O'LEARY: For the present.

Fitzgerald was not yet finished. Cruelly quoting from a letter of Stephens himself about treason, he expressed the hope that the sentence he was about to impose would deter others. After one final interjection from the still defiant O'Leary of 'I hope not', the sentence was imposed—twenty years' penal servitude.

The announcement was received by O'Leary without any trace of emotion. With a brief glance at his devoted sister Ellen, who had sat through the entire trial on a special seat beside him just outside the dock, and who was now observed by reporters to be trying to repress her feelings, O'Leary was hurried below.

WITHIN MINUTES OF HIS REMOVAL from the dock O'Leary was introduced to the rigours of life as a convict. In nearby Halston Street a prison van awaited him, surrounded by an escort of cavalry and mounted police. This time he was taken, not back to Kilmainham (to where all the IRB prisoners had been removed from Richmond jail the day after Stephens's escape) but to Mountjoy prison. Here his beard and hair were shaved off; he was put into the drab convict uniform with the hated broad-arrow design and, with a placard bearing his name and number hanging round his neck, he was photographed. After the prison rules had been read out to him he was taken to his cell.

Over two weeks passed slowly in Mountjoy while the rest of the trials in Dublin and Cork were being held. Meals—breakfast of gruel and milk, dinner and supper of bread and milk, with meat twice a week—were passed through a trap-door in the cell door, through which one's clothes had to be passed out at night. Sleep was impossible. The bed was of the hammock type, reminding one of the IRB prisoners of a coffin; every fifteen minutes during the night the trap-door was noisily opened and a bright light shone through on to the convict's face, so as to satisfy the warder that the inmate had not escaped in mid-winter in his flannels and shirt.

On 23 December the IRB convicts were wakened unusually early and, after a cursory examination by the prison doctor, pronounced fit for a journey. With handcuffs on their wrists, manacles round their ankles and chained together in groups of two or three, they set off in a closed prison van at 5.15 a.m. on a dark, wet December Saturday morning, with a detachment from the Fifth Dragoon Guards in front and mounted Dublin Metropolitan Police men behind. At the corner of Rutland (now Parnell) Square a second military escort joined them as the horse-drawn vehicle rattled through Sackville (now O'Connell) Street and out along the coast road to Kingstown, now Dun Laoghaire.

At Kingstown pier they were taken from the van and, passing between two more rows of armed soldiers, were put on board the steamer *Ulster*, by now occupied by a detachment from the Royal Marine Light Infantry. On board ship they were all placed, still chained, in one cabin and taken in charge by an official of Pentonville penitentiary.

Upon arrival at Holyhead on the Welsh coast the convicts were met by a large crowd as well as by yet another escort of armed marines, and given into the custody of a party of warders from

Pentonville under the deputy-governor—who declined to answer O'Donovan Rossa when sarcastically asked why the irons could not be removed now that they were in a free country. During the long train journey to London Rossa persuaded a warder to purchase a meat-pie at Chester for his guests. Upon arrival at Euston at 8 p.m. the convicts were transferred to a prison van containing iron cages; in this vehicle they crossed London to Pentonville jail.

In Pentonville the IRB men were ushered together into a large hall and told to strip naked. When their bodies had been thoroughly searched for hidden articles, they were ordered to don a new set of prison clothes, similar to those which they had discarded, but without flannels. Outside snow fell heavily. After supper, which consisted of a pint of gruel and four ounces of bread, the convicts were locked into their separate cells, seven feet square and containing a board-bed seven feet by three feet and covered by a half-inch mattress, two sheets, one blanket and a rug.

The following morning, Christmas Eve, the prisoners rose at six o'clock to a breakfast of $\frac{2}{3}$-pint of cocoa and eight ounces of bread. Since it was a Sunday, Victorian England did not require them to work; and since socialistic Fenians were not expected to be practising Catholics, there was no Mass. At mid-day dinner arrived—one pound of potatoes, one pound of bread (double the ration for a weekday), four ounces of meat 'in its own liquor', and four ounces of cheese, another Sunday speciality.

At 5 p.m. supper was served, the prisoners retiring at 7.30 p.m. to their separate cells. At 8 p.m. the bell rang for bed and the gas lights went out, plunging the cells into total darkness. None of the IRB men has told whether or not they were obliged to work on Christmas Day; but since Rossa's account of his Christmas dinner shows that he got the normal Sunday fare, it may be assumed that no work was done that day either.

Next day the real meaning of penal servitude became a little clearer. Fifteen minutes were allowed at the break of day for dressing, and for cleaning one's cell—washing the water-can washing-basin and cell-urinal, and polishing the brass tip of the gas burner. While this was going on, the orderlies, two convicts from each block chosen in rotation, were doing their chores—collecting the slops from each cell, sweeping the floor, dusting the doors, cleaning the toilets, brightening brasses and helping to serve breakfast.

The meal over, there came morning parade, followed by a search of each prisoner before they all marched off to work, which continued all day except during dinner period. Once a week the convict had to wash out his cell; twice a week he was permitted the luxury of a shave. In Pentonville, what was known as a close prison, the work was picking oakum, that is, tearing old tar ropes to floss; failure to complete three pounds daily incurred punishment.

Before and after work, exercise was permitted; this involved walking round the yard in groups. Talking was prohibited at work, at exercise or from one cell to another. No wonder, after deputy-governor Farquharson had read out the rules to the new arrivals, that O'Leary whispered grimly to Rossa: 'This is hell.'

'The history of one day,' said O'Donovan Rossa years later, 'contains the history of nearly every day of prison life; the same cheerless food, the same solitary confinement, the same dreary monotony; except that if you grew discontented with any of these things you could have a change for the worse in dark cells, bread and water, handcuffs or anything that way. . . .' Rossa while a convict did much to provoke many such changes for the worse; but even without provocation the jail officials habitually made the lot of the Irish political prisoner more miserable than that of the dregs of England's criminal world.

Clothes badly folded were scattered round the floor; the Irish accent was regularly mimicked aloud; soft slippers were worn to spy on misbehaving prisoners at night. The IRB men were frequently forced to work beyond their capacity. One was obliged to work for days while blood poured down his legs from piles, another long after his fingers had been broken by a heavy stone; a third was made to remain at work although he was literally dying of cold. Kickham was forced to do knitting and sewing though half-blind, and O'Leary to pick oakum although his hands were torn from the efforts of previous days.

Breach of prison rules or failure to complete the prescribed quota of prison labour resulted in punishment, the most frequent and the mildest form of which was a diet of one pound of bread and one pint of water daily for anything up to several days at a time. Other types of physical punishment included confinement in a darkened cell or in a totally dark cell, either on a bread-and-water diet or on a more severe penal-class diet, solitary confinement in handcuffs or manacles, or in both.

For mental punishment a convict might be refused visitors or letters or forbidden to write letters, often for years at a time; a convict undergoing punishment for a prison offence was not allowed to attend religious service on Sundays. In addition to all this, there was the system of marks and remission. One's sentence was automatically converted into so many thousand marks, including remission for good conduct. Each punished offence involved a deduction of marks and accordingly a shorter period of remission, possibly a total loss of remission as the marks deducted accumulated.

Yet even in such a grim régime there were rare light moments and occasional opportunities to evade rules with impunity. Once a week the convicts took a bath in a long trough of cold water divided into thirty-six cubicles, each big enough to hold one man, who shared the same foul water with the other thirty-five. Since the cubicle wall did not extend down to the floor, one could stretch one's leg under the wall into the neighbouring cubicle. One day the irrepressible Rossa managed to get a cubicle adjacent to that into which he had seen Kickham enter; he then succeeded in 'kicking up an acquaintance' with him. 'I spoke to him as intelligently as I could with my big toe, and he seemed to understand me, for he gave it a shake-hands.'

The prisoners' ability to see the humorous side of things was not shared by the officials. When Kickham commented in a letter home that 'if the girls go into convents at this rate, the Fenians may well become monks', the passage was erased as being of 'an idle or improper tendency'.[7] When Rossa cut himself while shaving and, with his own blood wrote (truthfully) on the cell-door *Le sang rouge d'Irlande coule en Angleterre*, he got forty-eight hours on bread-and-water, because it was alleged that this meant 'the red blood of Ireland *will rise* in England'.

Ingenious methods of communicating were soon evolved by the IRB men, who quickly learned 'the secret telepathy which is an occult science of jails'. Words were laboriously tapped out with eating utensils on cell walls; wives' letters were torn into shreds, tied to minute pieces of slate and thrown over cell walls to be pieced together again for re-reading. Newspapers and tobacco were secretly traded; in Chatham, Rossa had his poems passed round an entire cell-block for critical appraisal. At Mass while one group of apparently devout men prayed fervently aloud another also whispered aloud, but on topics far removed from religion.

Nor was the possibility of rescue overlooked. Early in 1866 a London engineering firm got a contract for iron work in Pentonville. Then in the firm's employment was a young Cork engineer named Jerome Collins, who had been clerk of works for the North Gate Bridge in Cork. Collins visited the jail several times in the course of his work and was introduced by the governor to the block containing inmates from his own country. Back in his lodgings each evening Collins made notes of a section of the prison lay-out he had memorised that day.

Having studied the complete plan of the jail he considered that a mass escape would be possible, given proper planning and some courageous men. His idea was to blow with petards the outer and inner gates, thus giving immediate access to the office between the two in which the cell keys were stored at night. But, before he succeeded in laying his scheme before any influential IRB man in

London, his employers got to hear of his project and informed the Government.[8]

Jerome Collins took the next boat to America, to become the founder of the powerful Clan na Gael organisation, and a pioneer of modern weather forecasting before dying mysteriously in the famous *Jeannette* Polar expedition of 1879–82. In Portland jail later, John Boyle O'Reilly made three attempts to escape, and Rossa, Hugh Brophy and Michael Moore all entertained the idea to the extent of planning for it.[9]

Although it was customary for penal servitude prisoners to spend nine months in the probationary prison, the stay in Pentonville of O'Leary and his comrades was cut short for a reason never made clear. Perhaps it was felt that a jail near London might offer other opportunities for rescue projects.

On 14 May 1866 the twenty-four IRB convicts in Pentonville were awakened even earlier than usual, chained together once more and taken through London in prison vans to Waterloo station, where they began a seven-hour railway trip. They were sustained during the journey by bread and cheese served in canvas bags, and, after some skilful negotiations by Mulcahy with their accompanying warders, they succeeded in securing permission to converse freely.

At Weymouth station the train was diverted to Portland convict prison. Here, in what the *Times* later called 'the bracing air and pleasant scenery of Portland', their condition generally was to take a turn for the worse.[10] Here, too, O'Leary and Luby were destined to spend the rest of their term in jail.

Situated off the coast of Dorset, the so-called Isle of Portland is joined to the mainland by a natural break-water known as Chisel Beach. Portland prison, a public works penitentiary, stands on the top of an exposed hill on this bleak treeless peninsula, noted for its extreme of weather. Here are situated quarries of an almost white stone which have been worked for several centuries.

Here in mid-1866 the IRB prisoners were introduced to a régime of slave labour as brutal as its successors in other countries a century or so later. 'It was,' said the Home-Secretary solemnly in the Commons in 1869, 'the most cheerful and the most healthy of all the convict prisons.' O'Leary in a letter to his sister three months after his arrival stated—and since the passage was not erased it must have been the truth—that he had so far been able to do all the work given him, 'but it only required one more turn of the screw and I will be overpowered'.[11]

As had happened at Pentonville five months earlier, the prisoners, immediately upon arrival, were obliged to strip naked and had their bodies searched. Having then been given a new uniform, three religious books, two educational books and one library book, they were lodged in basement cells which had never previously been occupied. Measuring seven feet by four and flagged, the cells had sides and a roof of iron; air came in and went out through two slits over and under the door, while indirect light from the central hall did its best to penetrate two panels of opaque glass on one side-wall. '. . . However we were boarded, we were not very comfort-ably lodged,' commented Rossa later.

The daily routine in Portland was similar to that in Pentonville, but with two important differences. First, both food and drink were inferior in quality. Breakfast and supper were the same as in Pentonville; for dinner five ounces of meat were served com-pared to four in Pentonville, while the weekly bread ration totalled 168 ounces as against 148 in Pentonville.

In practice the meat was tough and hard, often inedible and occasionally tainted; the bread was barely digestible, the soup almost water and an occasional pudding 'would take the stomach of an ostrich to digest', according to Rossa. Moreover, the food was always served in filthy unwashed tins, the drinking water often contained live tadpoles, and the soup was frequently flavoured with dead mice. 'On this food,' said John Devoy, 'big men and little men, without regard to height or weight, were to do a full day's work at stone-cutting, relieved by occasional confinement on "bread-and-water". Yet only three or four of them went mad.'[12]

By far the more important difference between life in Penton-ville and in Portland was the type of work which the inmates were required to do. Portland was a public works prison and the quarries on the island were worked entirely by convicts. The land had to be cleared, trenched and then excavated; the stone had to be quarried, lifted, carried and finally dressed.

All this entailed work out of doors in every type of weather; even in hot weather, without the normally biting sea-wind, the prevailing whiteness of the stone, combined with the glare of the sun, resulted in frequent damage to the strongest eyes, a complaint from which most of the IRB men, including O'Leary, were soon to suffer. In addition, some warders brutally ill-treated the Irish prisoners. They were forced to carry huge stones on their backs and at times obliged, yoked five or six to a cart, to pull cart-loads of material.

Probably because of their arrival sooner than expected, no special instructions had been received as to what work the Irish prisoners were to do. So for their first week or so O'Leary, Luby, Rossa and the rest were assigned to the wash-house, cleaning the garments of 1,600 of the lowest stratum of English criminal life. In due course, however, orders came from the director, William Fagan, a Cork-man, a Catholic and a former MP in the 1850s. The Irish treason-felony prisoners were to work in the quarries like everyone else, but as a separate party and under the strict supervision of reliable English Protestant officers. O'Leary, Luby and Rossa were put to work as one gang in a valley visible from the window of the governor's office.

Although over 300 of the Portland prisoners were Catholics, there was no priest to minister to them in 1866. Governor Clifton openly sneered at the rosaries and scapulars he found on some of the Irish prisoners, and caustically reminded them of their ex-communication by Archbishop Cullen. He had, however, no objection to one of their number reading aloud religious works to the rest.

Clifton's choice was Luby, who, although a Protestant, had allowed himself (as had O'Leary) to be entered on the jail records as a Roman Catholic. Luby felt that this was asking too much of him and, protesting that he was not 'orthodox', suggested Kickham as a more suitable reader. The task was in fact allotted to Mulcahy, who made the best of the Protestant Bible. Never, recalled Rossa later, had he heard such treasonable preaching from a 'chaplain'; passages which denounced tyrants and oppressors, perjurers and liars, and which invoked blessings on those who suffered persecution for the sake of justice, were repeatedly read out by Mulcahy in the hearing of the humourless warders.

After some weeks, however, a special room was fitted out as a chapel and an altar erected there from stone hewn by the Irish prisoners themselves. Then along came the stern cold Fr. Poole, English to the core although trained at All Hallows College, Dublin; his strict adherence to the letter of his instructions must have made him practically useless as a spiritual adviser, at least so far as the Irish prisoners were concerned.

How did O'Leary, the product of a well-to-do Irish provincial home, who had been to a university and travelled abroad, and who had mixed with writers and artists, cope with this drastic change in his mode of life? There can be no doubt that he suffered greatly. Curiously enough, prison food affected him least of all; apparently his lean frame was satisfied with far less nourishment than the average man needed.

Indeed, his thin figure seems to have alarmed the officials in Portland, for without any request from O'Leary the governor and medical officer approved his getting meat instead of soup for dinner daily from March 1869. No doubt he missed his choice wines, and he certainly keenly felt the total prohibition on tobacco; Rossa endured punishment for trying to pass to O'Leary tobacco which he had acquired in his trading transactions. Like so many others in Portland, O'Leary had serious eye trouble and for a time

feared that he was going blind; this proved not to be the case.[13]
Characteristically, it seems that his eye complaint was as much the
result of over-use of the prison library as of any other cause.

Above all, O'Leary suffered from the cold. Several of the IRB
men made the same complaint about Portland, and even a hardy
man like Rossa, used to an open-air life, admitted that the cold
in Portland was the most intense he had ever endured. 'The climate
here is considered good; yet I fear few of us will stand it towards
the Fall, not to speak of the Winter.' So O'Leary commented in
a letter to his sister Ellen shortly after his arrival.[14]

The prison garb—a hemp smock, coarse-cloth jacket, sun-
bleached fustian breeches, cotton shirt and drawers, waistcoat,
peakless cap, belt, stockings and fourteen-pound boots—was clearly
inadequate for such a severe and exposed place and never varied
in hot or cold weather. All the prisoners noticed that the British
garments were of a poorer and lighter quality than the Mountjoy
uniform. Although an extra blanket was supplied in Portland in
the winter, the bedclothes were far too light for men obliged to
sleep wearing only shirt and flannels. As ill-luck would have it,
the winters of 1866 and 1867 were exceptionally cold.

Not surprisingly, O'Leary, like Luby and several of the others
with well-to-do backgrounds, was unable to do the prison work
satisfactorily. According to Devoy, oakum-picking inevitably
caused blistered fingers for a long initial period; he noticed that
the long slender hands of O'Leary were badly torn from this work.
In Portland the principal stone-work given to O'Leary's group
was making 'knobblers', forming hexagonal blocks of rough stone
quarried by others. This also caused bad hand blisters, since it
necessitated constant handling of a pick; it was, said the sturdy
Devoy, painful to watch Luby and O'Leary trying to manage this
implement. A letter from one of the Portland prisoners, written
after he had left the jail, refers to O'Leary being punished because
of his inability to wheel a heavy barrow full of stones and bricks.[15]

But, as always with O'Leary, his personal feelings took second
place to his principles. Events which occurred towards the end of
his imprisonment strongly suggest that from the start he was
regarded by the rest of the Irish prisoners as their leader and spokesman. He soon made it clear how he believed they should all behave
while in jail. As political prisoners—they always referred to themselves as the Irish State prisoners—they would endure without
complaint whatever treatment their captors would mete out to them.

Prison rules would be strictly obeyed, and there would be no
open defiance of the prison authorities. Obedience and subordina-
tion were, according to Luby (who fully agreed with O'Leary in
this matter) above all in accord with the dignity of the cause for

which they had been imprisoned and must now suffer. 'The political prisoner . . . considers that his sufferings ennoble his acts,' commented an official visitor to the IRB men in 1870.

This rigid and high-principled self-imposed set of rules was by no means faithfully obeyed by all the Irish prisoners; in particular, it became impossible to adopt a common policy as the convicts gradually became scattered through a number of jails. But to the end of their term of imprisonment the great majority continued to accept O'Leary's leadership on all matters of importance.

The main exception among the men not prepared to carry out O'Leary's policy was O'Donovan Rossa. But his was a special case. Finding from the start that he was singled out for particularly brutal treatment, he responded with a remarkable one-man campaign against the whole prison régime, with the result that he was constantly undergoing punishment for his defiant attitude. In his first three years in jail Rossa spent 123 days on a bread-and-water diet, 231 days on penal-class diet in a darkened cell, twenty-eight days in a totally dark cell, and thirty-nine days in handcuffs, thirty-four of them with his hands handcuffed behind his back even during mealtimes.

By O'Leary's strict code Rossa's actions were undignified for a political prisoner, and O'Leary bluntly told him so in Portland on several occasions, addressing him as 'Mr. O'Donovan'. Once he openly tried to dissuade Rossa from refusing to clean out his toilet. Eventually, in February 1867, Rossa was removed to Millbank and thence a year later to Chatham.

Everywhere he went Rossa systematically broke the rules. He smuggled out letters to his wife and to Richard Pigott, the editor of the *Irishman* newspaper (who publicised Rossa's treatment), as well as memorials to the Home Secretary and a petition to Gladstone. Once he persuaded a friendly Protestant chaplain to make him a present of a Protestant Bible—in the Irish language. In the end he could claim that it was his one-man campaign which, more than anything else, led to the release of the bulk of the IRB prisoners.

In Portland, O'Leary continued to accept his humiliating lot without complaint. Forty years later John Devoy could still recall vividly the shock he got on the morning after his own arrival in Portland in February 1868, having already completed a year of his fifteen-year sentence in Millbank. When his cell-door opened:

. . . two prisoners . . . were carrying a large tub with a pole stuck through the two handles. As they got in front of a cell door the man in the cell emptied his night's 'slops' into the tub and the two prisoners, with a resigned look on their faces, took hold of the pole, lifted the tub full of 'slops' and wearily plodded on to the next cell.

The men engaged in this menial work were John O'Leary and Thomas Clarke Luby. . . . I had never seen O'Leary without his fine dark beard, but I recognised him and Luby at once. . . . The English prison system, we are told, has for its chief object the 'reform' of the criminal, rather than his punishment . . . this was the method by which O'Leary and Luby were being 'reformed'.

There came times when even O'Leary felt justified in committing a breach of prison regulations. Cornelius Dwyer Keane, the former centre of the IRB in Skibbereen, who had been brought up by Stephens to the staff of the *Irish People*, entered Portland a tall powerfully-built man in excellent health and weighing fourteen stone. Like so many others, he soon found himself over-worked and under-fed; after a while he took on the appearance of a gaunt skeleton. One day O'Leary tried surreptitiously to pass him his own bread ration but was detected; both men were punished and the loaf confiscated.

On another occasion, around Christmas 1868, a group consisting of O'Leary, Luby, Keane, James O'Connor, Rossa and John Kenealy of Cork were all reported for speaking at work. Rossa as usual got a severe sentence; O'Leary, Luby and Kenealy got twenty-four hours on bread-and-water. This was the last time O'Leary incurred punishment for breach of prison regulations.

Gradually the complement of Irish prisoners in Portland was reduced. Some had to be transferred because of ill-heath. The delicate Brian Dillon of Cork, only four feet ten inches in height, weighing only seven-and-a-half stone and with a deformed back, was removed to Woking invalid prison with the elderly 'Pagan' O'Leary as early as April 1866. Denis Mulcahy and William Roantree followed them, in November 1866 and February 1867 respectively; Kickham joined them there on a date now unknown.

Repeated bad conduct led to the removal from Portland of some. Rossa never returned after he was taken to Millbank early in 1867, while Devoy, John McClure, Charles Underwood O'Connell and James O'Connor were transferred to the same jail in May 1868, for having, against the express direction of Luby and O'Leary, organised what they called a strike but what the prison authorities naturally regarded as a mutiny.

Some time late in 1867, forty-five of the Irish prisoners in English jails, many of them from Portland, were sent to western Australia, whence most of them never returned. The group, which accounted for about half the total in English jails, included a strong Cork contingent (Thomas Duggan, John S. Casey, John Kenealy, Eugene Geary, Jeremiah O'Donovan and Cornelius O'Mahony among them) as well as Hugh Brophy, Stephens's confidant of the lean years of the late 1850s, Michael Moore the pike-maker, John Boyle O'Reilly, and the six men to be rescued in the memorable *Catalpa* expedition.

This move was made, it was claimed, with the consent of the men concerned. However, while Luby and Underwood O'Connell later indicated that each man had, the previous September, been asked individually to go but not pressed if he refused, there is also evidence suggesting that no choice was given.[16] Rossa was asked to agree to go also, but refused. Rumours reached him in Millbank to the effect that O'Leary and Luby had gone, but the visiting priest, Fr. Vincent Zanetti, declined to confirm the rumour. Death claimed three of the IRB convicts—John Lynch of Cork in Woking in 1866, Daniel Darragh in Portland in 1870 and Edward Duffy (who had been engaged to O'Leary's half-sister Mary) in Millbank early in 1868.

Letters and visits were the prisoners' only permitted links with the outside world, and even then only purely personal information was all that could be obtained. Depending on what class a prisoner belonged to (this in turn being dependent on his general conduct) he might every three, four or six months write and receive one letter and receive a visitor for twenty minutes.

Since the families of the Irish prisoners were almost invariably resident outside England, the practice seems to have been altered after a while to allow accumulation of visits, so that visits of an hour's duration were not unusual. Visits took place in a special room containing a glass cubicle divided into two, with a warder listening in to ensure that only personal matters were discussed. Thus did Rossa see for the first time his third wife's first child, a son born a few months after his father had got a life sentence.

As the years went on, a further relaxation of the visiting rules was apparently allowed, a visitor for one man being permitted to meet several others in turn, and presumably bring news from their families. Ellen O'Leary, who came to Portland as often as permitted, was allowed this privilege after at least one refusal; so was Rossa's wife. One prisoner was never allowed visit another who was ill in the same jail; Rossa's repeated pleas to see Duffy, who was dying, were all turned down, and even his offer to forgo normal visits in exchange for one to Duffy was heartlessly refused.

Letters had to be confined to two ruled pages of a special form, which, even in O'Leary's minute scrawl, allowed a mere 400 words or so. Although the rules printed on the reverse side of the forms did not so provide, nothing of a political nature or in any way critical of the prison régime might be mentioned in a letter. Breach of this unwritten law resulted in the offending passage being scored out by the governor or chaplain, who read all incoming and outgoing mail.

In serious cases an entire outgoing letter might be rejected and the privilege of writing forfeited for an indefinite period. Similarly, improper incoming letters might be withheld, without the intended recipients being so informed. Luby learned of the death of his aged widowed mother in 1870 from Governor Clifton, who held up in his hand a letter containing this distressing news, but refused to permit Luby to read it because he was not yet due his next letter.

Apart from two letters to Ellen, publication of which he specifically authorised in special circumstances, only one complete jail letter by John O'Leary has survived.[17] Written on 23 December 1868 to his uncle William in Tipperary, it is of some historical significance since it contains a revealing personal impression of his imprisonment, a subject O'Leary refused to discuss with even intimate friends in later life. ('I was in the hands of my enemy, why should I complain?' Thus did he dismiss the matter years later.)[18]

For more than three years I have borne, I trust not altogether unmanfully, much mental and physical suffering. How I have suffered I cannot tell; and even if I could, I would not. There was not a day or hour of all that time that might not bring forth its own peculiar pain, and perhaps the hardest thing of all to be borne was the constant fear lest something still worse remained to be borne. Comparatively speaking, however, I may still look upon myself as rather fortunate.

There follow two half-lines heavily scored out. But the scoring is not efficient enough to prevent the offending sentence being deciphered by a powerful microscope and a study of the handwriting.

For some of my companions are dead and some are mad, and many are invalids for life. To be sure, my hair is just growing grey, 'though not with years', and I seem to myself to have aged greatly, and the time may have told upon me in many more ways than even I can guess, but I still have the use of all my limbs and (I believe) of all my wits and for this, I say again, I thank God, and God alone.

The remainder of the letter is devoted entirely to more personal matters—references to Ellen's visits, to his aunt and her growing children, and some characteristic comments on a family dispute with the Loughrea cousins, in which neither 'the precious Eddy' (his half-brother) nor 'that pompous vulgar Val Dillon' (a brother of John Blake Dillon, and then a prominent Dublin solicitor) is spared.

The only letter written to O'Leary while in jail, that has been preserved, came from Charles Kickham in Woking invalid prison in 1867. He had recently learned that his friends had arranged for the publication in book form of one of his novels, *Sally Cavanagh*, and with memories of his major venture into journalism still fresh, he used his half-yearly letter as a convict to send to his former editor, now also a convict, a dedication of the forthcoming publication.

While the IRB men languished in English jails or in Australian penal settlements, they had not been forgotten by the Irish people. From the start the manly bearing of the prisoners and the severity of the sentences imposed on them gained them much sympathy, even from outside the ranks of their own supporters, which manifested itself in the generous help given to the fund set up to assist the dependents of the men in jail. Gradually, too, Rossa's dogged campaign made an impact on the outside world. With the help of Richard Pigott, whose care of and concern for Rossa's children revealed a tender side to the character of the future forger, Rossa's treatment was publicised in press and parliament.

Eventually things reached a stage at which the British Government felt that it had to do something to allay public suspicion about the treatment of the Fenian convicts. Its decision showed that combination of dishonesty and ineptitude which has so often characterised British handling of Anglo-Irish relations. On 8 May 1867 a two-man commission of inquiry was set up by the Home Secretary to investigate allegations made regarding twenty-nine Irish political prisoners in English jails. The members of this body were Alexander A. Knox, a well-known London police magistrate, and Doctor George D. Pollock, of St. George's Hospital, London.

Inside two months this body had produced and presented a report which was unsatisfactory in almost every respect. Superficially, they managed to create the impression of having done a thorough job. They visited all the jails concerned, examined the prisoners and officers privately, inspected the works and tasted the food.

To each prisoner they put a series of eight prepared questions concerning spiritual arrangements, medical attention, food, cells, clothing, possible cruelty of officers, conditions in Pentonville and treatment generally. Hearsay evidence was excluded, but no evidence was taken on oath. Prisoners were given no time to prepare evidence, to consult among themselves or to be represented. No prison records appear to have been examined and no record of evidence or meetings was kept.

Little wonder that the Government and the prison authorities were exonerated from all the charges made against them. Food and accommodation were found to be satisfactory; all the prisoners in Portland were bronzed despite its exposed position and the previous prolonged cold winter; in any event, their output was only half or one-third that of the ordinary convict. As for the allegations of cruelty, they had been concocted by half-a-dozen turbulent men and were without foundation—although Governor Clifton was revealingly described as 'a strong disciplinarian'.

A considerable portion of the evidence was taken up with the examination of the case of O'Donovan Rossa, the only prisoner to give detailed evidence. But the commission concluded that any punishment he had received was the natural result of his rebellious attitude since his conviction. The preposterous allegation of Clifton, that Rossa, because he had tried to smuggle out of Portland a letter clearly intended for his wife but addressed to Michael Moore's mother, was intriguing with Moore's wife, was accepted.

An indication of the depth of the inquiry and the credulity of Knox and Pollock may be gained from the fact that they reported as a serious statement the solitary remark which they had been able to elicit from 'treason-felony convict O'Leary', that 'he finds the state of things at Portland almost relatively perfect happiness'.

Nor was the manner of the publication of the Knox-Pollock report such as to inspire confidence. Apparently an authorised, but not full, version was released for reproduction by loyal journals; the complete report was nowhere published and is not obtainable to this day from official sources. The *Evening Mail* indiscreetly divulged, in an editorial, portions which are to be found neither in its authorised version nor in the edited version from its London correspondent. The *Irish Times* version contained substantial evidence by James O'Connor, of which not a line is to be found in either the *Evening Mail* or the *Nation*. Even the *Nation* itself has at least one quotation not to be found in either of the other two papers.

It fell to the *Nation,* however, to pass judgement in the name of the average Irishman on this whole shabby performance. Without anyone of Irish origin on it, the commission was dubious in its constitution and, not surprisingly, partisan in favour of the prison officials as well as contemptuous of the prisoners, whose only complaint it alleged to be 'that they cannot get out'. Since the inquiry merely whitewashed the authorities it was unfair, dishonest, biased and prejudiced; the report it produced was unworthy of credence or respect and as a document it was merely 'a juggle and a cheat'.

As might have been expected, the Knox-Pollock report did nothing to allay public disquiet about the treatment of the Irish political prisoners. Some twenty months later there came a sudden and inexplicable change in the British Government's attitude. An amnesty movement recently started had attracted some support and led to rumours in January 1869 of an impending release of the IRB men.

12. Fenian prisoners arriving at Cork jail, March 1866

13. Fenian prisoners exercising in a special 'cage', Mountjoy jail, June 1866

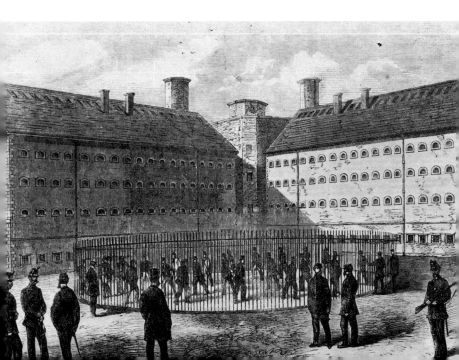

14. A flying column of British troops at Dundrum, Tipperary, after the 1867 ri

15. An amnesty meeting at Cabra, Dublin, October 1869

On the afternoon of Thursday 4 March fifteen men were ordered out of the work-gang at the quarries in Portland, marched back to their cells, where each was given a new tweed suit, £2 and his fare home. At four o'clock they were free men. At the same time at the other end of the world the same thing was happening to thirty-four other IRB convicts in western Australia, most of whom either settled in that country or made for the United States.

The group liberated in England included three former colleagues of O'Leary on the *Irish People*, Kickham, Haltigan and James O'Connor, as well as C. M. O'Keefe (the eccentric journalist whose crazy articles had provided the flimsy basis for the allegations in 1865 of a Fenian massacre plot), W. M. O'Sullivan of Kilmallock, later a prominent Irish Party MP, and William Moore Stack, father of the future patriot Austin Stack. Those freed in Australia included many of the Corkmen (but not the military prisoners or Cornelius Keane) as well as Hugh Brophy, Michael Moore and Cornelius O'Mahony, the former clerk in the *Irish People* office. At the same time Stephen Meany, one of the prisoners in Portland with American connections, received an unconditional pardon through the intervention of the United States Minister in London.

In Ireland tumultuous welcomes, marked by defiant and unrepentant speeches, particularly by Kickham, were the order of the day. When on 8 March the liner *Preussischer Adler* docked in Dublin with Kickham, Stack and O'Keefe on board, a huge crowd greeted them; a week later Kickham and Haltigan arrived in Kilkenny to find thousands packing the streets of this city which was the birthplace of the founder of the IRB. Soon the loyalist press was circulating rumours that there was to be no clemency for any further Fenian prisoners because of the ungrateful utterances of those just set free. In due course, however, Gladstone was to be compelled to change his mind once again.

The releases of 1869 proved to be the spark which set alight the hitherto flickering amnesty movement. At once the Central Amnesty Committee under John ('Amnesty') Nolan, a former IRB man and friend of Devoy, got to work organising meetings and petitions on a national scale. The Archbishop of Dublin, now a Cardinal, became so alarmed at what must have seemed to him a resurrection of the dreaded evil of Fenianism that he came out strongly against the new movement and even prohibited church-gate collections.[19]

As frequently happens in Irish politics a split occurred, out of which grew a rival organisation, the Amnesty Association, inaugurated at a monster meeting in the Rotunda, Dublin, in June 1869. In this, Isaac Butt MP, and Richard Pigott the journalist were prominent figures. The release of the remainder of the political prisoners now became for a time the main aim of Irish politics.

Even the veteran G. H. Moore MP, who after his retirement in disgust in the 1850s had been unsuccessfully courted by Stephens, spent the last year of his life advancing this new cause.

As the year progressed great meetings were held all over Ireland. One of the largest took place in Dublin in October 1869 after a week-long legal controversy between Butt and the police authorities, who had banned a planned march through the city; a week later London was the scene of another big demonstration. Shortly afterwards there came the election of O'Donovan Rossa as MP for Tipperary; when the news reached Chatham jail Rossa solemnly asked for a re-transfer back to Millbank, on the grounds that the proximity to Westminster would enable him to take his seat. As a convicted felon he was promptly unseated, and in the subsequent election Kickham failed by four votes.

By April 1870 rumour had it that Gladstone, dismayed by the continued detailed airing in press and parliament of the grievances of the Irish prisoners, was contemplating a second inquiry into their treatment. Indeed, it is now known that as far back as 1869 Dublin Castle had prepared a list of treason-felony convicts 'whose sentences might with safety be considerably reduced'. It included O'Leary, whose 'language in the dock was most intemperate'. When in May 1870 the membership, terms of reference and procedural rules of the Commission on the Treatment of Treason-Felony Convicts in English Prisons had become known, it seemed that this later investigation should prove a considerable improvement on the miserable efforts of Messrs. Knox and Pollock.

Its chairman, the Earl of Devon, was a well-known public figure in Britain and an extensive landlord in Ireland; his father had given his name to a more famous Commission twenty-seven years earlier, the Occupation of Land (Ireland) Commission of 1843, known to all students of the Famine period. Dr. R. D. Lyons of Dublin was the son of a former mayor of Cork, a professor in the Catholic university, a pioneer in Irish forestry and a fair-minded man of liberal views generally. Dr. E. H. Greenhow of London, a well-known figure in the medical world, was married to a daughter of the Scots radical leader and friend of O'Connell, Joseph Hume. The Honourable George C. Brodrick was a son of the seventh Lord Midleton and a successful barrister and then a leader-writer on the *Times*; although he was strongly opposed to Irish nationalist aspirations, at least he took an interest in Irish affairs. Finally, Stephen Edward de Vere of Adare (Sir Stephen from 1870 onwards), an elder brother of the poet Aubrey de Vere, came from a respected Limerick family.

By their letter of appointment the Commissioners were requested by the Home Secretary to inquire into and report to him on:

(i) whether there is anything in the treatment, diet or discipline of the convict prisons to justify any charge of unnecessary severity or harshness towards the prisoners confined therein, or of neglect of the conditions necessary for the due preservation of their health; and

(ii) whether the treason-felony prisoners had been subjected to any exceptional treatment in any way or have suffered any hardships beyond those incidental to the condition of a prisoner sentenced to penal servitude.

By advertisement in the Irish newspapers the Commission announced the facilities which would be available for the making of statements by the prisoners. They would first be allowed to make oral statements to the Commission in a private room, without any prison officials present and without prejudicing their future, for the preparation of which they would get three days free from work. Oral or written statements (or both) could also be made by any friend or agent of a prisoner, who would be allowed access to him. Finally, a shorthand note of the entire evidence would be taken and both the report and evidence would be published.

The shortcomings of the Commission soon became obvious. It was not empowered to administer an oath and, after an undignified correspondence in public with Butt, decided not to allow counsel to represent the prisoners. Most important of all, however, the majority of the prisoners themselves, doubtless with memories of Knox and Pollock, refused to co-operate. One of the Commissioners in his memoirs said: 'Some two-thirds of the prisoners . . . acting in concert utterly declined to make any complaint whatever, or to have anything to do with us. . . . Their patriotism . . . certainly enabled most of them to assume a certain air of dignity . . . very different from the bearing of ordinary criminals.'[20] In the adoption of this uncompromising attitude O'Leary played a leading part, and it is clear from remarks even of prisoners in jails other than Portland that he was still regarded as the spokesman of all.

When offered pen and paper by Governor Clifton to prepare a statement for the Commission, O'Leary refused them on each of the three days allowed for the purpose. Luby's reaction was to quote to the governor a remark of Daniel O'Connell about 'a jury of butchers trying a sheep'; another Portland prisoner said that if there were any Irishmen on the Commission they could be only humbugs.

When the Commission reached Portland in the course of its inspection of the jails, Lord Devon, on hearing of O'Leary's refusal to testify, and presumably being told that he was the ringleader, presented himself at O'Leary's cell-door. The exchange which followed has not been recorded, but O'Leary insisted that the Earl was rude to him. Devon then ordered him to be brought before the Commission in their room. Here it became at once apparent that five years' imprisonment had done nothing to weaken the defiance which O'Leary had displayed in Green Street courthouse in 1865.

After the chairman had explained the purpose of the Commission and its method of inquiry, he asked O'Leary if he wished to give evidence. He had asked for no Commission, answered O'Leary contemptuously, and he would make no statement of his grievances now—only in his own chosen time and place. He gathered, he continued, that they wished to know if he had been treated worse than ordinary penal servitude prisoners: 'I may complain that we have been treated no worse than murderers and thieves.'

After a sneer at Lord Devon's previous incursion into Irish affairs, O'Leary sarcastically remarked: 'You know the way convicts are treated, don't you?' O'Leary's own impression of this scene later was that 'the English doctor looked as if he regarded O'Leary as a very bad character, that Mr. de Vere seemed to consider the whole situation quite funny, and that Dr. Lyons appeared to regard O'Leary's predicament as a sad one.'[21]

To Dr. Lyons O'Leary volunteered the allegation that they had been treated much worse after the Knox-Pollock inquiry, but whether as a result of it he did not profess to know. He had, he added defiantly, seen the newspaper reports of the evidence given there—newspapers were forbidden in jail—and they were altogether false. Finally, when again asked by Lord Devon if he wished to say anything about the subject of the present inquiry, O'Leary answered: 'Did you think I was coming, like an Oliver Twist, to ask for more porridge?' He was led out.

As might have been expected from men so ill-treated and separated in different jails, there were deviations from the O'Leary line. In particular, some of the IRB men appear to have felt free to air their grievances about ill-health. Of the eight men in Woking prison, Brian Dillon, Denis Mulcahy and William Roantree testified at length on this aspect of their imprisonment.

But 'Pagan' O'Leary merely politely answered all questions put to him, emphasising that his only complaint was that his term should have started from his first trial in mid-1865. His last words to the Commission were: 'I have done the most of my time, sir; so I'll do the rest of it quietly and go away.' Both Bourke and Power, in identical prepared statements, declined to testify.

O'Donovan Rossa, then in Chatham, naturally refused to remain silent. His good name, he felt, still had to be cleared; accordingly, in a prepared statement (opening with an appropriate Latin quotation and interspersed with his own inimitable explanatory remarks) which took several days to deliver, he gave a detailed account of his prison experiences. Indeed, his patently honest testimony was to provide the Commission with material for its most scathing criticisms of the prison system, and its members frankly admitted how impressed they had been by Rossa's candour and fairness.

Nonetheless, the cases of these men were exceptions to the organised opposition of the Irish prisoners as a whole to the Commission. Devoy, as spokesman for the other five with Rossa in Chatham, in a well-reasoned statement repeated O'Leary's points in more polite language and was backed up by individual refusals from Underwood O'Connell, McClure, Halpin and Mulleda.

In the result one cannot but admire the persistence of the Commission and their success in piecing together a faithful account of the truth from unco-operative, and often patently untruthful, prison officials and from searching inspections of the jails for themselves. Lord Devon and his four colleagues pursued their investigations for the four summer months of 1870 until, by late September, they had completed sixty-three meetings, of which over one-third had been held wholly in one of the four jails concerned. It took a few months to sift the evidence, which filled over 500 foolscap-size printed pages and contained more than 16,000 questions and answers.

The fifty-page report which the Commission ultimately presented to the Home Secretary represented a notable victory for the Irish political prisoners, alike for those like Rossa who helped the investigation, as for those who followed O'Leary's lead and ignored its existence. The Commission's generally favourable finding in regard to the treatment, diet and discipline of the IRB men was so hedged about by important qualifications as to constitute a serious indictment of the entire prison system. There were reservations about the quality of the food, and a finding that its quantity was inadequate in severe weather.

The qualifications of the prison doctors were criticised, and a system of labour according to previous habits and individual capacity was recommended. The shortcomings of the so-called privilege of memorialising the Home Secretary and of the flagrant abuse of the rules regarding both incoming and outgoing mail were emphasised. Strong disapproval was voiced of the punishment practices of manacling, confinement in dark cells and reduction of food. The provision of peaked caps and of better shelters was suggested for Portland.

Similarly, in regard to the second head of the inquiry, the Commission's general finding was that no ground existed for the belief that treason-felony prisoners in English prisons were as a class treated more severely than ordinary prisoners. Nevertheless it was observed that the Irish prisoners had 'never ceased to protest against being classed with criminals, and every privilege confirmed their belief in the justice of their demands'. Finally, in a remarkable recommendation which was clearly outside the terms of reference but which fully vindicated O'Leary's stand, the Committee urged the setting aside of a separate part of each prison for political offenders.

It was no coincidence that, long before the publication in 1871 of this very human document, its findings were of merely academic interest to nearly all the IRB prisoners sentenced between 1865 and 1867. Shortly before Christmas of 1870 Gladstone, upon receipt of the report of the Commission, informed the outgoing Lord Mayor of Dublin by letter of the Government's intention to release the bulk of the treason-felony prisoners.[22] All, in fact, were to be liberated but a handful of the most recently convicted men; this group included Michael Davitt, with whom it seems unlikely that O'Leary was then able to become acquainted in Portland, since the Manchester men were strictly segregated from the Irish prisoners.

The apparent act of clemency was not to be unqualified. On the Sunday before Christmas O'Leary's native town of Tipperary (where 20,000 people had held an amnesty meeting in October) was the scene of yet another great amnesty demonstration, which was addressed by the parish priest, Dr. Howley, Ellen O'Leary's godfather. Naturally there were references to O'Leary, whom it was hoped would soon be among them once more. But with memories of the speeches of Kickham and his colleagues of 1869 still rankling, the British Government decided not to permit any of the liberated men to return to Ireland or settle in England until the completion of the term of imprisonment to which they had originally been sentenced.

In a delightful passage, penned almost forty years later, John Devoy summed up the situation:

It is said that there is no such punishment as exile known or recognised in British law, and some English newspapers denied at the time that any of the Fenian prisoners were exiled. British law and British political procedure are full of such equivocations and hypocrisies. The Fenian prisoners had frequently been told that they were not political prisoners. The political offence of which they had been convicted was called 'treason-felony', so they were treason-felony prisoners and ordinary convicts. By a similar jugglery of terms the thing called exile in other countries was a 'conditional pardon' in the case of the Fenians.[23]

But even in the playing of this shabby trick Gladstone and his ministers did not get things all their own way. Many of the IRB

men, including all in Portland, on hearing of the condition attached
to their proposed release, at first refused to accept the amnesty on
these terms. In Portland, after an official had read out a letter
from the Board of Prison Directors announcing the Government's
decision, O'Leary, on behalf of all the men, insisted on writing a
letter back to the Directors demanding a further elucidation, if not
a retraction, of the condition of exile. The reply he received satisfied him that there was no binding condition attached to the release,
and a comparatively pleasant Christmas passed enlivened by several
visits from Rossa's wife.

In Chatham on the other hand the enforced exile was apparently
accepted by all but Halpin, who later relented; Rossa expressly
agreed to remain out of Britain and Ireland and with the other
four (Devoy, McClure, O'Connell and Mulleda) set off for New
York in January 1871 on the liner *Cuba*. Devoy, on hearing of the
Franco-Prussian war, had first thought of getting back into French
uniform, but changed his mind.

Of the eight men in Woking six appear to have accepted the
conditional pardon and sailed for America in another liner. T. F.
Bourke, in a letter to Kickham, regretted his inability to spend
'a day or two in "the valley near Slievenamon".' Dillon, who was
seriously ill, having had to be almost carried into the presence of
the Commission some months before, was released unconditionally
and returned to die soon after in his native Cork. An unconditional release was also granted to the 62-year-old model convict
'Pagan' O'Leary, who returned to America to die—as was his right
—in an old soldiers' home in Georgia.

On Christmas Eve O'Leary wrote announcing the good news to
Ellen in Tipperary; a second letter followed within a week. Both
are full of sarcasm over the magnanimous gesture of Gladstone,
and when published in full by Pigott in the paper *Irishman* must
have made Gladstone realise that exile alone was not going to
silence a man with a spirit like O'Leary's.

The second letter showed that already he had decided on France
as his place of exile. But the war was then at its height with Paris
under siege and, though pro-French in his sympathies (surely the
only time himself and Cardinal Cullen were ever in agreement) he
remarked: 'You know I have no military taste, though far from
being Quakerish in my principles.' On the condition attached to
his release he was even more scathing than in his first letter.

I am unable to see how I could, even with the best intentions, do much
mischief to society at present. I couldn't hurl the Hill of Howth upon
the Pigeon House, or undermine Cork-hill, or even cut the throats of
Earl Spencer, or Archbishop Trench or Cardinal Cullen. . . . But no
matter how small I sing they will insist on taking me for a roaring lion. . . .

Soon his own actions were to show that here at least he was being naively modest.

On 12 January 1871, the day of the general release, O'Leary and Luby were removed to Millbank near London, from where arrangements were made for their departure from Her Majesty's United Kingdom. Both signed their conditional pardons 'unconditionally and without reserve', informing the authorities that they could not bind themselves regarding their future conduct. They were offered £5 each, a 'first-class kit' and free berths. O'Leary refused to take the money, and an offer by him to pay for the clothes was declined.[24]

On 21 January, some days after the IRB men on their way to America had received a great welcome during their brief call to the port of Queenstown, O'Leary and Luby, the one grey-haired at forty-one and the other stooped and aged at forty-nine, slipped quietly off unnoticed on the steamer to Belgium. It was another bitterly cold winter and, since the river Scheldt was frozen over, their ship was diverted to Ostend, whence the passengers were taken by train to Antwerp. Here Luby was re-united with his wife and family, and O'Leary in a few weeks joined by his sister Ellen.

CHAPTER FIVE

1

NO WORSE SELECTION than Paris could have been made by a political exile seeking a place of refuge on the Continent in early 1871. The previous summer the Franco-Prussian war had broken out, and for five winter months the French capital was besieged by German armies. On 29 January 1871, a week after the arrival in Belgium of O'Leary and Luby, Paris capitulated. The following month saw the final stages of the transition from the Second Empire (which O'Leary had known so well in his student days) to the Third Republic; and on 1 March the German troops entered Paris.

Within three weeks the city was in turmoil again. The proclamation of the Commune was followed by a second siege, this time by the French army. After six weeks the citizens were overcome and tens of thousands were massacred by French soldiers almost within sight of the German troops camped on the edge of Paris.

If Paris was inaccessible, Antwerp was cold and uncomfortable. Accommodation was poor. Luby and his wife stayed in Dietin's English Hotel on Van Dyck Quay; their young daughter slept with Ellen O'Leary, who stayed in a guest-house in an adjoining street with her brother John. All took their meals in Dietin's. In April the Lubys sailed for America, which they had chosen in advance as their future home. Ellen O'Leary, whose home was in Tipperary, probably returned to Ireland about the same time.

Left alone in his uncongenial surroundings, O'Leary must have doubted the wisdom of the decision which made him the only one of the Irish political exiles to remain in Europe. His thoughts would naturally have turned to America, whence most of his former colleagues in the movement had gone, the principal exception being the now discredited Stephens, who participated actively in the Commune rising. By a fortunate coincidence circumstances soon made O'Leary's presence in New York an advantage to the Irish revolutionary movement.

From the moment of his release, O'Leary had resumed his active interest in Irish affairs, interrupted by his arrest six-and-a-half years before. While in jail he would have learned of the failure of the home movement in 1866 and 1867, largely because of the split in the movement in the United States. As financial manager of the IRB during its most active period, no one appreciated better than he the need for a united and energetic movement in America to supply money to confederates in Ireland.

In pursuance of this objective O'Leary's former fellow-convicts, Rossa, Thomas F. Bourke, John Devoy, Harry Mulleda, Dr. Edmond Power and Patrick Walsh, had, shortly after their arrival to a tumultuous welcome in New York, set up the Irish Confederation. Intended to replace the various existing Irish-American groups, the Confederation (in which Luby had also eagerly participated after his arrival) was pledged to keep out of American politics. The old Fenian Brotherhood, still influential in New York though weakened by dissensions for several years, held aloof from the Confederation. Whether he was asked so to act or not is not clear, but it must soon have been realised that, because of his absence from America, O'Leary was in an ideal position to act as mediator.

Accordingly, for the second time in his life he set sail for the United States, not this time as the envoy of Irish revolutionaries but as a prospective peacemaker between rival Irish-American factions. Arriving in New York on 19 July, he found the city and its inhabitants in a state of tension after the bloody Orange riots of 12 July in which over fifty people, many of Irish origin, had been killed and twice that number injured.

Following the publicity which had attended his arrival in 1859, it would not be surprising to find that O'Leary in 1871 stipulated that news of both his arrival and his doings in the United States were, as far as possible, to be kept out of the press. This, indeed, is the impression one gets as one peruses the pages of the half-dozen or so Irish-American newspapers then flourishing.

Within six weeks apparent success attended O'L[...]
John Savage, whose controversial personality had b[...]
causes of the factional bitterness, was persuaded to resign from
the Council of the Fenian Brotherhood, and in mid-August 'a
lengthy and very agreeable conference' was held, in the Brotherhood's offices, between John O'Mahony and Generals Millen and
Halpin representing the Fenians, and Rossa, Luby and Bourke
representing the Confederates.[1] 'John O'Leary, Esqre, lately
arrived from Belgium' was also present, acting as mediator.[2]

After several such conferences under O'Leary's chairmanship,
proposals for a coalition of the two bodies were agreed on and a
formal settlement was announced after a final and cordial meeting
on 25 August. The press was told that 'the committees were kindly
aided in their deliberations by an Irish patriot, not officially
connected with either organisation', who had asked that his name
be not mentioned.

An Alliance Council was established consisting of two representatives from each body, with an agreed chairman as a fifth member.
A levy of twenty-five per cent of existing funds was to be paid by
both bodies to the Council, which would have the sole right of
contact with 'the directing body of the revolutionary organisation
in Ireland'. Remittances were to be sent regularly to the Supreme
Council of the IRB, but all attempts at insurrection in Ireland were
to be discouraged until proper preparations had been made.

It is clear, however, that this seemingly promising arrangement
did not work, and that O'Leary's efforts had been only partly
successful. The original intention had been to merge all the existing organisations in the Confederation; but, at its tenth annual
convention in March 1871, the Fenian Brotherhood had rejected
this plan, and the settlement reached in August under O'Leary's
auspices represented a compromise whereby the Brotherhood was
to retain its own identity. Despite support for the Confederation
from all but one of the Irish papers in New York, and from the
unpredictable but popular John Mitchel (then living in the city)
the new Allied Council collapsed after a few months.

Several factors accounted for this state of affairs. After the
dissensions of the previous few years complete apathy reigned in
Irish-American circles, which even the sincere and energetic efforts
of the banished IRB leaders could not dispel. Doubtless press reports
of the activities of revolutionary bodies, especially those engaged in
fomenting revolution in a distant land, are not the best guides to
the progress or otherwise of such organisations; yet the pages of
the Irish-American press of 1871 are almost totally devoid of any
indication of solid achievement.

Since one of the main causes of the split in the Fenian Brotherhood some years before had been the so-called invasion of Canada, a final, if minor and unsuccessful, raid into Manitoba from Minnesota in October must have revived bitter memories. In addition, the still semi-secret Clan na Gael was slowly but surely working to replace all other such bodies, though it had not yet reached the position of strength it was to occupy later in the century.

Nor can the sudden appearance in New York late in September 1871 of James Stephens, now an agent for a French wine firm, have been conducive to harmony. The former IRB leader had been deposed following his flight to France in 1866 and, at the instigation of the Senate wing of the Fenian Brotherhood, a provisional Supreme Council of the IRB had been set up a year or two later. Even in Ireland there was still (especially in Dublin and Munster) a strong dissident Stephenite wing of the IRB, and in the United States opinion was sharply divided on the handling of affairs by Stephens.

Early in October Luby delivered another of many lectures on recent Irish history which he gave that year in various parts of the United States. This one—like all the others, in reality a means of publicising the Confederation—was held in the Cooper Institute in New York. Before Luby's arrival in the hall Stephens entered and took a seat at the rear, to the accompaniment of cheers; but Luby prefaced his address with a bitter attack on him and 'the tide of popular favour turned and set dead against the faithless chief'. It is significant that O'Leary, who also attended this lecture, made no reference to Stephens in a brief speech made after Luby's address at the request of the audience, and that the chivalrous O'Mahony stoutly defended Stephens subsequently in the press, refuting allegations that he had been the sole cause of the decline of Fenianism.

This seems to have been O'Leary's only public appearance in America during this visit. He stayed in Rossa's house on Staten Island; it was from Rossa's offices at 263 Broadway that an address entitled 'Tipperary Election Fund', and signed by O'Leary and Bourke, was published in the press in October. Its purpose was to appeal for funds to meet the expenses of the parliamentary campaign fought in 1869 on behalf of Rossa and Kickham, and it expressed the characteristic sentiment of O'Leary—who believed that Tipperary people were a race apart and could do no wrong —that 'the man who cares little for his native town or county is not likely to care much for his native country'.

From Rossa's house O'Leary made occasional trips by steamboat into New York to visit friends like Mitchel (now residing at Brooklyn) and O'Mahony. One Sunday late in August the boat back to Staten Island after that in which O'Leary had travelled exploded, killing sixty passengers and seriously injuring over 100 people. Early in January 1872, his health much improved, O'Leary returned to Europe, arriving in Paris near the end of that month.

2

THE PARIS TO WHICH O'Leary returned in 1872, and in which he was to spend another thirteen lonely and frustrating years, was very different from the Paris he had last seen in the summer of 1860. Gone were the halcyon days of the Second Empire, before Napoleon III had embarked on his disastrous foreign adventures; instead, the newly-born Republic, under the leadership of the veteran politician Thiers, was fighting for its existence against rival royalist groups.

In the senseless destruction of the last days of the Commune rising a large part of Paris had been destroyed; the city was no longer even the seat of government. Still it was a lively place, full of political activity and the capital of an energetic nation which was already making an astonishing recovery from the shock of military defeat by Prussia, the first of two it was to suffer at the hands of German arms in seventy years.

There was much to do in Paris once one had found comfortable living quarters. O'Leary encountered some initial difficulty. November of 1872 found him out in the suburb of Batignolles, at 11 Rue Brochant; some time afterwards he was back in the centre of the city, and finally he settled in the Hotel Corneille in the street of the same name. Here he was to remain for the rest of his period in Paris; from here he was to make occasional excursions—to the French provinces, to Britain, to the United States, even to Tipperary.

Situated opposite the Odeon Theatre, the Hotel Corneille was a popular resort for Irish visitors to Paris. To a man with O'Leary's ascetic habits it had a more important advantage; not only was the charge for accommodation low, but one could also occupy a room indefinitely without taking meals at the hotel. And nearby were several excellent cheap restaurants.

O'Leary's daily routine varied little. Each morning at the same time he took the same seat in a quiet corner of the homely Cafe de la Paix. Having ordered the minimum of food and drink, he proceeded to his correspondence for the day; judging from the long letters of his which have survived, his outgoing mail must have occupied several hours. Next, the papers, provided free of charge by the manager, were read carefully, to the accompaniment of a glass of wine and a pipe. Interruptions from any visitor with Irish connections—a Fenian emissary from America, an IRB agent from Dublin, or a literary friend from any one of half-a-dozen countries —were always welcome; even to bitter political opponents he was always courteous, if formal.

From the cafe he went to a Duval restaurant, or to the old Cafe Voltaire on the far side of the Place de l'Odeon, for a cheap lunch of soup, meat and vegetables, and a pint of claret. Soon it was time for a stroll along the quays, not to take the air, much less to mix with the ordinary Parisian (whom he never got to know), but to indulge in his lifelong hobby of book-collecting. Several hours were spent carefully inspecting the contents of every bookstall— searching, reading, replacing, choosing and finally haggling over prices.

He became a proficient French speaker, with a pronounced Tipperary accent, never even attempting to master the difficult French 'u' sound. Eventually, as dusk began to gather, he made his way back to the Hotel Corneille, carrying an armful of seemingly valueless books and tattered magazines. His day's purchases were hurled carelessly to the farthest corner of his spacious room, to join an ever-growing and precariously balanced pile which soon covered tables, chairs, window-sills and a large area of floor space.

Finally he made a sparse evening meal—a single cup of tea or coffee and a slice of toast, followed by a heated glass of wine and an almost interminable series of pipes before retiring. To callers who inquired how he did not burn to death by going to bed with a lighted pipe in one hand and a newspaper or magazine in the other, he explained that the last pipe for the night he smoked as it hung from a string suspended from the ceiling; when he nodded off it remained in that position and slowly burned itself out.

O'Leary's existence in Paris was by no means that of a recluse. He was not long back in the city before he formed (or, in some cases, reformed) several valued friendships. Foremost among those he had known there in the late 1850s was John P. Leonard, Young Irelander, journalist, professor of English literature in the Sorbonne, Knight of the French Legion of Honour and a member of the French Academy. This distinguished Irish exile became one of O'Leary's closest acquaintances; through him O'Leary came to know some of the leading officers of Irish origin in the French army, most of them descendants of the Wild Geese.

In 1874 and 1875 O'Leary was amongst the attendance at the

annual St. Patrick's Day banquets held in the Vefour salon of the
Palais Royal.[3] At the 1875 function, which was presided over by
Commandant Corbet, with Viscount O'Neill de Tyrone as vice-
chairman, one of the guests was Fr. Logue DD, destined to become
an Irish Cardinal, and one of the speakers was Dr. George Sigerson.
In 1875, when the Irish feast-day fell on a Friday, those attending
this exclusive *Diners de St. Patrice* were given a special dispensa-
tion from the rule of abstinence by the Archbishop of Paris.

Another intimate companion of O'Leary in Paris in the early
1870s was Denis Dowling Mulcahy, the IRB man from Clonmel
who had been on the editorial staff of the *Irish People*. After an
initial visit to America Mulcahy, who had been a law student before
his imprisonment, settled in Paris, where he remained for some five
years studying medicine.[4] As an orthodox IRB man, a student of
literature and a Tipperary man, his friendship would have been
particularly valued by O'Leary.

Two other Tipperary people who made periodic calls to him in
Paris were his half-brother Edmund and his sister Ellen. Edmund
acted as financial agent of the IRB after his brother's arrest in
1865; he was now in medical practice in London.[5] Ellen's visits,
though probably less frequent, were apparently of longer duration;
she stayed in the Hotel Corneille and entertained John's visitors in
his room at night. During O'Leary's exile in Paris a half-sister,
Mary, died from tuberculosis in Tipperary on 24 May 1872, at
the early age of thirty.

To Paris for a five-year period starting in 1873 came the 21-year-
old George Moore, the future novelist. Arriving in the city with
the intention of studying painting, Moore soon turned to writing.
That O'Leary would have been interested in meeting a son of the
late G. H. Moore MP (whose views on Irish affairs had been similar
to those of the IRB leaders of the mid-1860s) goes without saying.
However, Moore, who was then writing his play *Martin Luther*,
can hardly have had anything in common with O'Leary other than
an interest in literary matters, and the acquaintance does not seem
to have meant much to either of them.[6]

A more congenial conversationalist by far would have been
Dr. George Sigerson. Now married and practising in Dublin, he
made frequent trips to Paris, perhaps to see his old professor, the
world-famous physician Jean Martin Charcot, or to study under
him, or possibly merely to maintain his lifelong contacts in that
city.

From time to time in Paris O'Leary ran across James Stephens,
then living in that city in extreme poverty with his wife. In a letter
to an IRB man in America Stephens told how O'Leary rescued
him from destitution and starvation in June 1874. Evicted from

their lodgings, their belongings having been impounded by their landlord, Stephens and his wife (who was in poor health) roamed the streets of Paris on a cold night until they found themselves, by a stroke of luck, near O'Leary's lodgings. After having struggled up six flights of stairs to O'Leary's sparsely-furnished two-roomed garret, they were touchingly welcomed by O'Leary, still sitting up over his books near midnight.

The following morning O'Leary, having assured Stephens that he had been planning a walking tour of Brittany, interviewed his landlord on their behalf, arranged for them to become new tenants of his rooms, generously paid a month's rent in advance—he was to send them in all nearly sixty francs by post in the next few months —and then set off for Brittany. On another similar occasion, when Stephens was nursing his sick wife, O'Leary it was who ran messages, visited the pair regularly, bringing newspapers and magazines and giving them sums of money to help defray medical expenses. Little wonder that, in a letter of 1 October 1878, Stephens apologised for not going to see O'Leary and pleaded poverty as his excuse.

It was in Paris that O'Leary became acquainted with two or three then notable, but today almost forgotten, Russian figures.[7] Ivan Sergeyevich Turgenev, the first Russian novelist to be widely read outside Russia, spent much of his time in and around Paris, where he was lionised by French literary circles. O'Leary read him extensively in French translations and, on his return to Ireland, always kept a set of Turgenev's novels on his bookshelf.

Peter Alexeivich Kropotkin, geographer and author, but better known as an anarchist, spent the year 1877 in Paris, having escaped from Russia the previous year. Two years earlier still, Sergius Stepniak had also fled his homeland, ultimately to settle in London, where O'Leary got to know him, presumably through the Waterford author and publisher Edmund Downey, who befriended Stepniak on his arrival in England.[8] In view of O'Leary's later attitude towards land agitation in Ireland, it is worth recalling that all three Russians were champions of the oppressed peasantry of Russia.

The most constant of all O'Leary's friends during his exile in Paris was neither an Irishman nor a man with much interest in that country or its affairs. Charles Henry ('Harry') Meltzer was an able and successful journalist of English birth and Russian parents. When he and O'Leary first met, Harry Meltzer was Paris corres-pondent of the *Chicago Tribune*; later he was employed in turn by the *New York Tribune*, the *New York World* and the *Daily Telegraph* of London.

Although Meltzer was many years younger than O'Leary, their common interests—literature, art in general and world affairs— formed the basis of an immediate and lasting friendship, which was

16. John Devoy

17. John O'Connor

18. O'Donovan Rossa

19. James Stephens

20. Henry Dixon

21. W. B. Yeats

22. 'Tricky Micky Hickie'

23. Arthur Griffith

continued by correspondence when thousands of miles separated the two. Although they differed widely on political topics, Meltzer became fascinated by O'Leary's personality and was genuinely attached to him, naming O'Leary as godfather to one of his children. O'Leary introduced Meltzer to Turgenev's writings and to the works of the great French novelists; they regularly exchanged news of events in Ireland and the continent. On one occasion Meltzer, in return for some valuable press cuttings, even persuaded the Irishman, contrary to a lifelong practice, to attend a music-hall performance. To Meltzer's consternation, O'Leary insisted on reading a newspaper all through the show.

O'Leary, while residing in France, explored much of the French countryside on foot. As a boy of nineteen he was prepared to walk twelve miles by night with a body of men from Tipperary to Cashel, and thence the same night a further twenty miles to Clonmel. It need occasion no surprise to find that in his forties he was still an enthusiastic walker. With Harry Meltzer on many a day in the mid-1870s he covered many miles in the outskirts of Paris; they also enjoyed numerous long tramps together through the woods of Fontainebleau.

It is evident that O'Leary's absences from Paris were often long and unexpected; a visitor from America seeking him in the summer of 1877 discovered that he had been missing for some time and was unable to ascertain when he would return. Always anxious to visit historic spots, O'Leary was noted for his interest in cathedrals, an odd hobby for one who for so many years was not a church-goer himself. When some years later a journalist friend in Paris was sent to cover an epidemic of cholera in Barcelona, he did not forget to send back to O'Leary a detailed description of that city's breath-taking cathedral.

In the spring of 1879 O'Leary and John Devoy attended a meeting for revolutionary purposes in Boulogne on the Atlantic coast. When their business was over, O'Leary insisted on returning to Paris through the old town of Arras, which he had never seen. Devoy, who reluctantly agreed to the detour—it enabled him to visit a battlefield on which his former commander in the French Foreign Legion had been victorious against the Germans—has left an unforgettable picture of O'Leary upon their arrival at Arras. Standing in the town square, wearing on the back of his head his favourite billycock hat turned up at both sides, and on his back a heavy knapsack—both always carried by him on a walking tour— he read out to Devoy passages from a guide-book which described the mediaeval houses in the square still occupied as residences.

Like most people when immersed in a favourite subject, O'Leary was completely unaware of the impact he was making on onlookers.

Soon a crowd of schoolboys on their way home swarmed around him, shouting repeatedly 'damned Ainglish-man'. For obvious reasons this was too much for Devoy, who quietly took refuge in a doorway from the excessive attention, the heat and the noise. Meanwhile, O'Leary, not realising that his adult audience had deserted him, continued to read aloud from the guide-book, altogether ignoring the screaming boys; he might as well have been alone in the square.

O'Leary had not been long in Paris before he got to know several well-known journalists of Irish origin. James J. O'Kelly, then on the *New York Herald*, was a Dublin-man, a connection by marriage of James Stephens, and had been on the Supreme Council of the IRB while O'Leary was in jail. Later his adhesion to the Home Rule movement—he was to be an MP for over thirty years—was to cause a breach with O'Leary; in 1871 he was fresh from his experiences as a war correspondent. Even more famous by then was John Augustus O'Shea, who had reported the recent war from Paris for the London *Standard* and then settled in Paris; he had the additional merit, in O'Leary's estimate of men, that he was of Tipperary origin.

Then nearing the peak of his career was Edmund O'Donovan, a son of the great Irish scholar John O'Donovan. Edmund, later renowned for his travels in the Near East, was in Spain in 1873 for the Carlist rising and in Bosnia in 1876 during the revolt there against Turkish rule; in 1883 he died in the Hicks Pasha expedition to the Sudan. His brother Willie was *Irish Times* correspondent in Paris during the 1870s; he died in America at a comparatively early age. Both were close friends of O'Leary, and both were IRB men, Edmund having been to America on a mission for that body after '67. [9]

Considering the company he kept, it is not surprising that O'Leary for some time after his arrival in France toyed with the idea of becoming a journalist. Once again his lack of energy seems to have got the better of him. As early as November 1872, he was considering a suggestion by James J. O'Kelly to contribute book reviews regularly to the *New York Herald*; nothing seems to have come of this.

By early 1874 O'Leary was correspondent in Paris for another American paper, the San Francisco *Irish Nationalist*, in which he often used the pen-name 'An Irish Exile'. [10] This paper was then edited by none other than Hugh Byrne of Tinahely, the former 'Hugo del Monte' of the *Irish People*. According to a prominent American Fenian who visited O'Leary in May of that year, this was then his only regular journalistic assignment. [11] Later, in the early 1880s, he contributed a feature each week for several years to John Devoy's *Irish Nation,* published in New York.

Such of this writing as has survived may not strike the modern reader as being of a particularly high standard. O'Leary's Parisian dispatches consisted largely of his critical comments on current Irish affairs, the trend of which was then rarely altogether to his liking. Although his writings frequently give the impression of having been composed in haste, the opposite is known to have been the case. Each contribution was the result of much thought and was produced only after considerable mental anguish. As with public speaking, writing for publication was something O'Leary never really mastered.

It was during his years of residence in Paris also that O'Leary acquired his reputation as a letter-writer, an achievement of his political career about which an entire chapter could be written. Although to O'Leary himself his private letters were at least as important as those he wrote for publication, it was as a regular writer of letters to the press that he became best known during his exile.

While he was likely to choose almost any topic—the failings of the Irish race, the latest book of poetry, an obituary of an Irish public figure—usually he dealt with strictly political matters. In particular, the Home Rule movement and the Land War were favourite targets for his unerring pen. Although he never descended to mere personal abuse, he could, by skilful analysis of the utterances of an opponent, effectively belittle even popular parliamentarians like Parnell and William O'Brien.

Nor was O'Leary concerned where his letters appeared in print. Apparently he took the view that, with a public organ denied to the IRB since the suppression of the *Irish People*, he was justified in using any outlet for his opinions. Thus during most of the 1870s he (like several associates) was content to write to Pigott's *Irishman*; when he had to attack Pigott he used the *Nation*.

In the 1880s, when the *Freeman's Journal* became a staunch supporter of Parnell, O'Leary sent his letters mostly to that paper; but when it changed sides in the middle of the Parnell Split he sent it no more letters. For a time his letters appeared in William O'Brien's *United Ireland*, and from about the turn of the century O'Leary took to having his then rare letters published in Arthur Griffith's *United Irishman*. But at any time a letter from O'Leary was likely to turn up in any paper in Ireland, England or America, others he chose from time to time being Davitt's *Labour World*, the *Pall Mall Gazette* and Mitchel's New York *Irish Citizen*.

As a rule, the shorter a letter from O'Leary the more effective it was. Unfortunately, when he felt the need to unburden himself on an important matter, he sat down to compose a long letter. Almost invariably this became far too long and too tedious, with rambling and involved sentences, frequent diversions off the main track, and numerous qualifications of the letter's main statement.

With his brief notes it was a different matter altogether. Such a letter was clearly dashed off in a hurry, or even in a temper, and never re-read or corrected. The result was always a spontaneity that the longer letters entirely lacked.

Both during his lifetime and after his death it was frequently said that O'Leary's letters were more of a hindrance than a help to the cause of Irish nationalism. In some ways this was true; his constant sniping at the Home Rule movement and its leading figures, with seldom a constructive idea, naturally irritated men who felt that they were making the best of a difficult job at Westminster.

But even this proves that O'Leary's letters were never ignored; and it is probable that most of the constitutional leaders, knowing his frankness and fair-mindedness, would have admitted privately that criticism such as O'Leary's kept them at their job. And none could deny that, when at his best, O'Leary's mastery of the English language produced some brilliantly apt comments.

For his part O'Leary could, of course, legitimately argue that his main purpose was to keep before the public the idea of physical force. To men like himself and Devoy, who all along held to the view that parliamentary agitation alone would never solve Irish ills, such letters to the press needed no justification. That they kept not only the idea of physical force, but also the existence of the IRB and what it stood for, before the Irish public for a period of some thirty years, during the whole of which that body and those principles did not enjoy the support of the majority of Irish nationalists, there can be little doubt. Looked at in this light, O'Leary's letters to the press served a very useful purpose indeed.

More revealing by far are O'Leary's private letters, of which a surprisingly small number have survived. Even the most trivial of these gives a more intimate picture of the man than all his letters to the press over a period of forty years. Such a private letter, particularly if written to a member of his family or to a lifelong associate like Luby or Devoy, is essentially an outpouring of O'Leary's private thoughts. Although usually unpolished and scrawled at high speed, it meant much to a correspondent long familiar with the writer's hand and style.

Reading a long letter of O'Leary to a colleague in the IRB, one feels one is listening-in on one side of an intimate conversation. There is a burst of short sentences, followed by a rambling paragraph; then comes a seemingly endless sentence, peppered with dashes and parentheses. And when something important has to be said there is a quite startling change-over to a telegraphic style, with verbs and definite and indefinite articles all missing and requiring to be filled in by the reader as he goes along.

As he became older and more eccentric in his habits, O'Leary's letters came to acquire even more unusual features. A date was rarely given; pages were never numbered. Frequently even the address was missing, or the letter was headed simply 'Paris' or 'Clontarf'; 'the height of affectation and irrationality' Luby called this. Gradually, too, the tiny scrawl became more and more difficult to decipher, especially when the Victorian customs of writing sideways in a margin, and even turning an already-filled page at right-angles and 'over-printing' it, were used to excess. 'It is a dee-dee shame,' wrote Kickham to Ellen O'Leary in the polite language then expected of a bachelor addressing a spinster, 'for a rational being to write in such a way. . . .'

When it came to ending a letter, O'Leary was anything but Victorian. Instead of the elaborate 'Believe me, I am, Your obedient servant' or the like, it was usually 'Yours in a frightful hurry' or 'Yours with any amount of bawling children about me'. And invariably there was a postscript, often half as long as the main letter, and sometimes written days later.

Related to his epistolary eccentricities were two other habits O'Leary acquired late in life—writing postcards instead of letters, and sending newspapers and clippings to friends. The postcard-writing was probably begun as an economy measure when O'Leary ran short of money; it led to the most extraordinary results. The scrawl became even more minute, and a card by O'Leary could contain more than a letter by an average person.

With the papers and clippings, too, came an equally blatant fraud upon Her Majesty's post. A heavy load of newspapers from O'Leary invariably carried only the minimum postage; inevitably, if the recipient resided in the United States, there was a charge to pay. Finally, when the paper-parcel was opened, a letter running to thousands of words, together with several dozen clippings from other journals, would all float out.

So famous did O'Leary become amongst his friends for his correspondence that they openly indulged in parody and sarcasm at his expense. Dr. Sigerson once ended a letter to him thus: 'Pray say where you are (if you are anywhere) and how and where a letter may reach you (if this reaches you).' And from the writer Richard Ashe King came this parting remark in a letter to O'Leary: 'I must close now as I have the rest of your postcard to read—I got through a bit of it in a few hours last night and this morning.'

NO MATTER HOW CONGENIAL his surroundings in Paris, it was in Ireland and her chances of achieving political independence that O'Leary was still primarily interested. For some years after his release the outlook remained bleak; Fenianism in the 'seventies met with one disappointment after another. Moreover, O'Leary deliberately remained aloof from the IRB for most of the 1870s, only taking—or getting—a seat on its Supreme Council as late as 1877.

Despite its astonishing growth and popularity a decade before, its promise of success around 1865 and its remarkable recovery after the arrests and trials of that year, the IRB had failed miserably in '67. By 1870 or so it had been reduced to an insignificant and disunited force, and was to remain so for several years. Its leader now was James F. X. O'Brien, O'Leary's former associate in the Queen's College, Galway, and fellow-student in Paris, and later the vigorous anti-clerical letter-writer from Cork to the *Irish People*. By now O'Brien and O'Leary appear to have parted company.

The other members of the Supreme Council, which had been set up following Stephens's deposition in 1866, lacked the ability and energy of Stephens's associates of the 1860s. One, John Leavy, proved to be an informer; another, John O'Connor Power, was, to put it mildly, unsuited for the executive of a secret society. Furthermore, there still flourished in parts of the country (notably Dublin, Cork and some of the southern and eastern counties) a dissident wing owing allegiance to Stephens. This group was strong enough to send its own envoy to New York in 1874, seeking recognition by the Clan na Gael; he was coldly received by the businesslike leaders of that body.

All this time the young Home Rule movement was repeating the pattern of events after the '48 rising, when the eclipse of the physical force party led to the gradual rise of a more moderate and strictly constitutional agitation. By 1871 Home Rule meetings were being held with increasing frequency, and were attracting gradually larger public support, in many parts of Ireland. Soon Home Ruler and Fenian became almost indistinguishable from one another, so vociferous had one become and so mild the other.

Nor could the rank-and-file IRB man be blamed for sympathising with Butt's movement when he saw IRB leaders apparently throwing themselves behind the agitation wholeheartedly. The establishment in 1873 of the Home Rule League, which superseded the earlier Home Government Association, had been with the goodwill, if not the encouragement, of O'Connor Power, Joseph Biggar and Patrick Egan, all then on the Supreme Council. Moreover, at a secret convention of the IRB that same year the society determined to lend its support to every movement calculated to advance the cause of Irish independence, consistently with the preservation of its own integrity.

Earlier still, another Council member, James O'Connor, had been present at the meeting in a Dublin hotel in May 1870, which led to the founding of the Home Government Association, the fore-runner of the Home Rule movement. In 1874 O'Connor Power became MP for Mayo, with strong IRB backing. The following year, when the veteran John Mitchel successfully fought Tipperary, one of his most prominent speakers was Charles G. Doran, then Secretary of the Council.

With the unseating and subsequent sudden death of Mitchel, rumours were current to the effect that Denis Dowling Mulcahy would contest the seat.[12] There was even another rumour linking O'Leary's name with the constituency.[13] But back in 1871, when he had been wrongly reported in the press as giving his blessing to Home Rule, the error had provoked a typical letter from O'Leary, in which he clearly showed that he, for one, still remained a firm believer in complete separation and in its achievement by physical force.[14]

In his first public statement since he had, to use his own words, 'emerged out of the deep obscurity, if not total darkness, of an English prison, into the comparative light of exile', he cynically asserted that if Home Rule should win, 'it would be because the British Government knows it has to reckon with others besides the Home Rulers'. This new agitation was obviously too polite for his liking; he remained convinced that, in dealing with the English, there was 'much to be gained from their fears and nothing from their love'.

With his old colleague Kickham apparently prepared to tolerate this open flirtation of parliamentary agitation by the IRB, in the vague hope that it might eventually lead to a group of Irish MPs deliberately refusing to attend Westminster, little wonder that O'Leary despaired of Irish affairs in the early 1870s. To John Devoy he wrote:

. . . the way things have been going on since I came out of prison has given me more pain than all the rest. I suppose I am getting less philo-sophical, though not more hopeful. I see little anywhere but honest incompetence or clever roguery. And then I feel nearly powerless for any good. I am eating away my own soul, and that's not a pleasant occupation.

To Kickham about the same time in Paris he conveyed much the same depressing view. The Irish wing of the movement he regarded as 'frauds and imbeciles', and those in America had 'but little honesty and no capacity'. He saw no hope for the cause and thought it should be left to future generations. The gentle Kickham rightly rebuked him for this approach; how pleasant, he joked, for those who could drop out when the humour took them. For himself, he would continue to do his best and 'ask nothing more from those who are tired . . . but give them credit for their past'. 'Unless somebody urge him on, and give him an opening as I did,' wrote Stephens of O'Leary to a friend in America in 1874, 'there is but slight probability of his being of much further use to his country. . . ; his . . . lack of faith in the people, if not in the cause, have increased.'

O'Leary at this period, and for some time afterwards, had two pet aversions, one on each side of the Atlantic. Towards John O'Connor Power he exhibited feelings of bitter hostility that at times exceeded the bounds of prudence. Power, a Galway man who had been a childhood friend of Davitt in Lancashire, was an IRB organiser from 1860 onwards and, after the arrests of 1865, a member of the Supreme Council. Able and ambitious, his unprepossessing appearance was compensated for by a natural gift of oratory. Leading the wing of the IRB which, from the early 1870s, favoured working openly with the Home Rulers, he eventually antagonised both the IRB and Clan na Gael as he moved gradually into the parliamentary movement himself—with whose leaders he also fell out later on.

O'Leary, who held firmly to the orthodox IRB view that no physical force man should touch parliamentary agitation in any form, became incensed by O'Connor Power's ability for several years to keep a foot in both camps and get away with it. To him Power, more than any of the many prominent IRB men who changed allegiance around this time, was the embodiment of all the evils implicit in parliamentary agitation.

Both in public and in private correspondence Power was relentlessly pursued by O'Leary, in language reminiscent of the most trenchant editorials of the *Irish People*. So obsessed did O'Leary become by the harm which he sincerely believed Power was doing to the cause of extreme nationalism that, in a letter to Devoy, he would, quite spontaneously, begin his latest tirade against Power with the phrase—'And talking of rogues reminds me of Mr. O'C.P.'.

Every bit as damaging outside Ireland as the harm he was convinced Power was doing inside that country was, in O'Leary's view, the project initiated in the United States by O'Donovan Rossa in March 1876, and to which he gave the lurid title of the Skirmishing

Fund. Always impatient to strike a blow at England, Rossa had found his first five years in America frustrating because of the lack of achievement and the wasteful participation by colleagues in American domestic politics, though he himself had committed this same sin.

In 1878 he announced the formation of the Fund, the object of which would be to make surprise and harassing attacks against England from time to time, while the revolutionary bodies continued to prepare for a general insurrection. What Rossa envisaged was not merely a series of sporadic guerilla attacks, but also more sensational operations such as kidnapping, assassination and reprisals where deemed justified.

To O'Leary, as indeed to the IRB and Clan na Gael leaders too, this was a disastrous scheme. It offended against the cardinal rule of the early IRB that careful preparation must precede any open action against Britain; it diverted money and energy from the essential preparatory work; and, in its advocacy of terrorism, it did great harm to the cause of Irish freedom in the eyes of sympathetic foreigners. As money began to pour into Rossa's new fund from all sorts of people (many not Irish) with old grudges against the British, and as the possibility of 'skirmishing' projects being pushed through increased, O'Leary became more dismayed.

From its start he denounced the Skirmishing Fund in language so vehement that Kickham, though also against the scheme, reacted strongly and refused to join the public condemnation. Yet in O'Leary's unceasing attacks on the Fund there is a different emphasis when compared to his onslaughts on O'Connor Power. Rossa had, after all, been up to then an orthodox IRB man, and a close friend of O'Leary; unlike O'Connor Power, the sincerity of his motives could not be questioned. Accordingly, an air of scorn and futility at the whole project was adopted by O'Leary: '. . . my friend Rossa,' he wound up patronisingly in his first public statement criticising the Fund, 'notwithstanding all this blood and thunder, is at bottom the most affable and best-natured of men.'

Across the Atlantic other Irishmen, or more accurately, those in one Irish revolutionary body, were planning and plotting once more on a long-term basis, and when O'Leary got to hear of their doings he responded constructively, if not with any great enthusiasm. Curiously enough, he found the ideas of the Irish in America more in harmony with his own views for some time than were those of the IRB itself. The Irish Confederation collapsed in the spring of 1873, after having held only one annual convention, and many of its members joined or rejoined the Fenian Brotherhood. This, too, was by now almost moribund; only sixty delegates attended the 1874 convention of what had once been a powerful and wealthy body. On the platform were Luby, Bourke and Rossa—but not Devoy.

Devoy had given his allegiance to Clan na Gael, now gradually becoming the most influential of Irish-American organisations and under Devoy's guidance progressing steadily year by year. By 1874 Clan na Gael was actively working for an alliance with the Supreme Council of the IRB, such as it was; for it is clear that Devoy and his colleagues thought poorly of O'Brien, Power and the rest and were only awaiting the opportunity to find more orthodox successors to them. By mid-1874 some sort of working arrangement had been concluded between the two bodies, providing for (amongst other things) the regular examination of the IRB accounts by a Clan representative, who could inquire into the expenditure of subsidies granted by his organisation. The following year O'Connor Power visited America as envoy of the IRB.

Disagreement over the necessity for the IRB leaders to sign the 1874 agreement prevented its coming into operation for a year or more, and by then Clan na Gael was thinking of a more ambitious project. What was now sought was the establishment of a Revolutionary Directory, a sort of provisional Irish government-in-exile, composed of nominees of the Clan, the IRB and a third smaller body in Australasia. It was felt that the years of open disagreement in America had discredited the Irish revolutionary movement; what was badly needed now was a central representative body to speak for all extreme Irish nationalists.

The most prominent advocate of the Directory was the remarkable Dr. William Carroll of Philadelphia, chairman of the Clan na Gael Executive, whom O'Leary was soon to get to know. An enthusiastic Freemason of Ulster Presbyterian stock, he was a relative of the famous Carroll of Carrolton, one of the signatories of the American Declaration of Independence. After serving in the Union army as a surgeon during the civil war, he settled in Philadelphia, becoming one of its most respected citizens and a successful doctor. A man of considerable ability, he was to place the cause of Ireland before his livelihood until his death in 1926 at the age of ninety-one.

O'Leary's largely negative role in the moves leading to the setting up of the Directory provides impressive evidence of his influential position in Irish affairs. He had now been out of Ireland for over a decade and supported no political group in the country. Yet Carroll and his colleagues in New York obviously felt that O'Leary's support for the proposed Directory was essential if it was to work satisfactorily. It was decided to put the whole idea frankly to him in Paris; for this purpose either Carroll himself or Devoy was to cross the Atlantic.

Neither was able to do so, however, and Carroll had to explain the details to O'Leary by letter. By late April 1876 he had got a favourable reply from Paris; O'Leary still thought poorly of the Clan efforts generally, but approved of the Directory idea and agreed not to attack it. He would assist in any plan to restore the IRB to its old revolutionary basis, but was not (to the relief of the men in New York) in favour of Stephens as leader. Moreover, he would even go the length of writing a column in Pigott's *Irishman* if it would serve the cause in any way—an astonishing concession from O'Leary.

It only remained for Carroll to continue his skilful game of negotiation with all the parties concerned. At its convention in Philadelphia in August 1876 Clan na Gael passed a resolution approving of the Directory. O'Connor Power came to the United States again that year, but neither he nor any member of the then Supreme Council was told that O'Leary for once thought the same as they on one important topic. Why in the circumstances it took yet another year for the Revolutionary Directory to be set up is not clear, unless the Clan leaders were taking their time in the hope that a new Council would take over in the IRB—as it ultimately did.

The establishment of the Revolutionary Directory in 1877 must have given some satisfaction to O'Leary watching events from Paris. The new arrangement worked well in practice for several years. Consisting of three delegates from Clan na Gael and three from the IRB, a quorum was obtained by the simple method of one man from one side meeting the three from the other. The Australasian representation became a dead letter because of the distance involved. O'Leary was a member of the Directory from its establishment, though not apparently, between 1878 and 1880.

Even more hopeful from O'Leary's point of view must have been the crisis in the Supreme Council, which came to a head in 1877 and led to the reconstruction of that body and the return to its leadership, after twelve years, of O'Leary himself. Although the details of this convulsion will probably never now be fully known, the general trend of events is fairly clear. As early as July 1876 Dublin Castle was told by its secret agents (of whose reliability one cannot be at all certain) that 'a crisis in Irish national politics is at hand'.

Later in the year it learned of a meeting of the Supreme Council at which Home Rule was discussed by the members, and Joseph Biggar, John Barry and Patrick Egan, who had publicly identified themselves with that movement, were called on to resign from the Council or sever their connections with Home Rule. Apparently, however, no firm decision was reached, possibly because the most prominent IRB man still in the Home Rule movement, O'Connor Power, is said to have missed this meeting through illness.

Around the same time reports reached the police of obvious efforts at re-organisation by the IRB in various parts of Ireland. There was also talk of a re-constitution of the body at its highest level, providing for a number of provincial directories with executive control in London. John O'Connor, Doran's successor as secretary of the Supreme Council, was followed round the country by police without their ascertaining what he was up to; he was reported also as moving to and fro between Ireland, England, New York and Paris.

All that can be said with certainty is that gradually the wing favouring support of the Home Rule agitation lost ground and the old orthodox men regained control. In the early part of 1877 plans were made to bring back the body of John O'Mahony, who had died in poverty in New York on 6 February, and to use his funeral as a demonstration of strength, following the precedent of the MacManus funeral in 1861, as that in turn had followed the precedent of the O'Connell funeral.

This event led to the temporary return to Ireland of some of the pre-1865 IRB men, Mulcahy and Roantree among them, and seems to have given an impetus to the purging of the parliamentary wing of the organisation. According to a secret source of the Castle authorities, an important meeting was held in the European Hotel, Dublin, after the O'Mahony funeral, at which a decision was reached to withdraw support from the Home Rule movement.[15]

Soon after this matters reached a climax at a meeting of the Supreme Council which marks a turning point in the history of the IRB. A resolution condemning parliamentary action by members of any rank was passed and, as a direct result, Patrick Egan and John Barry resigned from the Council, and Joseph Biggar and O'Connor Power were expelled from it. A few weeks later still, John O'Connor, Charles G. Doran, Denis D. Mulcahy and Charles Kickham crossed to Paris to confer with O'Leary on the re-organisation of the Council. From this time onwards Kickham figures as president of the Council in succession to O'Brien. O'Leary, though not apparently on the Council—he was offered a seat in May 1878 —clearly influenced its decisions from then onwards, and resumed his old post of chief financial manager of the movement, his residence outside Ireland making him a suitable custodian of the substantial sums regularly arriving from the Clan na Gael.

Considerable disagreement exists as to the date of the meeting of the Supreme Council at which four of its most prominent members parted company with it. The dates suggested by T. M. Healy and Richard Barry O'Brien, Parnell's biographer—1876 and

early 1878 respectively—are clearly unacceptable. Davitt, who
(since he was still in jail at the time of the meeting) was also relying
on hearsay, merely gives pre-December 1877. Biggar's sworn testimony subsequently to the Parnell Commission, placing the meeting
in August 1877, has been generally accepted.

Another source has, however, been curiously overlooked, which
throws more light on this point—Dublin Castle. According to
information dated 12 March 1877 from an informer whose identity
is not revealed, a meeting of the Supreme Council was held the
previous week at which Biggar, Barry, Egan and O'Connor Power
were 'compelled to resign'. Moreover, this fits in with the later
discussion of the changes with O'Leary in Paris, which an apparently
different informant of the Castle placed in late April 1877.

Despite its apparent recovery, however, the IRB was soon to
find its power threatened from a new and totally unexpected
direction, as a direct result of a train of events which commenced
within three months of the re-constitution of the Supreme Council.

4

JAMES J. O'KELLY, the son of a Dublin blacksmith, and John
Devoy, the son of a Kildare tenant-farmer who had moved to the
city, were friends from their childhood days, having been at school
together in Marlborough Street. Both joined the IRB in the same
place on the same day in January 1861; then their ways parted.
Devoy became the chief organiser of James Stephens's daring
scheme to seduce Irishmen in British uniform; O'Kelly joined the
French Foreign Legion. He was serving in Mexico when a letter
reached him from Devoy revealing the plans for a rising.

O'Kelly came home and opposed the rising. Devoy got fifteen
years for treason-felony. O'Kelly was elected to the Supreme
Council and played a major part in the re-organisation of the IRB
after Stephens's deposition, resuming his post as Head Centre of
the London district. In 1870 he returned to French service, and
tried to recruit an Irish brigade during the Franco-Prussian War.

After the collapse of the French Empire he sailed for the United
States. He joined the editorial staff of the *New York Herald*,
becoming in turn drama critic, art editor and war correspondent

in Cuba. When, early in 1871, Devoy reached New York following his release from Portland jail, his appointment to the editorial staff of the *Herald* cannot have been a coincidence. He soon rose to the post of foreign news editor.

If anybody knew Devoy's mind, it was O'Kelly. And, since he was regularly on assignments in Europe for his paper, he would have been in an ideal position to keep Devoy informed on political affairs in Ireland. Unlike Devoy, who was required by the terms of his pardon to remain out of the United Kingdom until 1882, O'Kelly could visit the country, and did so frequently in the 1870s. Only an intimate acquaintance like O'Kelly had a chance—if anyone had—of influencing the views of the headstrong Devoy. It is not at all improbable that O'Kelly was the real schemer behind the main political events in Ireland between 1877 and 1880.

In May 1870, shortly before the meeting in the Bilton Hotel, Dublin, at which Butt founded the Home Rule movement, O'Kelly —then still on the Supreme Council—met Butt at the lodgings of another leading IRB man (probably O'Connor Power) and promised (with what authority, if any, is far from clear) that the attitude of the IRB towards the new movement would be one of benevolent neutrality. Already O'Kelly, to use his own words in a private letter to Devoy some seven years later, was looking forward to 'the creation of a political link between the conservative and radical nationalists', although in the pre-'67 days he had been strongly opposed to parliamentary action.

The events of the early and mid-1870s—the support given by prominent IRB men to the Home Rule Confederation started in 1873, the election of Power as an MP, and the open sympathy of rank-and-file IRB men with the Home Rulers—must all have seemed to O'Kelly to bring his dream nearer realisation. Most significant of all was the impact Parnell had made on the popular mind by 1877. The obstruction tactics in Westminster of Parnell, Biggar and Power were the talk of Ireland between 1875 and 1877; in the last week of July 1877, in two almost unprecedented scenes in the House of Commons, Parnell made a laughing stock of parliamentary procedure.

The following month O'Kelly met Parnell at least twice. He was immediately impressed by him and found that Parnell too had ideas on co-operation between the two wings of Irish nationalism. Probably it was O'Kelly who mentioned the subject first and then took Parnell's silence as meaning approval; if so, it was not the last time this was to happen in the next few years. According to John Daly of Limerick, a well-known IRB figure later, Parnell had mentioned to him as early as 1873 the prospect of such co-operation.[16] Perhaps Parnell may have interpreted O'Kelly's conversation in 1877 as an approach by the IRB.

Across the Atlantic, Devoy (like Rossa) was impatient at the lack of results from the revolutionary movement. A letter or two came from O'Kelly telling of his meetings with Parnell; at once Devoy, the professional revolutionary, got to work. He consulted Dr. Carroll and both appear to have agreed that, with a man of Parnell's calibre likely to lead the Home Rulers soon, the idea of a coalition between physical force and constitutionalism was at least worth exploring. It was hardly a coincidence that in October Carroll was appointed by the Clan na Gael Executive as envoy to the IRB, with a general mandate to remain in Europe until that body had been re-built on firm foundations.

At this stage O'Leary once more enters the picture. On 8 November Carroll sailed in the liner *Vaderland* from Philadelphia, reaching Antwerp on 20 November and Paris four days later, having spent three days in Brussels. It was his first meeting with O'Leary; each seems to have been impressed by the other. After having been introduced (presumably by O'Leary) to the Irish colony in the French capital, Carroll began his various assignments.

Before leaving America he had met in New York O'Donovan Rossa, who had authorised him to tell James Stephens that, until the split in the IRB had been repaired, the Fenian Brotherhood (now under Rossa's control) would not support him. Stephens, whose wine agency had collapsed some years before, was now living in poverty in Paris. Carroll brought a letter of introduction to him from O'Leary. The two men met and talked, but failed to reach any agreement on unity within the movement in Ireland, Carroll coming away with the impression that he was dealing with an eccentric.

From Paris Carroll travelled south to Spain in an attempt to further one of those lunatic schemes which the Irish-Americans were periodically planning in the second half of the nineteenth century. This time it was hoped to seize Gibraltar with a force of picked IRB men and American mercenaries, and hand it over to Spain. In Madrid in mid-December Carroll met O'Kelly by appointment and the two went to see the Spanish premier, who would not hear of the plot. One wonders what O'Leary thought of all this.

By mid-January 1878 Carroll had reached Cork. He was to spend some five or six months in these islands, and to travel the whole of Ireland investigating the state of the IRB. His native Donegal was the only county of the thirty-two which he did not enter.

At first he was shocked by the dissensions he found. 'Dear Charlotte,' he wrote to Devoy a few days after his arrival, using a code intended to foil any attempt by the Castle to tamper with the post, 'You will be sorry to learn that our dear friend is in even

worse health than we had been informed, for with characteristic
modesty he had not written fully the extent of his sufferings.' But
by early March the position had improved. 'Dear Carrie—I hasten
to tell you that Miss Brunnell is rapidly regaining her health.'

Now it was Carroll who was being modest. He succeeded in
winning back to the Supreme Council both the 'provinces' of
Leinster, which had seceded to Stephens, and that of the north of
England, which had broken away following the Council expulsions
of 1877. He organised and supervised secret elections of the IRB
all over the country, had Doran replaced by John O'Connor as
secretary of the Council, and had the three 'home' members of the
Revolutionary Directory appointed. Finally, he arranged for a
grant of 10,000 dollars from the Skirmishing Fund (long since out
of Rossa's hands) and a grant of 7,000 dollars from the Clan
Executive, all to be spent on arms. The money was safely lodged
with O'Leary in Paris.

In March 1878, while Carroll was in London, Parnell and F. H.
O'Donnell MP got in touch with him, requesting a meeting. At a
celebration in Dublin in January to mark the release of some IRB
prisoners, Parnell had asked that Carroll join him in his hotel.
When Carroll declined, Parnell went to Carroll's hotel, where the
two met for the first time, in a friendly atmosphere, but without
anything passing between them except vague hopes of co-operation.

The IRB still held aloof from such contacts. But, by a stroke of
luck, a prominent IRB man not yet on the Supreme Council arrived
in London incognito the very week in which Parnell had asked to
see Carroll. The previous summer O'Leary's uncle, William, had
died in Tipperary; his affairs could not be properly wound up
without the presence of his nephew. Accordingly, permission was
given to O'Leary, on the representations of friends, to return
privately, solely for the purpose of attending to family business.

Some time in March the first of a series of meetings took place
which led ultimately to the New Departure, the name given to the
co-operation in the 1880s between the extreme nationalists and the
two movements of Davitt and Parnell, the one agrarian and the
other parliamentary. O'Leary was present at both the first and
the last of these conferences. This first one was held in the privacy
of Carroll's room in the Surrey Hotel, off the Strand, London.

There were present the three MPs, Parnell, O'Donnell and
O'Kelly, and Carroll, O'Leary and John O'Connor. Different
versions of this meeting conflict on the details; but all concur that
no definite agreement was reached between the two sides. Since
O'Leary had undertaken not to engage in politics while in the
United Kingdom, he must have regarded this as merely a social
gathering. Had he known that Castle spies followed his every

movement (and that of Carroll) he might not have gone to the hotel at all.

The accounts of the Surrey Hotel meeting are of interest for what they reveal of O'Leary at the time. To bring O'Kelly, a former Supreme Council member, now a parliamentarian, was a blunder by Parnell. O'Kelly and O'Leary could not be expected to agree on Irish affairs. Nor did they.

According to Devoy, whose source was probably Carroll, a violent argument developed between O'Leary and O'Kelly over O'Connor Power. This seems to have brought the proceedings to an abrupt and inconclusive end, to the disappointment of Parnell. O'Leary spoke so loudly that a person in an adjoining room shuffled his shoes on the floor to indicate that they could be overheard; later it transpired that this was the future Lord Ashbourne, then a high Castle law official.

O'Donnell later claimed that most of the talking was done by himself and O'Leary; this is substantially confirmed by Barry O'Brien, Parnell's biographer and later a close friend of O'Leary. O'Donnell has recorded the following illuminating exchange:

O'LEARY: Nine out of ten Irishmen entering the British Parliament with honest intentions are corrupted soon. It is the same even in Dublin; when once they get drawn into the whirlpool of British corruption in Dublin, with the West British society, the jobbery, the servility, very soon all the manliness goes out of them. If Irishmen are to save their honour, they must keep aloof from everything English.

O'DONNELL: What, even from English literature, Mr. O'Leary?

O'LEARY: If England had only Shakespeare and Milton and the rest, the Fenians would not be against her. It is her Cromwells and Castlereaghs and that vile brood which are the trouble.

O'DONNELL: Very well answered, Mr. O'Leary. But if you were an Edmund Burke, you would defend the oppressed Indians and make things unpleasant for Warren Hastings?

O'LEARY: If the Indians gave the English just a touch of Brian Boru, that would be far better than any Edmund Burke in or out of Parliament.

PARNELL: I am afraid that Mr. O'Donnell has no chance against you, Mr. O'Leary.

O'LEARY: I am not saying that good members would not be better than bad ones, if they could keep right. George Henry Moore meant well.

Shortly before nine o'clock on the night of 19 March 1878 a stranger entering Tipperary town would have assumed that all the townspeople had retired for the night. The streets were deserted and, curiously, hardly a window was lighted. But at nine o'clock John O'Leary alighted from the train on his first visit home for thirteen years.[17] Gladstone might muzzle O'Leary; but he could

not silence O'Leary's fellow townsmen. Much to his embarrassment, arrangements had quietly been made to welcome him.

As he entered the yard at the back of the railway station, the
Amateur Band struck up a national air. This was the signal the
town had been awaiting; in a flash every window in the town was
ablaze with light. People poured out of their homes and made
their way down Bridge Street to meet and greet the visitor.

The visitor did not lose his head: quite the contrary. He firmly
declined to be paraded through the town, insisting on going on
foot and along the pavement, while the crowds, headed by the
band, climbed the hill to Main Street, turned past O'Leary's childhood home and followed him into James's Street, where he put
up at a private hotel. No amount of persuasion could force him
to make a speech. It is even said that he made some uncompli-
mentary remarks about the sincerity of his reception, and said that
he would have preferred to have heard 'The Wearing of the Green'
instead of 'God Save Ireland'.[18]

The disappointed crowd remained in the streets for hours. The
Amateur Band was joined by the Mitchel Brass Band. Bonfires
were lighted on the outskirts of the town. The startled constabulary
was strengthened by a troop of soldiery. But the people were well
behaved, apart from two exuberant youths who threw a stone each
through the window of a bank.

O'Leary remained for several months in his native town. He
stayed with Ellen in her cottage up opposite the church, venturing
out only to visit friends—Dr. Jeremiah Dowling, the Tullochs, and
his half-sister's family, the Kings. He could not resist the temptation
to linger in the bookshop at the foot of the street; soon IRB men
began to gather there too. But mostly O'Leary kept to his sister's
house, reading his newspapers and going through his books, which
Ellen had so carefully stored for him while he was in jail.

Up the road was the convent school, whose pupils idolised Ellen
O'Leary. Any excuse was good enough to call on her. One fine
spring morning of 1878 a few of the small girls, playing in the
school yard, developed a thirst. Where better to get a glass of
water than at Miss O'Leary's? Down they went and knocked on
the door; to their astonishment it was opened by a tall, stern-
looking man with a long beard. But the stern-looking man was
fond of children. Yes, of course he would get them a drink of
water. And so, for fifteen minutes, the principal advocate of armed
revolution in Ireland went in and out from the kitchen of the
cottage, filling and re-filling his tumbler of water as the crowd of
thirsty school-girls grew; for everyone wanted to see this strange
but gentle man who was staying in Miss O'Leary's. And doubtless
the bearded man was glad of their company for a change.

One of those who was at the Surrey Hotel meeting the week before has left an impression of O'Leary. He was now a 'singularly noble-looking man, acquiline-featured, dark-eyed, tall, in the prime of life. He looked like a scholar who wore a sword'. Dr. Dowling's nephew, then a small boy, recalled seventy-seven years afterwards this private visit of O'Leary to Tipperary.

Reclining in an armchair, his fine head (with its abundant hair, handsome acquiline nose and deep-set eyes) bent on his chest, over which his long beard was spread, he would occasionally remain silent for a few minutes, apparently brooding. Then, when something interesting or amusing was said, he would grasp the arms of his chair, sit upright and become animated and join in the conversation. His conversation was always interesting, but he was not a good talker, for he often paused, hesitating for a word or phrase.[19]

Meanwhile in Dublin a new factor had entered the movement for a New Departure in Irish politics. In December 1877 there had emerged from Dartmoor jail, after serving seven years of a fifteen-year sentence, the one-armed IRB arms agent, Michael Davitt. According to himself, he had been doing a good deal of thinking about Irish affairs while in prison; certainly, from the moment he was released, he began to express sentiments quite different from those he carried with him into jail in 1870.

Within a short time he met, either in Dublin or London, Parnell, Carroll and Egan; all were impressed by him and he by them. He at once resumed his seat on the Supreme Council of the IRB, although he went about openly advocating tolerance between the various nationalist groups and preaching support by the physical force movement for the parliamentary movement.

Davitt probably had other ideas too; but these he kept to himself until his arrival in America in July 1878. There he met John Devoy, apparently for the first time in his life, and found that Devoy had been thinking along lines similar to his own. The land question, both felt, should be the basis of a new coalition between physical force and constitutionalism. Not only Devoy, but some (though not all) of the Clan na Gael leaders, seemed also to agree. So did John Boyle O'Reilly of the Boston *Pilot*, Patrick Ford of the *Irish World*, the *New York Herald* and the whole of the Irish-American Press.

The Clan na Gael secretly organised a lecture tour for Davitt at their expense. For six months he travelled the States expounding his version of the New Departure. Devoy was with him for much of this time, expounding his version, in which much greater emphasis was laid on the land question than by Davitt. Perhaps the numerous opponents within the Clan of any open agitation did not at this stage think the thing would develop. Possibly the IRB leaders in Ireland did not take it all too seriously either; they had more important tasks in hand.

In October something happened that must have made such people realise how much in earnest were both Devoy and Davitt. Interpreting the re-election of Parnell, as president of the Home Rule Confederation, as his replacement of Butt as leader of the parliamentary group, Devoy sent a now historic cable to James O'Connor, offering to Parnell the support of the Irish-American nationalists on five conditions. Self-government should be substituted for federation as the main aim of the party; the land question was to be vigorously prosecuted until a peasant proprietary had been won; sectarianism should be banned; the Irish MPs should vote together in an aggressive anti-coercion policy; and they should support all struggling nationalities.

This cable has always been regarded as having had the express approval of the Clan na Gael Executive, some of whose names were appended to it. But, according to the Executive's report to the Clan Convention held in Wilkesbarre, Pennsylvania, in August 1879, the organisation had taken no stand on the matter. The first the Executive knew of 'the so-called New Departure' was when the cable, together with interviews with prominent Irish-Americans approving of it, appeared in the *New York Herald* the day after Devoy had sent the cable to James O'Connor.

The reaction from all relevant quarters was such as to dampen the enthusiasm of anyone but Devoy. Kickham, to whom Devoy had directed that the cable be shown for his approval, disapproved of the plan. Parnell did not bother to reply; he even pretended later on that he never heard of the message in the telegram. O'Leary, both in private letters and in public statements, expressed dismay at the ideas implicit in the cable; once more he considered dropping out of the movement altogether. Davitt, still on his lecture tour, was furious because he regarded it as impolitic to come out so openly at this stage.

For the New Departure to have any chance of success, the support of the IRB was essential. Davitt pressed Devoy to accompany him to Europe to overcome the anticipated IRB resistance. Only when the Clan na Gael appointed him as envoy to the IRB did Devoy consent to go. He sacrificed his career on the *New York Herald* to help his new policy over what seemed the principal obstacle. That Parnell would agree to lead the new movement he had little doubt.

Early in January 1879 Devoy and Davitt, having crossed the Atlantic separately, met again in Paris to attend a conference with the Supreme Council. At least eight of the eleven members (if not all eleven) attended this momentous meeting, which took place in a private room in a small hotel near O'Leary's lodgings and went on for four days.

From the accounts of the proceedings which have survived, it is obvious that there were some stormy scenes as the two visitors from the United States were heatedly attacked for their suggested new policy. Davitt came to Paris expecting strong opposition and, being a sensitive man who could not bear any criticism of his ideas, took offence where none was intended.

First, he and Devoy were obliged to sit through the normal agenda of the Council; this may well have made Davitt more irritable than usual. Nor can the physical disabilities of Kickham have made for an orderly meeting; everything had to be relayed to him by the deaf-and-dumb alphabet, which cannot have been much help to a man like Davitt with only one arm. In any event, Davitt found himself brusquely waved aside by Kickham whenever he tried to reach Kickham's ear-trumpet.

O'Leary found himself acting as mediator in a clash which occurred on the first day. Davitt and John O'Connor, the Council's secretary and Kickham's 'interpreter', were by now barely on speaking terms. Davitt's attitude was seen by Kickham as an attempt to belittle him. When he replied harshly to Davitt, Davitt burst into tears, picked up his hat and coat, and rushed from the room, followed by the understandably worried Devoy.

All that night Davitt, who had walked back to his hotel sobbing openly in the streets, talked with Devoy. Early next morning O'Leary arrived and persuaded the two to return to the discussions. They agreed; but Kickham was still adamant. The New Departure, as advocated by Devoy, found only one supporter on the Council, Matthew Harris of Ballinasloe, later an MP.

This meeting has been regarded as marking the parting of the ways for the physical force men and the constitutionalists. Yet, with the support of O'Leary, Devoy persuaded the Council to sanction the participation by members of the IRB in the open movement, provided they did not enter Parliament. It was not until over a year later, by which time the mainly agrarian aspect of the new policy had become clear, that this permission was withdrawn and all connection between the IRB and the Home Rulers and Land Leaguers ended—in so far as the Supreme Council was in a position to end it.

O'Leary's attitude to the New Departure is worth examining. Essentially a tolerant man, he considered with interest Devoy's startling ideas. After so many years with nothing to show for the work of the secret movement, it is obvious that O'Leary was attracted by the suggestion that the IRB should come out into the open. Yet there remained his immovable hostility to the idea of genuine nationalists working in the British parliament.

Against this, however, must be placed the fact that O'Leary admired Parnell personally from the moment they first met. When in March 1878 the Surrey Hotel meeting broke up, F. H. O'Donnell pursued Dr. Carroll and engaged him in a long private discussion, which led to some more meetings between the two in the following few days. O'Leary remained with Parnell; the two struck up an immediate friendship, even discussing their respective families. Perhaps O'Leary recalled young Fanny Parnell's visits to the *Irish People* office with her mother some thirteen years before.

That O'Leary, unlike the rest of the Supreme Council, did not summarily reject the New Departure is proved by his later actions. Upon the conclusion of the meeting in January 1879 he and Devoy had agreed to travel with Kickham and John O'Connor as far as Dieppe; they went by Amiens and Rouen, so that O'Leary could inspect the cathedrals of those cities. Devoy, recalling this trip some quarter of a century later, referred to discussions on the train between the four (all of them on the Revolutionary Directory) on the new policy, and even suggested that a sub-committee had been set up, with O'Leary on it, to formulate the precise line the policy would take.

Devoy, having now (at least in his own estimation) been partly successful in his approach to the Council, decided to meet Parnell himself to ensure that he would accept the leadership of the new movement. An appointment was made for the two for Boulogne for 7 March 1879. When Devoy intimated his intention of bringing along O'Leary (against the express wish of Davitt) in order to forestall any possible later misrepresentation, Parnell countered by bringing Biggar.

It is impossible to accept as the whole truth this explanation by Devoy of O'Leary's participation in the Boulogne discussions. It seems likely that he realised, probably to his surprise, that O'Leary was more receptive than any of the other IRB men to the idea of co-operation with the parliamentary group. In addition, having presumably learnt of the friendship that had sprung up between O'Leary and Parnell, he would naturally have regarded O'Leary's presence in Boulogne as conducive to harmonious discussion.

He was not wrong. When Parnell and Biggar disembarked, it was O'Leary who effected the introductions at this first meeting between two of the greatest figures of modern Ireland. As the four walked along the quays, it was O'Leary who made the party feel at ease by informally inquiring after Parnell's mother and sisters. Doubtless, too, it was O'Leary who led the other three down to the quayside park, to which he and Luby had led James Stephens nineteen years before upon his return from the United States.

Before they went to lunch in a nearby fashionable hotel, Devoy and Parnell did some serious talking while O'Leary, a lapsed Catholic, and Biggar, a Presbyterian converted to Catholicism, discussed the doctrine of predestination. Parnell, recalling O'Leary's starting a hare (to use his own phrase) about O'Connor Power at the previous meeting in London, hoped he was not going to do the same again. Devoy jestingly accused Biggar of having, by his conversion, injured the cause of Irish nationalism in the eyes of Orangemen. When Biggar asked if he should not consider his soul before the Orangemen, Devoy, with a smile and a shrug, replied: 'Oh, I'd be willing to see you damned for the sake of Ireland.'

Even after Boulogne and the progress which Devoy believed he had made there, he was still not certain of Parnell. So, when he heard from Davitt that Parnell was hesitating on the land question, he crossed to Ireland secretly, the conditions of the Queen's pardon notwithstanding, and met Parnell several times again. After the last of these meetings, held in Morrison's Hotel, Dublin, in Davitt's presence on 1 June 1879, Devoy regarded the New Departure as an accomplished fact.

How can his support of the New Departure be reconciled with O'Leary's hostility to parliamentary action? Parnell obviously measured up to his requirements as a national leader, under whom O'Leary was prepared to tolerate a limited form of co-operation between the IRB and the Home Rulers. Yet, according to Devoy, this co-operation excluded action in Westminster.

There can be only one explanation of this apparent paradox. O'Leary, like some other leading men of the time, must have visualised a mass abstention policy by a strong and united party of Irish MPs who would ultimately, probably on a signal from a fully-prepared physical force body, declare themselves an independent Irish parliament. This idea was not new. It had occurred to Kickham and Davitt. It was mentioned by both Carroll and Devoy as one of the main aims of the New Departure. It had even been discussed by the IRB in the early 1870s. It later became one of the planks of the Sinn Féin platform.

'The revolutionary organisation,' said a prominent American Fenian in a conversation in mid-1880 with the British consul in Philadelphia, which the consul dutifully reported to London, 'was deluded by false representations of Parnell and others, claiming to start an organisation in Ireland and the United States powerful enough to elect sufficient members of parliament (as well as representatives on local boards) to command a controlling vote. This force would then, at a given time, withdraw in a body, return to Dublin and there organise an Irish parliament, which would, at a fitting opportunity, declare the absolute independence of Ireland.'

Such a symbolic action, backed by a physical force movement, would make a strong appeal to O'Leary. At any rate, he undoubtedly left Devoy under the impression early in 1879 that he supported the main idea behind the New Departure and, presumably convinced that a re-united IRB would have an important role to play in the planned train of events, co-operated enthusiastically with Devoy in re-organising that body.

Devoy, however, seriously misjudged the support for his ideas. It is clear now that he wrongly took Parnell's silence or cordiality to signify assent to his project, whereas Parnell was merely skilfully gaining that assistance of the extreme nationalists which he had so casually sought from John Daly of Limerick in 1873. The new policy as planned by Devoy became impossible to execute when the Land League under Davitt renounced a resort to arms.

Within a year of the Boulogne meeting the IRB leaders had also repudiated the New Departure. To idealists like Kickham and O'Leary, to start a land agitation was to lower the aim of the the separatist movement; it would mean substituting a social or economic objective for the political aim of all Irish nationalists since Wolfe Tone. In the words of a famous Irishman who was deeply influenced by O'Leary's ideas a decade later: 'And so was founded an agitation where some men pretended to national passion for the land's sake: some men to agrarian passion for the nation's sake: some men to both for their own advancement.'[20]

On the land question—and no other—Devoy and the IRB parted company, even though it meant the beginning of an eclipse of that body that was to last for twenty years. If they bitterly resented the new agrarian movement, begun by Davitt under Devoy's guidance and with the active co-operation of the Home Rule MPs, it must be remembered that the IRB leaders had good reason for resentment. As recently as January 1878 Devoy was as vigorous an opponent of parliamentarianism as any of the IRB men. Nobody had been more critical than he of O'Connor Power's watered-down version of Fenianism when Power visited the United States as IRB envoy in 1876.

Yet by the summer of 1878 Devoy had completely reversed his own ideas on co-operation between physical force and constitutionalism, and proceeded to try to force his new views on a Supreme Council which, with the encouragement of Devoy and the Clan na Gael leaders, had rid itself of Power and his supporters. The Council could point out that in 1870, and again in 1873, the extreme nationalists had agreed not to obstruct Butt and his party, but in both cases had imposed a time limit on this period of tolerance.[21] Now in effect they were being asked by Devoy to extend this time limit indefinitely.

Convict Establishment, *Portland*

Near Weymouth

Convicts are permitted to write one Letter on reception and also at intervals of 3, 4 or 6 months, according to the class they may be in. They may also receive one Letter (prepaid) at the above named periods. Matters of private importance to a Convict may be communicated at any time by Letter (prepaid) to the Governor or ~~Chaplain~~, who will inform the Convict thereof, if expedient.

In case of misconduct, the privilege of receiving or writing a Letter may be forfeited for a time.

All letters of an improper or idle tendency, either to or from Convicts, or containing slang or other objectionable expressions, will be suppressed. The permission to write and receive Letters is given to the Convict for the purpose of enabling them to keep up a connection with their respectable friends, and not that they may hear the news of the day.

All Letters are read by the Governor or Chaplain, and must be legibly written on the ruled lines, and not crossed.

Neither Clothes, nor any other articles, are allowed to be received at the Prison for the use of Convicts, except through the Governor. Persons attempting otherwise to introduce any article to or for a Convict are liable to Fine or Imprisonment, and the Convict thereof is liable to be severely punished. Convicts are not allowed to have Money, Books, or Postage Stamps sent to them while in Prison.

A Visit of twenty minutes duration allowed every 3, 4 or 6 months, according to class, between the hours of 2 and 4 P.M., not on Sundays.

F & P 3000 2-65

My Dear Uncle

Dec. 23rd 1868

25. A letter from John O'Leary from Portland jail, December 1868. The lines in italics on the transcript opposite were scored out by the prison censor

Dec. 23rd 1868

My dear Uncle,

For more than three years I have borne, I trust not altogether unmanfully, much mental and physical suffering. How I have suffered I cannot tell, and, even if I could, I would not. There was not a day or hour of all that time that might not bring forth its own peculiar pain, and perhaps the hardest thing of all to be borne was the constant fear lest something still worse remained to be borne. Comparatively speaking, however, I may look upon myself as rather fortunate. *For some of my companions are dead and some are mad, and many are invalids for life* while I am still in the possession of that greatest of all earthly blessings—'a sound mind in a sound body'. To be sure my hair is fast growing grey, 'though not with years', and I seem to myself to have aged greatly, and the time may have told upon me in many more ways than I can even guess, but I have still the use of all my limbs and (I believe) of all my wits and for this, I say again, I thank God and God alone. But I have given enough of my short space to myself. 'Tis very hard to avoid egotism in such a place as this; 'tis not easy to avoid it in any place. I heard all about my aunt and her young ones from Ellen. Probably some of her young ones are ceasing to be young and will soon force her to feel almost venerable herself. I am sorry to hear that you are still at feud with the Killeen people. Upon this subject I scarcely know what to say, and for this among many other reasons, that I know nothing of the details. You must forgive me, however, for saying that in these affairs the fault is scarcely ever *all* on one side. There is far more of folly than anything else in family quarrels, and I cannot easily believe that there is anything much worse in this. If that precious Eddy had much to do with the business I could believe that there might be much that was wrong, and I can conceive that pompous vulgar Val Dillon meddling mischievously in the matter; but of the Killeen people themselves I cannot think ill. They may not be over nice, but I am sure they are not ill-natured.

Love

J. O'Leary.

26. John O'Leary
and Dr. George
Sigerson in the
Contemporary
Club, 1886—a
pencil sketch by
J. B. Yeats
(senior)

If Kickham warned Devoy—as he did in Paris—that the new movement would undermine the recently re-organised IRB, no doubt Devoy could reply that in time both the Home Rule party and the Land League would be in the hands of the IRB. That clearly was what his own colleagues in the Clan na Gael Executive visualised. But all too soon the IRB men were to be proved right and Devoy wrong. Rank-and-file members went over wholesale to the League and the party, and the very existence of the IRB, the *raison d'être* of the Clan in America, was threatened. Devoy found himself outwitted by Davitt and Parnell, both of whom succeeded in exploiting the IRB for their own interests without in any way allowing their movements to be used by the IRB.

5

ALTHOUGH HE WAS as politically active as ever during his last few years in exile, O'Leary's efforts produced no worthwhile results. With the growth of the land movement the IRB was almost wiped out and its ideal forgotten; the influence of O'Leary and his colleagues grew steadily weaker. In addition, to the dismay of O'Leary, the violent deeds of the extreme wings of both the Irish and American physical force movements alienated public support.

In Ireland the secret meetings between Devoy and Parnell in April 1879 had hardly concluded before the New Departure began to take an unexpected turn, which was soon to arouse even greater hostility than before from the Supreme Council of the IRB. As he followed powerlessly the events of that year, O'Leary must have become more and more disheartened.

Now assured of the backing of the rank-and-file of the extreme nationalists, Davitt pushed ahead vigorously with his land agitation. Only a month after the Boulogne conference between Devoy and Parnell, at which O'Leary had been present, came the historic meeting in Irishtown, county Mayo, which Devoy is said to have attended incognito. This marked the real beginning of the Land League. In August the Land League of Mayo was founded by Davitt, and the following October came the establishment in Dublin of the Irish National Land League, with Parnell as president.

In the summer of 1879 O'Leary was again allowed home by the

British Government to attend to family business.[22] He was to remain for three months. This time, presumably on his own insistence, there were no public demonstrations. Nor does he appear to have taken part in political discussions.

One cannot have passed through rural Ireland in the summer of 1879 without feeling the tension which was steadily mounting, as the tenant farmers became more restless and a widespread failure of crops became apparent. It was clear from the start that the new movement was semi-Fenian in both outlook and support. Davitt, Egan and Thomas Brennan, its leading figures, had been well-known IRB men. In the western counties, where the Land League was strongest, the IRB had been accustomed to operating in the open since the emergence of O'Connor Power fifteen years earlier.

This turn of events was one which O'Leary could not be expected to countenance. It was one thing to support a movement like Home Rule, which at least had some form of self-government as its ultimate aim. But to switch to an agitation having as its object merely the reform of the land system was, in his view, wholly wrong for a purely military conspiracy which had always concentrated on strictly political activities. To permit the IRB to be used in such an agrarian movement he regarded as indefensible.

O'Leary was not alone in this attitude. Kickham, still president of the Supreme Council, was probably a keener observer of rural Ireland than anyone else. But despite his undoubted sympathies for the farmers, he also strongly held that political independence should precede any reform of the land system.

The IRB soon showed that it was prepared to fight back. Its leaders, while sincerely believing the Land League to be bad for the country, doubtless also appreciated that it would undermine their own organisation. In particular, O'Leary, as the former financial manager of the organisation, must have realised that, with funds from the United States now being diverted into the Land League, the IRB would soon feel the pinch and have to restrict its activities.

In the first three months of 1880 Parnell toured the United States. His visit proved a resounding success. He covered 10,000 miles, spoke in sixty-two cities, addressed Congress, and collected 200,000 dollars. On the day he sailed for home he established the American Land League, with Devoy on its committee.

On his arrival in Cork, however, Parnell was presented with an address by spokesmen of the IRB, who once more put the case against parliamentary agitation and announced their intention not to take any part in the forthcoming general election. Charles G. Doran, recently displaced from the post of secretary of the Supreme Council, but still an influential figure in the IRB, addressed the crowds who had gathered to welcome Parnell, first from the steps of the Victoria Hotel and the following day at the railway station as Parnell left for Dublin.[23]

Parnell's American tour was quickly followed by one by Davitt, which lasted six months. Parnell's action in setting up the American Land League had led to renewed opposition within the Clan na Gael to the New Departure. Dr. Carroll, who seems never to have thought much of the idea at all, was now leading the opposition. One of Davitt's principal reasons for this visit was to support Devoy in defeating, once and for all, their opponents in the Clan.

To counteract the presence of Davitt, to put the IRB case against the New Departure, and to attend a meeting of the Revolutionary Directory, the Supreme Council despatched O'Leary from Paris to New York. He arrived in June 1880 and, like Davitt, remained for six months. His mission was to prove a failure.

Shortly before O'Leary's departure from Europe, the Supreme Council had shown its teeth twice to the supporters of the New Departure. It expelled Davitt from the Brotherhood and, on O'Leary's advice, it vetoed a proposal, put forward by J. J. O'Kelly with the backing of the Clan na Gael (in the form of a grant of £1,800 to him), to revive the Arms Bureau, the underground arms-import agency which Davitt had been managing up to the time of his arrest in 1870.

Some time after O'Leary's arrival in America, O'Donovan Rossa, who had for some time past been at loggerheads with the Clan, announced a convention of the Irish Race for Philadelphia, his aim being to canvass support for a counter-blast to the Clan. Dr. Carroll, in whose house in Philadelphia O'Leary stayed, appears to have considered supporting Rossa and the newly-founded Society of United Irishmen, the main outcome of the Philadelphia convention. Although it is not clear whether or not O'Leary attended the convention, it is probable that Doran did so as the envoy of the IRB.

Unlike Rossa, O'Leary by no means severed all connections with the Clan na Gael. He went with Devoy, who had strongly resented the action of the IRB in sending out O'Leary at this juncture, to a big Clan re-union in New York. There he addressed the assembly, pleading once more for the old policy of abstention from all parliamentary action. According to Devoy, he got a cold reception and was answered by several Clan speakers. Finally, after Devoy also had spoken, O'Leary tried to reply; but, as always, his effort at an impromptu speech was poor.

Some weeks after O'Leary's arrival the Clan executive met to hear the opposing sides and come to a definite decision on the New Departure. Once again, as at Paris the previous year, the whole question was gone into in great detail. Dr. Carroll spoke first, urging the severance of all connection with the parliamentary movement, and alleging that Parnell's sole aim in seeking their co-operation was to use them for his own purposes.

Davitt countered by claiming that Fenianism had lost ground by keeping aloof from public movements. They should, he said, try to influence all movements and obtain support from every quarter. The land was the question of the hour; were they going to leave it all to the parliamentarians? Finally, he reminded them that no national movement could succeed without the support of the farming class, a point Devoy never tired of stressing.

O'Leary was last to speak. The New Departure, he asserted, was immoral and impolitic. He did not believe in pretence; but the New Departure involved a pretence of loyalty while there was 'treason all along the line'. The only result of that would be 'sham loyalty and sham treason'. 'If I were to stand absolutely alone,' he ended in an impassioned appeal, 'I will resist this dishonest and unholy alliance. "Freedom comes from God's right hand," and I believe in righteous means as well as righteous ends.'

But the Clan executive decided in favour of Davitt, who reported exuberantly to Matt Harris by letter on 10 July 1880. 'Perhaps you are aware that John O'Leary is out here. He came from Paris to upset my Land League endeavours but he will go back a wiser though a sadder man. . . . O'Leary failed completely to get up a crusade against the Land League in America.'[24]

Undaunted by the Clan decision, O'Leary continued what had now become almost a one-man crusade. He went to Chicago and met the new leader of the Clan, Alex Sullivan. They disagreed on almost everything—on the calibre of the Supreme Council, on its expulsion of Davitt, on its hostility towards the Land League. It is safe to assume that O'Leary disliked this sinister figure, whose gangster methods some years later did such harm to all Irish-American bodies, and with whom Devoy and the Supreme Council later quarrelled.

Of Boston, O'Leary would have had more pleasant memories. There he went several times to renew his acquaintance with Robert Dwyer Joyce. There, too, he became intimate with that noble figure John Boyle O'Reilly, by now one of Boston's most prominent citizens.

O'Reilly, in a letter to Devoy, has left a vivid, but far from favourable, impression of O'Leary. As a literary man both he and Joyce found O'Leary most charming, 'most interesting and extensively read', and a remarkably keen and perceptive literary critic. But on politics he was, in O'Reilly's view, utterly unrealistic.

To his dismay O'Reilly found that, in judging politics, O'Leary merely applied his critical mind to existing politics, without being able to advocate a plan of his own in substitution. He disapproved of everything that had been done in Ireland for twenty years. He insisted that nobody but a university graduate was fit to rule a nation, or even to control a revolutionary movement.

He argued in favour of a campaign to convert to Irish nationalism the moneyed Protestant classes who had been bribed into becoming West Britons by the corrupt patronage of the Castle. He was against any positive action in Ireland for the time being. And what O'Reilly regarded as the most staggering discovery of all, O'Leary was not, and had never been, a republican.

It would be wrong to accept as accurate or unbiased in every detail O'Reilly's portrait of O'Leary. The letter to Devoy is typical of this impulsive man, full of energy, impatient to strike a blow for his country and even prepared to countenance the dynamite projects of Rossa. O'Leary's refusal to countenance violent action in unarmed, unprepared and half-starved Ireland of 1880 must be set against the more unrealistic action of both O'Reilly and Joyce when Devoy returned to America in 1879—with the New Departure in his head and Parnell in his pocket, as he thought. The two residents of Boston straightway settled their affairs and prepared to sail for Ireland at a moment's notice to fight in the insurrection which both were convinced was imminent.

That O'Leary's hyper-critical mind could irritate those who disagreed with him is easy to appreciate. That he loved to argue for argument's sake is well established. It is easy to imagine the impact he must have made on O'Reilly and Joyce, two literary men with no experience of participation in politics or in a revolutionary movement, and both of whom were completely out of touch with the Ireland they had last seen some fifteen years earlier.

O'Leary, on the other hand, had remained in close touch with the movement from his release from jail in 1871. He had also kept himself informed on Irish affairs generally. His opposition to action represented the old IRB line of careful preparation for an insurrection. His desire to win back the Protestants was an indication of his (and the IRB's) adherence to the principles of Tone. His disapproval of the trend of Irish affairs since 1865 was in line with his (and the IRB's) opposition in principle to parliamentary agitation.

Finally, O'Reilly's discovery that O'Leary was not a republican would not have surprised anyone closely connected with the leaders of the extreme wing of Irish nationalism at any time in the previous twenty years. O'Leary had never concealed his preference for a form of constitutional monarchy for Ireland. It will be recalled that, as early as 1859, Stephens had considered it prudent to warn

O'Mahony of O'Leary's views on this subject. Much more recently, when shortly after his release he had visited the United States, O'Leary had once more publicly repeated his liking for a constitutional monarchy.

> I am not a republican by conviction . . . but, on the contrary, incline to think, that for countries in the same condition as most of the European ones at present, a constitutional monarchy would be the best and safest form of government—the one that, in my opinion, gives the strongest guarantee for the greatest amount of freedom of individual action which is compatible at the present time and in most countries, with the existing social order. [25]

John Boyle O'Reilly probably assumed also that, because O'Leary was not a republican, he was therefore against a republic for Ireland. This was not the case at any time in his life. As a youth of nineteen he had formed a secret society whose members bound themselves by oath to establish an Irish republic. According to Devoy, O'Leary saw little difference between a moderate republic and a constitutional monarchy.

In his later years O'Leary was in favour of an Irish republic because that was the aim of the IRB and there was no prospect of an Irish monarchy. 'I am not a doctrinaire and would have no objection to a moderate republic, either in Ireland or elsewhere,' he had written publicly as early as 1871. Like most Irish separatists he would, in Devoy's words, 'take any kind of a free Ireland in preference to the most liberal form of connection with England'.

On 4 December 1880 O'Leary sailed for Europe with John O'Connor, reaching Paris towards the end of the month. Although he was to make still another trip to the United States two years later, the failure of his mission in 1880 marks a decisive point both in the history of the IRB itself, to which O'Leary remained faithful to the end, and in his own influence on Irish and American revolutionary affairs for some years.

In America Alex Sullivan rose to the top in the Clan organisation and, during the notorious 'Triangle' regime (so called from a sign used on Clan documents) the power of Devoy waned and the support both for terrorism and for Land League policy increased. In August 1881 a Land League convention was held in Chicago which O'Connor attended as IRB delegate. Here it became clear that the desire of the Americans was for younger men to replace Kickham, O'Leary and others of the older school.

On this side of the Atlantic the Phoenix Park assassinations of May 1882, and the series of sensational explosions in British cities in the next few years, were all wrongly attributed to the IRB and led to a serious loss of prestige by the Irish body. Furthermore, the death of Kickham in August 1882 caused a vacuum in the IRB leadership which was not effectively filled for many years.

Nevertheless attempts continued to be made to establish a basis for co-operation with the Clan na Gael. For this purpose O'Leary once more crossed the Atlantic in May 1883, and remained in America for another six months. While there he met Devoy and most of the other leading figures, but does not appear to have taken part in the Land League convention in Philadelphia in August, which led to the capture of the American Land League by the Clan.

Doubtless the Clan leaders observed that the new blood which they had hoped for had not, so far, flowed into the Supreme Council. Although the constitution of the Council was altered in 1884 so that its members thenceforth consisted of seven elected members and four co-opted members, O'Leary appears to have become one of the co-opted members from the start, and was the only remaining figure of the pre-1865 era to hold office for so long.[26]

To the friction between the IRB and the Clan na Gael over the New Departure can be largely ascribed the failure of a promising project to start a newspaper to serve as an organ of the extreme nationalists, on which O'Leary was to have played a leading part. Ever since the seizure and suppression of the *Irish People* in 1865, leading Fenians on both sides of the Atlantic had used the Dublin weekly paper *Irishman* when occasion arose for presenting their views to the public.

But while Richard Pigott, the editor, was pleased to get this patronage, it was given with considerable reluctance by the IRB leaders. Pigott's reputation as a journalist was always low and his dishonesty notorious. The IRB naturally resented the fact that, as editor of the only paper with physical force sympathies, he had a virtual monopoly of their support.

To O'Donovan Rossa while in jail Pigott had shown many kindnesses. Upon Rossa's release he returned these favours by contributing a regular American letter to the *Irishman*. James O'Connor found employment on the paper after his release, and Kickham on occasions even wrote its editorials. But the upright O'Leary and the forthright Devoy had no time for Pigott, although both were at times also obliged to use his paper in order to publicise their views on matters of national importance. 'I used his paper as I might a placard on a wall,' said O'Leary crudely in 1883.

As early as 1876 the plan to publish a Fenian paper had been widely discussed by Carroll, Devoy and others, and a campaign for subscriptions had begun in the United States under Clan na Gael auspices. The idea was much talked of for several years. At one stage it was to be an American venture; later it was felt that a paper in Ireland would do more to further the cause. The possibility of a paper on both sides of the Atlantic was not ruled out.

By 1879 the project was being pushed vigorously by the Clan leaders. Davitt, incensed at the attacks on the New Departure by Pigott, was now enthusiastic. Since sufficient money does not appear to have been forthcoming, the chances of buying out Pigott were considered. Carroll was in favour of this; so was O'Leary.

It is clear that O'Leary was to have been one of those in charge of the proposed paper, and probably its editor. Kickham, Luby and Davitt were also mentioned. In the event of an American edition, O'Leary was to be its European correspondent. Information reaching the Home Office in London suggested that a fund of 5,000 dollars had been set aside by the Clan na Gael to finance the new paper.

Following the Supreme Council meeting in Paris in January 1879, negotiations were opened with Pigott for the purchase of his interest. Pigott, however, demanded what all concerned regarded as an excessive figure; he seems to have been convinced that it was Davitt who was trying to put him out of business, and he determined to make it as costly as possible for him.

Finally the talks with Pigott were broken off, and the plans for a paper began to be forgotten. Eventually in 1881 Parnell achieved what the IRB and the Clan had failed to do, and Pigott's papers became the organs of Parnell's movement.

O'Leary at this stage was still interested in writing. When in 1881 Devoy started the *Irish Nation* in New York, O'Leary became a regular contributor. Early in 1883, however, O'Leary made some outspoken, but bitter and unpopular, comments in public about two Kerrymen, Barrett and Poff, who had been hanged for an agrarian murder. His articles then ceased to appear in the *Irish Nation*, which later that year itself ceased to appear when its equally outspoken editor was sent to jail for some comments on the banker Belmont.

To Devoy's credit he allowed O'Leary complete freedom of expression in the *Irish Nation*, with the curious result that at a time when the voice of the IRB was silent in Ireland its official policy was being advocated almost weekly by O'Leary writing from Paris to New York. 'It is not a Land Act that we need,' he wrote in May 1882, 'but the right to make our own acts and mould our own lives as our own thoughts and feelings prompt us.'

When IRB policy warranted no exposition, O'Leary ranged over a wide field—French politics, Davitt's support for the American economist Henry George, and the debates at Westminster. When dealing with personalities O'Leary wrote in a style reminiscent of his best editorials and replies to correspondents in the *Irish People* nearly twenty years earlier.

Of Davitt at a stormy meeting he said: '. . . he showered "cowards" and "dogs" and "drunkards" upon his audience with a volubility worthy of a fishwoman, and a taste, let us say, worthy of himself.' Of some of the most prominent Irish MPs who, at a meeting in Wexford, had lauded the men of '98 O'Leary acidly commented: 'We must always be prepared to find plenty of men in Ireland, as elsewhere, combining a certain moral regard for brave men with the most absolute physical regard for their own skins.'

On top of his failure in Philadelphia and the loss of his correspondence in Devoy's paper, O'Leary suffered a serious personal blow in the death in 1883 of his half-brother Edmund. Eleven years John's junior and a child of their father's third marriage, Edmund had been educated in St. John's College, Waterford, and after having obtained a surgical diploma in London in 1863, became a ship's surgeon, travelling as far as Australia and America.

For some time after the 1865 crisis in the IRB Edmund had resided in Paris, where he had acted as financial agent for the IRB. Later he graduated in medicine in Scotland and became medical officer in the workhouse in Dunmore, county Waterford. Finally he settled down in London, where he had a surgery in Fetter Lane; 'a place of drudgery and small fees, . . . cheerless at best' a friend described it. Dissatisfied with the life, and encouraged by his friend Edmund Downey the publisher, Dr. O'Leary had been planning to move out to a fashionable suburb in London.[27]

His sudden death from gastritis on 12 June 1883 must have been a shock to his elder half-brother, then in the United States. Their sister Ellen crossed from Tipperary for the funeral, which was private. Like so many other Irish residents of London, Edmund O'Leary was buried in Kensal Green Cemetery.

Although finding himself almost wholly out of sympathy with the trend of events in Ireland, O'Leary continued even in his last few years in Paris to keep himself well-informed. Fundamental differences of opinion did not prevent himself and Devoy from corresponding regularly. In their detestation of the dynamite campaign approved by the ruling Triangle clique of the Clan na Gael, in their hostility to Rossa and his wild plans and in their resentment of Davitt's undermining of the IRB, they had much in common as well.

Nor did O'Leary lose sight of the possibilities of Parnell as a national leader, perhaps of a physical force movement if the occasion should arise. Early in 1881 at the height of the land war Devoy and O'Leary were in touch with Parnell, who had a mysterious meeting in Paris in February with O'Leary. He left

O'Leary under the impression that he was still prepared to go much further than constitutional action, should that not suffice to achieve his aims.

Yet keeping oneself informed of events is one thing; being in a position to influence those events is another. It is all too obvious from his letters that the failures and frustrations of the early 1880s made O'Leary even more critical than usual of men and policies of the national movement. He complained bitterly of his own feeling of isolation, and from time to time suspected that plans were being made behind his back—as, indeed, they were on occasions.

To make matters worse, O'Leary found himself for the first time in his life short of money. A small income which he had acquired on the death of his father in 1849 had grown steadily through premature deaths in his family, and by the late 1870s amounted to about £200 a year, a tidy sum in those days for a thrifty bachelor. Ironically, however, as the amount of house property (from which this income derived) grew, worsening economic conditions made it increasingly difficult for tenants to pay rents promptly.

It does not seem likely that he inherited much property from Edmund, who had made a holograph will in John's favour in Paris in 1872, but had subsequently sold some valuable property acquired from his mother in 1851. Edmund also had been noted for his charity towards many poor patients in London; and the O'Leary family had, at the time of the 1865 crisis, advanced £1,000 to the IRB which had never been repaid.[28]

By November 1882 we find O'Leary bluntly suggesting to Devoy that he be paid for his articles in the *Irish Nation*. How badly off he was at this time may perhaps be gauged from a remark he made (in a letter to Devoy), with what seriousness it is difficult to say, to the effect that since the death of O'Mahony he could now claim the Belmont fund. This was a sum of money, originally over 25,000 dollars but whittled down by legal costs, representing drafts from the Fenian Brotherhood to the IRB and payable to O'Leary, which had been seized and 'frozen' by the British Government in 1865, and to recover which O'Mahony had unsuccessfully litigated against the New York banker, Auguste Belmont.

As the end of his exile in Paris drew near, O'Learly eagerly looked forward to returning to Ireland. In his old age he admitted privately to having experienced a feeling of loneliness for most of his period in Paris. He was cut off from regular contact with his family, to which he was devoted; half-a-dozen or more of his closest relatives died while he was debarred from entering Ireland or England.

Impatient at his exclusion from public affairs, he felt seriously handicapped by having to learn of public events at second-hand. Inevitably, after his success in attracting public support while editor of the *Irish People*, he must have felt that, had he been in Ireland during the 1870s, things might not have gone so disastrously for the movement of which he was a leader.

Finally, during his exile O'Leary acquired new and stimulating friends by correspondence. It may suffice to mention two to indicate the wide range of O'Leary's interests and acquaintances. Alfred John Webb, the son of a Dublin printer and a Quaker, had, while compiling his great *Compendium of Irish Biography* (published in 1878), come into contact with O'Leary. Webb was one of the earliest supporters of Home Rule, but parted company with Parnell long before the 1890 split. Although politically poles apart, he and O'Leary became firm and lifelong friends.

Born Ada Ellen Bayly, the novelist Edna Lyall was the daughter of an English barrister and led a comparatively secluded life, mainly in Lincoln. She first attracted public attention with a massive three-volume novel, *Donovan*, in 1882; later Michael Davitt was to figure prominently in one of her best books. A champion of oppressed peoples in various parts of the world, she corresponded with O'Leary for several decades.

CHAPTER SIX

1 Triumphal Return

2 Willie Yeats

3 Troubled Years

1

ON THE MORNING OF 19 JANUARY 1885, nineteen years and one month after his conviction and twenty-year sentence for treason-felony, John O'Leary disembarked at the North Wall, Dublin. Probably at his own request, he was met by only a small party. All were members of the Young Ireland Society, which had elected O'Leary president for the coming year. Already this recently-formed literary group had displayed obvious IRB sympathies; one of its vice-presidents, Fred Allan (later for many years on the Supreme Council) had been unsuccessfully tried for treason-felony only a short time before.

That evening a packed audience awaited the arrival of O'Leary in the Round Room of the Rotunda. The huge crowd overflowed out into the street and up on to the platform, where a distinguished group, representative of all shades of Irish nationalist thought, greeted O'Leary enthusiastically as he entered to the cheers of the audience. Letters from Archbishop Croke and Joseph Biggar MP were followed by a formal address of welcome, the uncompromising terms of which must have pleasantly surprised even O'Leary.

As the subject of his inaugural address the new president of the

172

Young Ireland Society had chosen 'Young Ireland—the Old and the New'. In an inspiring speech—in content one of the best he ever made—O'Leary outlined the programme which he wished the society to follow. Young Ireland, he recalled, had tried to free Ireland but had failed; and Ireland was still unfree. But the work of Young Ireland had been the basis of all subsequent movements, and Young Ireland's outstanding achievement had been in literature. By comparison Fenianism had done little for Irish literature, and the Land League less.

It was accepted, he continued, that a knowledge of the past was necessary in order to help mould the future. Yet we were a non-reading people, and the supply of Irish literature was poor. Young Ireland had got out of this vicious circle by providing good reading matter. The Young Ireland Society could do nothing better, he suggested, than to imitate the movement from which it took its name. Literary meetings should be arranged regularly, rather than debates; the society should extend its activities by founding branches all over these islands, each branch having its own library of Irish books.

A fortnight after the Rotunda meeting O'Leary accompanied to Manchester Patrick Neville Fitzgerald; here both spoke at a public meeting of Irishmen in the Free Trade Hall. A native of Midleton, Fitzgerald had been, since the death of Kickham, the leading advocate of physical force in Ireland and, like Fred Allan, had a few months earlier been acquitted by a Dublin jury of a charge of treason-felony. As a youth Fitzgerald had participated in the rising of '67 in his native Cork; later he was to be for many years a prominent figure in both the IRB and the Gaelic Athletic Association.

From Manchester O'Leary travelled north to Glasgow. There, in the City Hall on 3 February 1885, after having received formal addresses of welcome from the Irish nationalist communities of that city and Stockton-on-Tees, he addressed the newly-established Glasgow branch of the Young Ireland Society.[1] Back in Ireland the following month O'Leary accompanied P. N. Fitzgerald to Limerick where, on St. Patrick's Day, the nationalists of the city presented Fitzgerald with a gift of 100 sovereigns to mark his triumph over British justice. At Limerick railway station the two IRB leaders were met by the mayor and a crowd of 10,000; behind a procession of bands the visitors were escorted to their hotel and that night, at a banquet in their honour, O'Leary again spoke.

Four months later O'Leary and Fitzgerald completed their tour in symbolic fashion. After having attended and addressed a reception in Waterford the previous evening, given by the local branch of the Young Ireland Society, they proceeded on 22 August 1885 to a monster demonstration in the Tipperary village of Mullinahone, to mark the third anniversary of the death of Charles Kickham. Here, by Kickham's grave, the nationalists of the south had assembled in their thousands to welcome O'Leary home to his native county. Fitzgerald took charge of the proceedings, and the principal speech of the day was delivered by O'Leary amidst great enthusiasm.

February 1886 saw O'Leary in Cork city where, in an address entitled 'What Irishmen Should Know', he outlined his views on modern Irish literature to the Cork Young Ireland Society. Of recent Irish authors he recommended especially Davis, Mitchel, Gavan Duffy, Standish O'Grady and George Sigerson; A. M. Sullivan's *New Ireland* he described as 'superficial, sensational and grossly inaccurate'. The writers who, in his opinion, most faithfully portrayed the Irish character were Griffin, Banim, Carleton and Kickham. In a characteristically trenchant contribution the following month to a press controversy on 'The Best One Hundred Irish Books', sponsored by the *Freeman's Journal*, O'Leary expanded the views he had expressed in Cork and extended his opinions to cover Irish historical writers.

But if literature remained a major interest of O'Leary's life, politics were not forgotten. 'I have come back from exile with the same opinions and feelings I carried with me into prison,' he declared defiantly in the Rotunda on his first day on Irish soil. He could not, he admitted frankly, promise freedom in the near future; but he still believed it to be 'the duty of every Irishman to live and, if needs be, to die, that Ireland might be free'. Little wonder that the *Freeman's Journal's* editorial on the following morning, after remarking that 'John O'Leary on a platform in the Rotunda is like a vision from the days of twenty golden years ago', agreed wholeheartedly with his views on national literature, but ignored his references to Irish politics.

As for his own plans, O'Leary told his audience in the Rotunda, he intended first merely to look around him at the country and its people, from both of which he had been separated for so long. Should he find himself out of harmony with existing movements, he would either remain silent or use his pen in the furtherance of Irish literature—for which last subject he felt much better qualified than for politics.

In the circumstances then prevailing this was a wise decision. Although O'Leary's own principles and aspirations might be unchanged, it was evident that those of the majority of the Irish people were. It is true that there had recently been superficial signs of a revival of support for physical force. In September 1884 over 15,000 men, headed by banners, had marched in military style through the centre of Dublin at the funeral of Denis Duggan, who

had taken part in the rescue of Stephens in 1865, in the rising of
'67 and in the *Catalpa* expedition to Australia in 1876. This had
been followed a month later by the trials for treason-felony of
Fitzgerald, Allan and P. W. Nally; and early in 1885 the expulsion
from France of James Stephens, at the instigation of the British
Government, led to a national testimonial which, in little more than
six months, realised almost £2,000.

It is equally true that by 1885 the so-called Fenians on both
sides of the Atlantic had become associated in the public mind with
fantastic, if exaggerated, projects to dynamite world-famous English
landmarks. O'Leary himself on more than one occasion at this
period complained in public of the erroneous public equation of
physical force with dynamite; so strongly did he feel on this topic
that at least twice in 1885 he publicly referred to his old friend and
associate in the movement, O'Donovan Rossa, as a madman.

On the other hand, the previous half-decade had shown that
Irish nationalists could achieve something by constitutional means
—even if, as O'Leary would insist, any concessions wrung from the
British were so wrung partly through fear of what might replace
the constitutional agitation. Especially since the passing of the
Land Act of 1881, Charles Stewart Parnell had become the undisputed leader of nationalist Ireland. To use his own metaphor,
he was now the man on the horse; and in O'Leary's view, as publicly
expressed at Mullinahone, Parnell 'should now be allowed to decide
when and how to take the fence'. Obstruction of Parnell in his
impending struggle for self-government was, according to O'Leary
at this stage, unworthy of patriotic Irishmen.

O'Leary's advice to the extreme nationalists was sound. Apart
altogether from the fact that the physical force party had never
considered itself bound to trim its policy to suit the constitutionalists, O'Leary, probably better than any other advocate of physical
force just then, appreciated the need for restraint. It is safe to
assume that, largely through his friendship with Gavan Duffy,
O'Leary, in the three-year period ending in December 1886, was
fully aware of the various private meetings and secret negotiations
between British and Irish politicians concerned in the campaign for
Home Rule. Duffy, now retired from the premiership of the
Australian state of Victoria and having achieved the unique (but
to O'Leary, dubious) distinction for a '48 leader of a knighthood
from Queen Victoria, had settled in the French Mediterranean
resort of Nice, whence he followed Irish politics and corresponded
with, amongst others, O'Leary.

In 1883 Duffy resumed an acquaintance with the Conservative
politician Lord Carnarvon, whom he had first met in Australia in
1874; in the winter of 1884 both had discussed the prospects for

a settlement of the Irish question, Duffy arguing that what had been achieved in colonies like Victoria could surely be copied nearer home. In February 1885 a leading Conservative journal published an article, written by Duffy in agreement with Carnarvon, urging the Tories to include in their policy the restoration of some form of Irish legislative independence similar to that which had existed in the time of Grattan.

There matters rested, the Conservatives being then out of office. In June 1885, however, Gladstone's administration was overthrown and replaced by a Tory ministry under Lord Salisbury, in which Carnarvon found himself overnight in the unenviable post of Lord Lieutenant of Ireland. Since the new government could not afford to lose the votes of Parnell and his party, it at once became clear that the five-year period of coercion would not be extended; it is even possible that Parnell's siding with the Tories to defeat Gladstone was the result of hints of favourable treatment he had received beforehand from some leading Conservatives. Gradually also, as the new Viceroy's sympathy with at least the principle of Home Rule became widely known, an air of hopeful expectation began to pervade the nationalist camp.

On 6 July Carnarvon met in London Justin McCarthy MP, a leading member of Parnell's party; the same day he came out openly in the House of Lords in favour of Irish self-government. There followed on 1 August a secret meeting between Parnell and Carnarvon; on the same day Duffy met Sir Robert Hamilton, the permanent Under-Secretary at Dublin Castle, another influential convert to Home Rule.[2] Later that month Duffy met the Marquess of Ripon, a prominent Liberal.

Meanwhile Parnell, satisfied that the Tories were angling for his support, sought better conditions from the Liberals. Failing to make any impression on Gladstone, he issued a manifesto in November urging Irish voters in Britain to oppose the Liberals in the forthcoming general election. The Conservatives won the election but promptly announced that coercion was to be renewed in Ireland; within a week Parnell switched to the Liberals and, by late January 1886, Gladstone was back in office again.

The events of the following five months are known to every student of modern Irish history. Gladstone, now unequivocally converted to Home Rule and totally dependent on the Irish members' votes, introduced the first Home Rule Bill despite considerable opposition within his own party. By June this opposition had led to a secession, which ensured the defeat of the Bill on 8 June by thirty votes.

Looking back at the proposed terms of settlement of the Irish question in 1886, particularly in the light of what was achieved thirty-five years later, it is difficult to see what attractions it held for Irish nationalists. The Irish assembly of two orders (each with a veto on the other), the reservation to Westminster of such vital matters as defence, foreign policy, customs and currency—all this was very little to emerge from a movement as powerful as that which Parnell had led for several years. It would in fact have represented somewhat less than the status which the six counties of Northern Ireland have enjoyed since 1921.

Yet the great majority of Irishmen would have been satisfied; the proposed settlement undoubtedly amounted to a repudiation of the centuries-old claim of Britain to decide the destinies of Ireland. Parnell himself expressly accepted the Bill as a final settlement; and the indications are that the influential Irish-Americans would also have approved. Duffy had created the impression early in 1885 that what was sought was a return to Grattan's parliament; and Parnell, in a speech in Cork soon after, had indicated that this would be acceptable to him. Since a parliament on the lines of Grattan's was what O'Leary had said, as far back as 1871, that he looked forward to, it should not occasion surprise to find him, in his Mullinahone speech of August 1885, expressly supporting Parnell.

One way or another it is clear that, from mid-1885, it was widely believed for a year or so in Irish nationalist circles that some acceptable form of self-government was on the way. Gavan Duffy was so convinced that Home Rule was imminent that he strongly urged O'Leary to prepare for a career in parliament by educating himself in economic and financial matters—an idea which would have brought a smile to the lips of many of O'Leary's close acquaintances. O'Leary himself is said to have admitted privately years later that he would have accepted a seat in the Irish Parliament under the Bill of 1886, had it become law; but, since this would almost certainly have involved some form of oath of allegiance, the story is not easy to believe.

How imminent he believed Home Rule to be in 1886 is evident from an article O'Leary contributed in December of that year to a non-political Dublin periodical. Dealing entirely with the question of guarantees for the Protestant non-nationalist minority in an independent Ireland, it is impractical and vague in its approach, tending to suggest that the fears of this minority were unfounded. But the whole tone of the essay clearly postulates a situation in the near future in which such guarantees might be required.[3] That a public figure like O'Leary, whose views might still influence some Irishmen, should suggest that Parnell be permitted without obstruction to work for the attainment of Home Rule should not occasion surprise. Neither, perhaps, is it surprising to find that O'Leary's appeal did not find favour with an orthodox IRB man like P. N. Fitzgerald.

On a smaller scale than Gavan Duffy, O'Leary also engaged in some private lobbying himself on behalf of his country's claim to independence. In the autumn of 1885 there came to Dublin on a private visit James Bryce, then a Liberal MP but now chiefly remembered as the great jurist, Viscount Bryce.[4] Like Carnarvon, Bryce, who was of Belfast Protestant stock, had been feeling his way towards support of Home Rule and had sufficient integrity to espouse such a cause even if it conflicted with his party's policy. Bryce and Carnarvon met and lunched together in Dublin; in February 1886 Bryce suddenly found himself Under-Secretary for Foreign Affairs in the Gladstone ministry pledged to give Ireland self-government.

Exactly when and how O'Leary and Bryce became acquainted is not known; but they were in correspondence early in 1886 and had met in London before April of that year. They became firm friends and remained so for at least ten years, if not considerably longer. It is obvious that Bryce was impressed by O'Leary's intellectual powers and was strongly influenced by his assessment of the Irish situation; but the claim, which Ellen O'Leary proudly made to her friends, that her brother had converted Bryce to Home Rule, seems a little exaggerated.

Bryce, whose introduction a year or two later to Gavan Duffy was almost certainly effected through the good offices of O'Leary, had several meetings with O'Leary in the spring of 1886, both at Bryce's residence at Bryanston Square, London, and (of all places for an IRB leader) in the Foreign Office. Both were agreed on the necessity for Irish nationalists to avoid further violence if Home Rule was to succeed, and Bryce argued with O'Leary that what was being offered by Gladstone to Ireland was 'a species of colonial system', rather than federation with Britain, that aversion of O'Leary from the days of Isaac Butt.

It ought not be inferred from all this that O'Leary had in any way modified his lifelong preference for physical force. Apart from those sponsored by the Young Ireland Society, all the meetings he addressed in the year following his return to Ireland were demonstrations by the physical force party. To his Manchester audience in February 1885 he said pointedly that he could see 'no moral difference between the rescue of an Irish leader in Manchester and that of a Polish or Italian leader in Vienna'. At Mullinahone in the following August he recalled that Kickham's creed had been that of Tone and Davis; in spite of all the events of recent years, continued O'Leary, it was still his too.

Addressing Irish nationalists in Newcastle-on-Tyne in December 1886, he concluded by commenting on the fashion of recent Irish leaders to be constitutional in words, if not always in deeds. For himself, however, he still preferred Davis's view that:

> Nor peace itself is safe but when
> The sword is sheathed by fighting men.

That he still firmly believed in the political separation of Ireland from Britain is abundantly clear from the manuscript of an un-delivered lecture which O'Leary had prepared in the late 1880s under the title 'The Irish Question: Unionist and Home Rule Delusions'. 'The path of safety for England lies in Repeal of the Union, pure and simple; if she stops short, she runs the risk of Irish discontent. . . . Better wait another century for the right sort of Home Rule than take an altogether wrong sort in a much shorter period.'

It was to his political teacher Davis that O'Leary also appealed in another argument he never tired of making around this time. There was, he believed, an urgent need for a return to decency in the conduct of Irish nationalist affairs. Expediency had, he regretted, taken over as the principal criterion of nationalist policy, with an inevitable lowering of standards of public conduct. To O'Leary the end never justified the means, even when the end was the attain-ment of his country's right to nationhood.

In particular, the violence to man and beast, the boycotting, the withholding of rents and all the other features of the land agitation he regarded as indefensible breaches of the moral code which he believed Irish nationalists should observe. The policies and actions of the Land League and its powerful successor the Irish National League, to which O'Leary remained unalterably opposed, had (he claimed in the unpublished lecture already mentioned) been respons-ible for that spirit of envy, hatred and malice which pervaded Ireland in the late 1880s.

England might break promises, he told his audience in Limerick on St. Patrick's Day 1885; but that did not justify Irishmen meet-ing fraud with fraud and cruelty with cruelty. He and those he represented still belonged to the school of Davis, which associated patriotism with morality. Another leg of the same argument, which O'Leary pleaded repeatedly in the 1880s, was the right to differ. Tolerance as a virtue in public life, he found, had disappeared while he had been in exile.

Here again he appealed to the Young Ireland movement for support, probably realising that tolerance of another's point of view had not been a notable feature of the IRB leadership in the '60s. In Davis's day, O'Leary recalled, a man was not required to be right, merely upright. Nowadays, however, he found that one was expected to agree with the ruling party in every detail, a state of affairs which stifled discussion of policy and to which he would never agree. Though Parnell, O'Leary remarked in his Mullinahone

address of August 1885, might be 'the uncrowned King of Ireland,
he was not the infallible Pope of Rome'.

2

UPON HIS RETURN TO DUBLIN IN 1885, O'Leary took rooms at
40 Leinster Road, Rathmines. Apart from the more congenial
surroundings, in comparison to what he had been accustomed to
for fourteen years in Paris, the standard of his domestic comforts
rose substantially through the presence of his sister, Ellen. In
March she sold her cottage in Tipperary and early in the summer
joined her brother in Rathmines, bringing with her all his books—
'John's treasures' she called them—which she had stored for twenty
years.

Their joint incomes from the house property in Tipperary permitted the comparative luxury (judged by the austere standards of
the O'Learys) of a maid. But when Ellen failed to solve satisfactorily the mystery of how apparently sealed bottles of wine were
found to contain pure water when opened, she dispensed with the
young lady's services and settled down cheerfully to the task of
housekeeping for her bachelor brother.

O'Leary himself no less enthusiastically began at once to participate in a variety of activities, chiefly of a literary character. From
the start he took an active interest in all the proceedings and projects of the parent Young Ireland Society, presiding at committee
meetings, attending its public lectures and speaking at its regular
debates. In June 1885, when he presented the society's prizes in a
competition for historical essays by Dublin schoolboys, the winners
included a 14-year-old youth with whom, fifteen years later, O'Leary
was to be associated in the last Irish separatist movement of his
lifetime. The boy's name was Arthur Griffith.

That the presidency of the Young Ireland Society was not without its risks was proved by the case of Charles McCarthy Teeling,
one of its vice-presidents. Teeling, a bombastic nationalist who had
fought for the Pope and since then had specialised in attending
physical force demonstrations on a white horse and making warlike utterances when it was safe to do so, refused one night to
accept a decision of O'Leary, ruling out of order a vote of censure

by Teeling on O'Leary himself for criticising the dynamiters. Teeling then tried to hurl his chair at O'Leary but was seized and ejected.

Thereupon the committee decided on Teeling's expulsion, and Teeling determined to prevent such a decision from being put into effect. On the night of the vital vote Teeling's supporters gathered in noisy force outside the society's rooms in York Street. But they failed to force an entry.

His evenings O'Leary spent chiefly in a first-floor room at the corner of College Green and Grafton Street. Here, shortly after O'Leary's return to Ireland, Charles Hubert Oldham, a Trinity College graduate and a Protestant with nationalist leanings who had established a Protestant Home Rule Association, had founded the Contemporary Club. Within a short time this room was resorted to by a remarkable assortment of intellectuals—painters, writers, poets, politicians, lawyers, doctors and professors.

Here, in an atmosphere of frank informality, mixed Parnellite and Unionist, Land Leaguer and IRB man, Christian and agnostic. Here, as a famous member later put it, political opponents interrupted and insulted each other 'without the formal and traditional restraint of public speech'. Literature and the arts were also discussed, the contents of the highbrow journals analysed, and members' paintings and poems examined and freely criticised.

At first membership of this club was confined to fifty, but this was later increased to seventy-five. Amongst the original members were Dr. Sigerson, Douglas Hyde, William Stockley (later a professor in University College, Cork, and a member of Dáil Éireann), John F. Taylor (a well-known barrister and Dublin correspondent of the *Manchester Guardian*), O'Leary and Davitt. The two last named were introduced by James Walker, a Dublin printer who was a Presbyterian and a Parnellite. Visitors were frequently introduced; amongst the earliest was the famous artist, poet and socialist, William Morris.

'It is one amongst the many misfortunes of Ireland that she has never yet produced a great poet,' remarked O'Leary in his lecture in Cork in February 1886. 'Let us trust that God has in store for us that great gift.' Already, without knowing it, he himself was playing an important part in the conferring of that gift. For, through a famous friendship which probably began in the middle of 1885, O'Leary was to become a major influence in the development of a young Dublin man, who in time would become the greatest poet writing in English. With this poet's name O'Leary's was destined to become linked forever in the story of Ireland's literary renaissance.

Amongst those who came regularly to the Contemporary Club was a 46-year-old eccentric painter, John Butler Yeats. He and

O'Leary at once became firm friends. His father had been a student in Trinity College with Isaac Butt, who defended O'Leary in 1865; and J. B. Yeats himself had as a young (but briefless) barrister devilled with Butt.

Yeats had more recently studied at the Academy School in London under Poynter (later Sir Edward Poynter, and president of the Royal Academy), whom O'Leary had known thirty years earlier. Yeats was also a keen student of English literature, and just then proud of the fact that his son Willie looked like making a name for himself in the literary world.

Early in 1885 a new literary magazine entitled the *Dublin University Review* had appeared in Dublin. Its editor was T. W. Rolleston, the 29-year-old son of a QC who became County Court judge for Tipperary, and grandson of Baron Richards, a judge who had tried several of the '48 leaders. Rolleston, a brilliant graduate of Trinity College with literary leanings, was to become within a few months one of O'Leary's most devoted disciples and to be associated with him in his later literary projects.

It was in this new journal that the first of Willie Yeats's published poems had appeared in 1885; and it was in the Contemporary Club that some more of his earliest poems were read aloud to a critical audience about the same time and voted on by the members. Then only twenty years of age, Yeats was a tall, dreamy, sallow-complexioned short-bearded youth, unsure of himself in public. He had gone to the Club, presumably at his father's suggestion, in order to try to overcome his shyness and to acquire some self-confidence. His visit was to have far-reaching results.

From the start Yeats was strongly attracted to O'Leary, whose personality fascinated him. The very appearance of this tall, thin, ascetic-looking man with the flowing beard was calculated to make a deep impact on the mind of an impressionable youth. When he heard about O'Leary's romantic career—his participation as a boy of eighteen in the Young Ireland movement, his editorship of the organ of a secret revolutionary society, but most of all his imprisonment and long years of exile—Yeats listened eagerly to his views on literature. And, although their literary tastes thus far had little in common, it helped when Yeats found that O'Leary thought highly of his writings so far. 'Young Yeats is the only person in this room who will ever be reckoned a genius,' O'Leary prophesied in the Club.

Yeats was also agreeably surprised to discover that O'Leary resided in the same part of the city as he. From Leinster Road to 10 Ashfield Terrace, Terenure, was less than ten minutes' walk. One evening Yeats, on some pretext or other, called to O'Leary's; but O'Leary was out. Ellen persuaded the shy visitor to await her brother's return and, in order to make him feel at home, dealt him a hand of cards in a game being fiercely contested by a few other women for the sum of sixpence. Yeats naturally lost, but was consoled by a glass of strong sherry, the effect of which took several days to wear off.

A card-party was not, however, the usual form of entertainment in O'Leary's. This was the era of the 'At Home', and a literary circle of men and women met once a week in Miss O'Leary's parlour. Here gathered the poetess, Katharine Tynan, daughter of a Clondalkin 'strong' farmer, the writer Rosa Mulholland, later to marry Sir John Gilbert, the Sigerson girls and Rose Kavanagh, a gifted young writer from Tyrone whose premature death in 1891 led to the almost total neglect of her work.

To his house, too, came John O'Leary's own literary associates. These included Douglas Hyde, Rolleston, Richard Ashe King, John F. Taylor, Dr. Sigerson, George Russell (later AE), Stephen Gwynn and William Stockley—all men destined to play leading roles in the revival of Anglo-Irish literature round the turn of the century. Here in this Rathmines drawingroom was hatched many a literary plot as O'Leary, unable for the moment to achieve anything effective as a revolutionary, instead played the role of literary patron and sponsor. Here he urged ceaselessly his talented disciples to try their hands at writing prose and poetry with a national content, without which he believed no political revolution in Ireland would bring lasting results.

To Willie Yeats this was to be O'Leary's main advice. But first he had to make the promising young poet aware of Ireland's literature. This O'Leary did chiefly by giving him the run of his magnificent collection of Irish books—'the best I know' Yeats called it in 1889. From this library he borrowed freely for several years, meeting for the first time Davis, Mangan, Carleton, Banim, Ferguson, Kickham and Mitchel. From their works he discovered for the first time that such a thing as Irish literature existed, and that all the themes he had been seeking elsewhere had been treated of by his own country-men, Catholic and Protestant, nationalist and loyalist.

From O'Leary and his books it was that Yeats first became aware also of the great store of Irish legend and fairy lore and semi-historical stories, then becoming available in translations and editions through men such as Ferguson, Hyde and Standish O'Grady —material which Yeats was to work into his poetry for the greater part of his literary career. 'From that great candle of the past we must all light our little tapers,' he wrote around this time. Through O'Leary it was also that he came into touch with the ordinary Irish nationalist (whether member of the IRB or merely adherent of the constitutional movement) by frequent attendance at the debates of the Young Ireland societies.

The invigorating effect on the young poet of the new friends gained through his association with the O'Learys and their acquaintances Yeats himself has described. He who had made few lasting friendships, even among those of his own class and religion, now found himself accepted in Catholic and nationalist homes. He who had felt shy in the company of women experienced an equality of sex which was taken for granted by the O'Learys and their guests. He whose father had so often impressed on him that politics was a low form of human activity became caught up in the endless arguments about Irish affairs—about the very possibility that Ireland might sustain her claim to separation from England—which in O'Leary's circle both preceded and followed discussions on literature.

It was in O'Leary's house in Rathmines that Yeats first became friendly with a vivacious red-haired girl, whom he first met briefly in his father's studio in York Street and who was to be his literary confidante for many years. Katharine Tynan, who by 1885 had already had a book of poetry published, remained so late on several occasions with Ellen O'Leary that, rather than face the lonely journey out to her father's house near the village of Clondalkin, she stayed the night in O'Leary's. This generosity was more than amply repaid by Andrew Tynan, who every week-end kept open house both for his daughter's literary friends and for his own political associates.

O'Leary was always the guest of honour at the Sunday 'At Home' in Whitehall, Clondalkin. The other guests usually took the Blessington tram from Terenure to Tallaght, or cycled; O'Leary generally walked the full six miles from Rathmines. In his pocket he carried a bottle from which he occasionally refreshed himself; he would have the Tynans believe it contained merely tea.

In the spacious dining-room of this thatched farmhouse, once the home of Emmet's beloved Sara Curran, dinner was eaten in the late afternoon after all save Yeats had argued about the progress of Parnell and his movement. Outside in the flower garden Willie Yeats, in an idyllic setting which he himself later described, declaimed poetry or hastily penned articles for John Boyle O'Reilly's *Pilot* of Boston, while sitting under the shade of an apple tree and using a sundial as his writing table.

All the time, while immersing himself in Irish literature, Yeats was also learning from his countless conversations with O'Leary on the same subject. O'Leary held first that neither nationality nor literature could live without the other. To him a political revolution could not succeed unless it was backed by a cultural revival;

he believed that, in point of time, a literary renaissance in Ireland should precede the attainment of nationhood. But he was convinced that the Irish nation was a separate cultural unit, and on this premiss he based his lifelong belief in the necessity for the political separation of Ireland from England.

A corollary to this principal article of O'Leary's creed was that Irish literature should be Irish in content. Irish writers who went abroad for their themes—and this was almost an accepted practice for most of the nineteenth century—he put on the same level as the West Briton in politics. For example, even Thomas Moore, whom O'Leary never tired of criticising for what he regarded as the spurious patriotism in his work, would rate higher in O'Leary's estimation than a good poet like 'young Willie Yeats' who, before he met O'Leary, had gone to Greek and Persian and Indian mythology for his themes.

What O'Leary wanted Irish writers to write about was not merely contemporary Irish life. As a student of Irish history and a revolutionary who always dreamed of—and for long periods plotted for—the day when the Irish nation would be restored, he wished to see Irish writers making use of the vast fund of Irish legend and folklore of which he himself was only partly aware. He was a keen supporter of men like Hyde who, through patient research, collection, translation and editing were helping to unlock this treasury of native raw material for Irish literature. So strongly did he feel about this that he regarded a writer like Sir Samuel Ferguson, a Unionist to the core, as a better Irishman than himself because of Ferguson's work in this hitherto largely neglected field.

Nor would O'Leary be satisfied to find Irish writers merely imitating the purely patriotic writing of men like Davis or Kickham. He admitted frankly that much of the Young Ireland literature was of a poor quality; this he attributed to the fact that too many of Ireland's writers and poets had been content merely to complain of Ireland's misfortunes. He deplored the fashion whereby the standard of Irish prose and poetry was judged solely by reference to its political content. He held strongly that Irish writing should be purged of politics, and believed that Irish literature stood to gain if this should occur.

Thus did Willie Yeats spend his vital formative years, his period of apprenticeship for the creative work on which he was to be engaged for the rest of his life. During these last few years of the 1880s he was making the friends, reading the books and forming the ideas which were to affect his whole life. And in the making of these friendships, in the selection of these books and in the formation and development of these ideas, the views of John O'Leary predominated. 'From these (i.e. Young Ireland Society) debates, from O'Leary's conversation, and from the Irish books he lent or gave me has come all I have set my hand to since,' acknowledged Yeats years later.

To judge of the impact of O'Leary's ideas on Yeats one has only to study some of his literary output at this period. In the *Dublin University Review* for 1885 and 1886 a number of poems by Yeats appeared. All were either love poems or dealt with foreign themes; not one was Irish in content. Then in the November 1886 issue came a long prose article entitled 'The Poetry of Sir Samuel Ferguson', in which the conversion to Irish topics is immediately obvious.

Ferguson is called 'the greatest poet Ireland has produced, because the most central and most Celtic'. Of the need for an Irish literature Yeats says that 'Irish singers who are genuinely Irish in thought, subject and style must . . . nourish the forces that make for the political liberties of Ireland'. On the source of this literature he commented: 'Of all the many things the past bequeaths to the future, the greatest are great legends . . . I hold it the duty of every Irish reader . . . to study those of his country till they are familiar as his own hands, for in them is the Celtic heart.'

Around the middle of 1888 Yeats began to contribute articles to the *Pilot* of Boston, and for over four years both prose and poetry by him appeared intermittently in this and the *Providence Journal*, another American publication. In the case of the articles it is evident that not a lot of care or thought went into their composition; but for that very reason they reflect faithfully the ideas then forming in Yeats's mind. O'Leary is always in the background, and at times the phraseology strikes one as being an actual quotation from him.

Of an Irish poetess who had written on German topics Yeats commented in August 1889: '. . . she should go over to Ireland and see what she can find there to write about. After all, Ireland is the true subject for the Irish.' In the same publication on 17 May 1890 he complained: 'We peer over the wall at our neighbours instead of making our own garden green and beautiful.' Reviewing some poems of William Allingham a little later, Yeats claimed that this poet's 'want of sympathy with the national life and history has limited his vision, has driven away from his poetry much beauty and power—has thinned his blood'. In the same paper, later still, comes this declaration: 'You can no more have the greater poetry without a nation than religion without symbols. One can only reach out to the universe with a gloved hand—that glove is one's nation, the only thing one knows even a little of.'

John O'Leary's intervention at a critical stage, his conversations between 1885 and 1888 and his continuing influence over a period of fifteen years changed the whole course of Yeats's career as a poet, writer and playwright. It was O'Leary who fired Yeats with the ambition to become a national poet, and probably O'Leary also who put into Yeats's head the idea of an Irish national theatre. Through Yeats alone O'Leary is entitled to a prominent place amongst the sponsors of Ireland's literary renaissance down to the foundation in 1904 of the Abbey Theatre. That Yeats, within a couple of years of meeting O'Leary, had already considered the possibility of establishing such a theatre is evident from his contributions to the *Pilot* and the *Providence Journal*.

Through his association with O'Leary, Yeats became almost overnight a nationalist and, despite considerable misgivings about the trend of Irish nationalism in a later period, a nationalist he was to remain to the end of his life. So deep an impression did O'Leary's political philosophy make on him that he soon even came to regard himself as a member of the IRB—for no student of that movement can accept the story that O'Leary swore either him or Rolleston into the IRB.

When in his old age he recalled in poetry the heroes of his youth, 'O'Leary's noble head' came first in his list of memories. And, within a few weeks before his death in 1939, he proudly described himself as 'a nationalist of the school of John O'Leary'. Moreover, Yeats's belief in later life in the rule of the educated classes, his preference for an oligarchy of the best personalities, and his dream of Ireland as a sort of replica of Grattan's era, all have an unmistakable ring of O'Leary about them.

Having discovered such a talented and promising disciple, O'Leary was not content merely to preach to him and lend him books. In the course of the eight or ten years following their first meeting in 1885, and especially after Yeats had moved to London in 1887, he helped the poet in countless practical ways, big and small. O'Leary it was who secured him introductions to the *Pilot* newspaper of Boston in 1887 and to the *Providence Journal* in 1888, for one or other of which Yeats wrote until the end of 1892. O'Leary it was who, almost single-handed, organised the collection of the funds needed to secure the publication in 1888 of Yeats's first book of poetry, *The Wanderings of Oisin,* which contains 'The Stolen Child', regarded as one of his best poems, as well as 'The Ballad of Moll Magee' and 'An Old Song Re-Sung', better known by its opening phrase 'Down by the salley gardens'.

That a substantial proportion of the poems in this book had been composed before Yeats had come to realise that Ireland was to be his main source of inspiration mattered little to O'Leary. Yeats, he felt, was a great Irish poet in the making, and, now busy and short of money in London, could not ensure the publication of his poems unless he could guarantee a given number of purchasers beforehand.

O'Leary got to work in Dublin and, for many months, made the collection of subscriptions his main task. Bundles of the necessary forms he carried with him everywhere; nowhere—in the Contemporary Club, in the houses of his hosts, in the Young Ireland rooms, even in the drawing-rooms of Tipperary town—did he consider it inappropriate to produce an order form for Yeats's book and secure a signature on it.

Nor was this by any means the end of O'Leary's assistance and influence after the Yeats family had resumed residence in London in 1887. In 1888 appeared Yeats's *Fairy and Folk Tales of the Irish Peasantry*, in 1889 his selection of *Stories from Carleton*, in 1890 his edition of *Representative Irish Tales* and in 1892 his *Irish Fairy Tales*. In the preparation of all four books O'Leary had a hand—posting across from his own library, or purchasing specially for Yeats, books unobtainable in London, as well as advising, encouraging and criticising. Whenever Willie Yeats's interest in literature showed signs of flagging, O'Leary it was who, with a stream of postcards, urged him not to desert his chosen subject.

When Yeats seemed in danger of devoting his whole time to the study of the occult, O'Leary remonstrated with him and questioned first the bona fides of the eccentric persons engaged in this pursuit, and then doubted outright if such study would in any way benefit Willie's literary career. When Yeats ran short of money O'Leary made frequent loans, and this at a time when his own sources of income were beginning to run down. And when life for Willie had become almost unbearably dull in London, O'Leary it was who, through a chance introduction, caused the beautiful Miss Gonne to alight from a hansom outside the Yeats residence on a spring day in 1889, and thus started one of the notable love affairs in modern English literature.

Yeats for his part eagerly kept in touch with O'Leary after his return to London in 1887. Indeed, he appears at this period to have been on terms of more intimate friendship with O'Leary than with his own father, his earlier confidant with whom he is known to have by now disagreed on important topics. From London Willie responded regularly to O'Leary's flow of letters and cards with the latest gossip of the English literary scene, often enclosing book catalogues, always of interest to O'Leary. Lively arguments were conducted by post on such matters as the advisability of paying Miss Gonne's hansom fares, Yeats's style, even his grammar and spelling. O'Leary, despite his strong disapproval of the whole movement, appears to have been inordinately curious about the activities of Madame Blavatsky and her disciples in occultism.

It would be wrong, however, to think that all O'Leary's literary activities in the decade or so following his return to Ireland centred round Willie Yeats. On the contrary, had he never met Yeats at all O'Leary would be entitled to a place in any history of the early years of the literary revival in Ireland. Yeats was only one of many, if undoubtedly the most promising, of his disciples to whom O'Leary during the late 1880s and early 1890s expounded his views on a national literature and his hopes of a literary, as distinct from a political, nationalism in Ireland.

In social clubs, in sedate parlours, at meetings of revolutionaries and in public addresses, in private correspondence and in letters to daily and periodic publications—everywhere he went, and whenever an opportunity arose, O'Leary preached his gospel of a cultural Home Rule which politicians, constitutional, agrarian and physical force men alike, had hitherto almost totally neglected. That Willie Yeats was by no means his only notable convert is evident from the case of Katharine Tynan, whose second book of poetry, *Shamrocks*, published in 1887 after she had joined the O'Leary circle, is much more Celtic in content and theme than her *Louis de la Valliere* in 1885.

Nor was O'Leary content merely to preach to others without making any effort himself to start a literary revival. He participated actively in several of the more prominent movements and productions of writing around this period. In 1888 there appeared a little volume entitled *Poems and Ballads of Young Ireland*, edited in all probability by Rolleston, though Yeats's name has also been mentioned in this connection. The title of this anthology is significant, because none of the authors had any connection with Davis's movement. The book was in fact the work of the literary clique centred round O'Leary, to whom it was dedicated, and who is known to have played a major part in its production.

This book, which has been called 'the first offering of the Revival', marked the break with the hitherto fashionable form of patriotic poetry. Hardly a line in its thirty-three poems could give offence to the most sincere loyalist; for political matter there were substituted mainly legends and folk and fairy tales. In addition, the simple language of most of the poems has a surprisingly modern ring to twentieth-century ears.

Taken as a whole the *Poems and Ballads of Young Ireland* contains poetry of a high standard which augured favourably for future writing from the poets there represented. Yeats, Hyde (whose poetry in English is now sadly forgotten), Sigerson, Rolleston and Count Plunkett are included, as are Rose Kavanagh, Katharine Tynan and Ellen O'Leary. The first verse of Rolleston's dedicatory poem to John O'Leary could aptly have been chosen as his motto:

> Because you suffered for the cause;
> Because you strove with voice and pen
> To serve the Law above the laws
> That purifies the hearts of men;

A year after the appearance of this book of poetry came another with which O'Leary was also closely associated. In 1888 there had been founded in Dublin the Pan-Celtic, a literary group, non-political and non-sectarian in outlook, confined to those who either had already made an original contribution to Irish literature or had a knowledge of the Irish language. The two O'Learys joined this body and Ellen was one of the contributors to its *Lays and Lyrics of the Pan-Celtic Society,* which appeared in 1889.

The editor of this anthology cast his net wider than Rolleston had done in the case of the earlier book, some of the fifty-two lays and lyrics coming from publications ranging from the Boston *Pilot* to the *Lyceum.* The result naturally is a lower standard generally, even in the case of poets who had also contributed to Rolleston's collection. Hyde and the Misses O'Leary, Kavanagh, Tynan and Sigerson are to be found in this book; so also are poets of a lower rank like A. P. Graves and the ballad writer P. J. McCall.

Another now forgotten literary project with which O'Leary was connected in the late 1880s concerned the Gaelic Athletic Association. This organisation, which has been the leading amateur sports body in these islands for threequarters of a century, was founded in Thurles on 1 November 1884. In its origins the GAA formed an essential part of that Irish cultural revival of which O'Leary had been a leading advocate, and of which the literary renaissance and the later movement of Hyde to foster the Irish language attracted more public attention than did the campaign to preserve native games.

To a movement which aimed at restoring Irish sporting pastimes and at giving Irishmen control of their own athletic pursuits, to the express exclusion of English games and West British-controlled sports organisations, O'Leary naturally gave his wholehearted approval. On Easter Sunday 1886 he was present in Thurles at one of the first big public demonstrations of the GAA.[5] Along with Archbishop Croke of Cashel, Parnell, Davitt and William O'Brien MP, O'Leary proudly consented in 1886 to become one of the earliest patrons of the GAA; from then to his death he remained a supporter of the principles of this body.

As was natural for such a national organisation, the GAA, once it had got on its feet, decided to publish an official organ. Thus there appeared in the spring of 1887 *The Gael,* a weekly journal priced at one penny, which at first was merely the organ of the

Executive Council but soon became the official organ of the whole GAA. Since its editor was Patrick T. Hoctor, an IRB man and well-known as a journalist and leading official in the GAA, it is not surprising that the literary page of this paper came from the start under the control of John O'Leary.

Here were published, amongst other items, poems of O'Leary's own circle—some by Rolleston, Hyde, Katharine Tynan and Ellen O'Leary—as well as his own public lectures. Unfortunately *The Gael* suspended publication early in 1888, either through lack of funds or because of internal differences in the GAA in 1887, and not a single entire copy of any issue is known to have survived. All that are available now are a few cuttings of editorials, some interesting poetic and prose contributions of these pioneers of our literary revival being lost to students of the period.

Any new Irish literary project of this period was certain to number John O'Leary amongst its enthusiastic supporters. In London there had flourished as early as 1883 the Southwark Irish Literary Club, which for almost a decade did most useful work in that city and proved to be the forerunner of two similar bodies, which between them gave a special impetus to the progress of the literary revival in the mid-1890s. The Southwark Club, under the control of an energetic committee, became a valuable centre of Irish culture at which frequent lectures of a high standard were given; O'Leary became a regular visitor to the club premises and was one of its many distinguished lecturers.

In 1891 the Southwark Club, largely at the instigation of Yeats, was transformed into the Irish Literary Society of London, with Gavan Duffy as president and a new programme formulated, aimed at making it a more efficient instrument in the furtherance of Irish writing. The following year the same impulse produced in Dublin the National Literary Society of Ireland, which was planned at a meeting held in O'Leary's home early in the summer of 1892.[6]

This Society was placed under the presidency of O'Leary who, with Yeats, Maud Gonne, Dr. Sigerson and Fr. Thomas Finlay SJ, was one of the speakers at the formal inaugural meeting in the Rotunda, Dublin in June 1892. With the formation of these two allied societies the Irish literary revival had definitely taken shape. It was under the auspices of the National Literary Society that there was founded in 1899 the Irish Literary Theatre, which through its successor in 1902, the Irish National Theatre Society, led to the foundation in 1904 of the Abbey Theatre.

Within a few months after the establishment in 1892 of the National Literary Society still another literary group had sprung up in Dublin, the Celtic Literary Society, having as its main aims the study of Irish literature, the spreading of a knowledge of the

Irish language and the popularisation of Irish music. This body
published its own manuscript journal, conducted Irish classes, built
up a library and published poems by its members in the Dublin
journals. Although actively supported by a few prominent figures
like O'Leary and Count Plunkett, its two leading members from
the start were two young Dublin men in their early twenties, William
Rooney and Arthur Griffith, both of whom had also been the prime
movers in an even earlier society, the Leinster Literary Society.

Long before his association with these literary societies of the
'90s, however, O'Leary suffered two shattering blows in his private
life; and his major interest had once more switched from literature
to Irish national affairs.

3

A QUARTER-OF-A-CENTURY LATER, when writing her memoirs,
Katharine Tynan nostalgically recalled John O'Leary's life shortly
after his return to Ireland. 'They were the few golden, tranquil
years, between wilderness and wilderness, in which the brother and
sister were together.' Superficially these would appear to have been
pleasant years, for after the long, lonely and frustrating period in
Paris O'Leary was home again, eagerly engaged in literary pursuits,
mixing in the social life of nationalist Dublin, tactfully encouraging
the latent revolutionary movement, and paying frequent calls to
Paris and London.

As the 1880s came to a close, however, O'Leary's old feelings of
disappointment must have returned. The further one moved from
the expectant days of 1886 the more the hopes of achieving Irish
self-government must have receded in the mind of such a sanguine
man. Worse still, with the opening of the Plan of Campaign late
in 1886 came the revival of that agrarian agitation to which O'Leary
was so bitterly opposed, since it necessitated the campaign for
political freedom receding into the background.

Moreover, O'Leary's domestic happiness was threatened from
two directions in the period between 1885 and 1890. For some
time before his return to Ireland his sister Ellen had been in in-
different health. Probably unknown to her brother, she had consulted a Dublin specialist, who had diagnosed cancer of the breast

and abdomen. Although she had undergone an operation, it had not been wholly successful.

From time to time between 1885 and 1887 Ellen suffered painful relapses. As the years progressed references to her ill-health became more frequent in the letters of O'Leary's acquaintances. His lifelong friend, Denis Dowling Mulcahy, now a successful doctor in New Jersey, recorded his alarm at her decline when he visited Ireland around this time. Although most of his intimate friends seem to have realised how near the end was, John O'Leary does not appear to have been fully aware that his sister was sinking fast.

Ellen herself, a deeply religious woman, was concerned only for her brother's future. She regretted that he had never married and would soon be left alone in the world. 'We are a most unmarrying family,' she wrote once to Luby's wife: 'I sometimes wish John were married lest I should be taken from him.' Most of all she was saddened by his failure to become reconciled with the Church.

In the summer of 1889 O'Leary left Dublin for a prolonged visit to Paris, where his old friend of the '50s and '70s, J. P. Leonard, now lay dying. After his departure Ellen made what was to prove a final round of calls on relatives. In Cork city she stayed with her nephew John King, now in business as a grocer at 9 Castle Street. There late in the autumn her condition suddenly deteriorated, and on 15 October the end came painlessly.

Aged 57, Ellen O'Leary had led a full life. Her loyalty to the Church had not prevented her being equally devoted to the movement of which her brother was a leader. Especially during the crisis of 1865 she had proved her worth, working closely with Edward Duffy, organising the relief campaign for prisoners' dependents and heavily mortgaging her house property to provide funds for the IRB.

From an early age she had shown promise as a poet, and over a period of almost forty years had contributed to the *Nation*, the *Irish People*, the *Irish Monthly* and other national journals. Much of her work was religious in content, but she also wrote some stirring patriotic poems. At her death a selection of her poems was in course of preparation for publication; on its appearance in 1890 it attracted wide publicity and confirmed her reputation as both the poetess of the Fenian movement and one of the more gifted of the early verse writers of the literary revival.

Because she had been a notable figure in her own right, the death of Ellen O'Leary was widely regretted in literary Dublin, the more so as it was unexpected save by intimate friends. Nobody was more shocked by the event than her brother, then in Paris. Although he hurried back at once through London, he was unable to arrive in time for the funeral, which took place to the family burial-ground in the old cemetery behind their childhood home in Tipperary.

To close friends O'Leary confided his sense of loss. To Willie Yeats he wrote: '. . . a horrible calamity has come and the light of my life has gone out.' To one of the Tulloch family in Tipperary he admitted: 'I thought I was much of a stoic, but I feel myself weak as a child under this blow. . . . Her death has, as it were, cut me adrift from my past.'

It is easy to imagine the grief which his sister's death must have caused to O'Leary. From the death of his mother when he was still a child to the day he left home for Carlow College, Ellen had helped their aunt to rear John and Arthur. Later during John's student days she had shared lodgings with her two brothers in London and Dublin.

During John's trial she sat by his side in Green Street court-house; for twenty years she had awaited his return to Ireland, visiting him regularly both in jail and in Paris. For five short years she had provided him with the only home life he had known for over forty years. She had enthusiastically shared all his literary projects and had entertained his associates.

Now she was dead, her literary career cut short just as her book of poems was about to be published. Her death left John the last survivor of their father's second family. Little wonder that seven years later Ellen's death was referred to by John in language so touching as almost to suggest it had occurred only recently.

So stunned was O'Leary by Ellen's death, and so slow was he to recover from the shock, that his friends became concerned and got together to devise ways to assist him in resuming a normal life. C. H. Oldham, Maud Gonne and Dr. Sigerson took charge of the arrangements for Ellen's book, which appeared within a year of her death and was widely acclaimed, a short selection of Arthur's poems being included in the volume.

O'Leary's associates also resumed earlier unsuccessful efforts to persuade him to write his political memoirs. Eventually he agreed to undertake this task, and former colleagues of the early days of the IRB were consulted on both sides of the Atlantic and asked to furnish material for a chronicle of events of the 1850s and 1860s. As a result of pressure by John Devoy detailed statements were soon on their way across the Atlantic from Luby, John Savage and Joseph Denieffe, while from France came material from Gavan Duffy on the events of 1848 and 1849.

Well aware of O'Leary's occasional lethargy, his Dublin friends decided to put the matter on a formal basis which would act as a stimulant to him. A committee was established which issued a circular inviting subscriptions to the forthcoming book, the treasurers being Alfred Webb and Richard Barry O'Brien MP, and its secretary George Coffey, later an official of the National Museum. Others associated with the appeal were Stephen Gwynn, Sir Charles Russell QC, Joseph Cowen MP, Michael Davitt and William O'Brien.

It is clear, however, that this device was principally an attempt by his friends to help O'Leary financially. Shortly after Ellen's death, he was confronted with a crisis in his financial affairs which he was never wholly to surmount, and which was to involve him in an unfortunate political controversy.

The shortage of money which had begun in his last few years in Paris worsened shortly after his return to Ireland, when his Tipperary tenants, probably taking advantage of the feeling against landlords, became erratic in their payments. O'Leary, who all his life had been generous to friends in need, now found it necessary to secure the repayment of loans he had made to close friends. To this shortage of money may be traceable the various changes of residence O'Leary made in the late 1880s; between 1885 and 1889 he and his sister moved at least four times—from 40 Leinster Road to 134 Rathgar Road in 1886, from there to 30 Grosvenor Road in 1887, and across to a now unknown address in Drumcondra in 1889.

As early as August 1886 Harry Meltzer sent him the first of two sums of money from Paris, and in the following three years Mulcahy made three repayments (one of 100 dollars) of a substantial loan made by O'Leary as far back as 1871. Late in 1888 negotiations for O'Leary to write for the *Newcastle Chronicle*, whose editor, Joseph Cowen MP, was a friend of his and a sympathiser with Home Rule, broke down. In December of that year O'Leary obtained from Dr. Mark Ryan of London a loan of £300, giving him as security a life-insurance policy which had passed to him from his father.[7] Perhaps he thought matters would sooner or later improve; he was in for a shock.

Since his youthful association with Fintan Lalor's movement, but more particularly from the days of the New Departure, O'Leary had been implacably opposed to all forms of land agitation by Irish nationalists. The Tenant League campaign of the 1850s cannot have affected his personal position at all, and the early stages of the Land War he was obliged to witness from the isolation of Paris. When, however, the agitation flared up again in the late 1880s his own position as a small property-owner brought him into head-on collision with its leaders.

The story of the Plan of Campaign is well known to students of the period. The essence of the scheme was a concerted refusal by tenants to pay more than what they (or their leaders) considered a

fair rent, and the paying into a special fund of such rent when
refused by the landlord, the reserve thus created to be used to
relieve any tenants evicted. To O'Leary this idea was wholly indefensible morally; it also seriously damaged a pet plan of his to
convert to nationalism the moneyed classes, including the landed
gentry, and thus removing one of the main props of the English
conquest.

That the Plan could ever hit his own pocket O'Leary probably
never foresaw for a moment. When early in 1889 the principal
landowners formed a syndicate at the instigation of Dublin Castle,
William O'Brien and John Dillon accepted the challenge. On the
Ponsonby estate near Youghal a settlement of a dispute had been
virtually reached between the landlord and the tenants' spokesman,
Canon Keller, when, through the intervention of a powerful member
of the syndicate, the talks broke down.

Encouraged by Canon Keller's public statements, O'Brien and
Dillon determined to teach a lesson to the man who had interfered.
He happened to be none other than Arthur H. Smith-Barry MP,
the landlord of by far the greater part of the ground on which
stood the town of Tipperary, out of which he enjoyed an income
of nearly £12,000 a year—and out of the buildings on which ground
O'Leary derived his sole income.

In June 1889 O'Brien visited Tipperary to organise resistance to
Smith-Barry; soon he had won an influential ally in the person of
Archbishop Croke of Cashel. The following week, when a deputation from the tenants demanded of Smith-Barry that he cease assisting Ponsonby he, presumably confident of the strength of the
Castle-backed syndicate, refused. A week later came the day for
the payment of the rents of Tipperary town; all were withheld.

These preliminary skirmishes were followed a month later by a
declaration of war by the townsmen. Under the guidance of
William O'Brien and led by two militant priests, Canon Cahill
and his curate Father David Humphreys, the tenants formally
demanded a twenty-five per cent reduction of their rents from
Smith-Barry and agreed to pay a 'tax' amounting to ten per cent of
the valuation of their holdings to go as relief to the Youghal tenants.

Smith-Barry next took ejectment proceedings in the courts, but
quickly discovered that a tenants' syndicate could match that of
the landlords. Two sales in Thurles of the interests of evicted
Tipperary tenants proved almost total failures, and Tipperary town
became the scene of the most prolonged and most bitter episode
in the whole Land War. Riots followed bomb attacks; squads of
police and detectives were drafted into the town, which attracted
publicity in the press of the world for two years.

The leadership of the priests alienated a small number of the

Protestant tenants, who allied themselves with a minority of others who refused from the start to join in the agitation against Smith-Barry. The climax of the whole struggle came with the erection by the evicted tenants in 1890 of New Tipperary, the nucleus of a second town on the outskirts of the now almost deserted old town. When completed New Tipperary contained two whole new streets of shops and dwelling-houses, with an impressive glass-roofed mart 200 feet long and eighty feet wide, in which it was hoped to revive the long-established prosperity of this market town.

In the midst of the excitement of this modern peasants' revolt, however, the interest of the middle landlord was wholly forgotten. It so happened that one of the most extensive members of this class was John O'Leary who, leaving himself open to obvious accusations from the tenants' side, denounced the whole scheme from the start. Convinced of the moral righteousness of his stand, O'Leary ceaselessly criticised in public and in private what he called 'the patent fiction of New Tipperary'.[8] In letters to the press and from public platforms he repeatedly alleged that the tenants had been coerced by O'Brien and Dillon, for the sake of achieving a victory over landlordism, into deserting their property; and he pointed to the undeniable cases of boycotting of recalcitrant tenants to prove his assertions.

New Tipperary was, he wrote on one occasion, a 'beautiful example of the cut-off-your-nose-to-spite-your-face policy'; in order to make Smith-Barry, who (O'Leary claimed) was worth £40,000 a year, lose £3,000, the National League spent between £25,000 and £40,000, and the town of Tipperary lost business to the tune of about £200,000.[9] And a few months later he said: '. . . there has never been, in the whole history of Irish agitation, anything so reckless, ruthless and utterly ruinous as this Tipperary affair from beginning to end.'[10] His personal interest in the outcome of the controversy O'Leary made no attempt to conceal. Tipperary he regarded as the supreme folly of the Plan of Campaign, out of which in his view no good could possibly emerge, either for the inhabitants of Tipperary or for the cause of Irish nationalism. For once he was wrong.

It was all very well for O'Leary to insist, as had his IRB colleagues at the time of the negotiations on the New Departure, that the land problem was a subsidiary matter, to be settled after and not before the winning of political freedom. New Tipperary did achieve something, both for tenants and Irish nationalism. If the final settlement appeared unfavourable, in the long run rents came down and the agitation ensured further ameliorative legislative measures.[11] Moreover, to this success may be ascribed at least in part the fine record of this area in the subsequent political struggle.

To his fellow-townsmen of 1889-91, however, O'Leary's pleas counted for little. In the circumstances it could not have been otherwise. Things might, perhaps, have been different had O'Leary been a kindly landlord; but he was not. Down the years not only he, but also other members of his family (including Ellen), had acquired a reputation for requiring strict adherence to the letter of their agreements by their tenants. By older folk in the town, dead within the past decade, John O'Leary was remembered principally, not as an Irish patriot, but as a 'hard landlord'.

When, some years before the New Tipperary agitation, the Irish National League (the successor of the Land League) had set up branches called house leagues in various towns, one of the earliest and most formidable opponents of the Tipperary House League was the O'Leary family. For most of 1886, to give only one example, this body was concerned solely in combating hardships alleged to have been incurred by some of its members who held as under-tenants from O'Leary or his sister.

In December of that year a resolution was passed at the con-clusion of the dispute condemning the treatment of their tenants by the O'Leary family. The tactful approach of the League to the O'Learys contrasts unfavourably with the brusque and provocative attitudes of the Misses Ellen O'Leary and her niece Eliza King, who managed her uncle's property affairs. As for O'Leary himself, he did not even bother to reply to courteous communications from the League.

Long before the New Tipperary episode had finally concluded in the autumn of 1891, O'Leary had lost by far the greater part of his only source of income. Smith-Barry, who had indeed treated the O'Leary's with leniency for a start, could not be expected to be tolerant for long of a tenant who took such an extreme line in Irish political affairs. So desperate did O'Leary's position become, and so strongly did he feel about the whole matter, that he risked a visit to the town at the height of the trouble, and had great difficulty in finding anyone to give him accommodation. And the affair led to an estrangement with his niece Miss King, because for a time she appeared to waver before finally closing her shop and thereby losing her entire livelihood—out of premises of which, incidentally, it was rumoured locally, the real proprietor was her uncle John.

O'Leary's opposition to New Tipperary annoyed and dismayed many of his sincere admirers and staunch followers. In particular, it was freely used to suggest that his lifelong antipathy to agrarian agitation was based on his personal interest. A close friend of his old age, the writer D. J. O'Donoghue, blandly assumed that O'Leary was against the Land League only because he was a land-owner. Even John Devoy commented curtly that O'Leary's position as a landlord prevented his taking a dispassionate view of the Land War.

To hold such views, however, is to ignore both facts and prob-abilities. Apart from his support as a youth for Fintan Lalor, O'Leary all his life held tenaciously to the view that reform of the land system should take second place to political independence. On several occasions he publicly expressed his sympathy with the principle of tenant right. Moreover, although he depended entirely on property for his income, he did not come to acquire a substantial amount of property until late in life, and then only through the premature deaths of brothers and sisters—long after he had first opposed agrarian agitation.

Furthermore, the various land agitations all concentrated prin-cipally on the abuses of rural landlords. All the evidence now available suggests that O'Leary never in his life owned a single acre of farmland, his entire interest in property coming from his position as a middle landlord of houses in Tipperary town. Finally, to suggest that his views on the Irish land problem were coloured by his own personal position is to accuse him of a prejudice which he never showed in any other aspect of Irish affairs.

After Ellen's death, his sense of loneliness, combined with his straitened financial circumstances, forced O'Leary to decide to cut all his links with Dublin and to settle elsewhere. For a time he hesitated as his friends tried to dissuade him from starting a new life at the age of sixty. Eventually, however, early in March 1890, he moved to London. To Katharine Tynan he explained that he was going 'in a certain sense to seek my fortune . . . and . . . to live in a quieter and cheaper way than would be easy in Dublin'.

For the next six months or so little is known about O'Leary's activities. One may assume that he read a good deal, probably in some badly-lit garret where the rent was lower than that demanded by the landlords of Dublin. It is known that he settled down to what must have been to him the tedious job of writing his memoirs, and one may assume that he visited friends like Dr. Mark Ryan and Edmund Downey. But almost the only traces of him are a visit of some duration to the Yeats family, where he would have been especially welcome, and a call on Bryce in the House of Commons.

His stay in London was suddenly to be cut short. Perhaps he came gradually to realise that, after all, his roots were in Dublin, that London in 1890 was far different from the city he had known as a student forty years before, and that he was in fact too old to start a new life abroad. But almost certainly the most cogent reason was that he found himself too far from the centre of Irish affairs. And when, in November 1890, the Parnell-O'Shea triangle at last became public news through the divorce court, O'Leary knew his place. He made straight for Dublin.

CHAPTER SEVEN

1 The Parnell Split

2 The Social Round

3 1898 and Sinn Fein

4 Last Years

1

BOTH DURING HIS LIFETIME and after his death it was commonly
assumed that John O'Leary took little or no part in Irish political
affairs after his return to this country in 1885. The picture was
frequently drawn of a man who, because he found little to his
liking in the trend of Irish politics, deliberately buried himself in
his books, turning his back on the movement of which, before his
imprisonment and after, he had been a leading member.

Nothing is further from the truth. Upon his return to Ireland
O'Leary went out of his way to announce that, in spite of the turn
of events in Ireland during his absence, he still pinned all his hopes
on the physical force movement. At a series of public meetings in
Ireland, England and Scotland, at which he was accompanied by
recognised leaders of the physical force party, he threw cold water
on the constitutional agitation at a time when it was solidly backed
by the majority of nationalists, and advocated the use of physical
force by Ireland in her dispute with England.

Not for a moment did O'Leary allow his literary interests to
interfere with his work in and for the IRB, the fortunes and prestige
of which had probably never been lower than at the time of O'Leary's

27. John O'Leary in Belfast, 1898
—a photograph taken in Alice Milligan's house

28. John O'Leary in 1900—a painting by J. B. Yeats (senior)

return from exile. By the death in 1882 of Kickham the Brother-hood had lost the last of its leading pre-1865 figures, his place as president of the Supreme Council probably having been taken by the comparatively unknown John O'Connor, who was a mere youth in 1865.

The movement itself never died. In conditions of great secrecy its leaders continued to meet regularly, and an IRB delegate usually attended the annual conventions of Clan na Gael in the United States.

If O'Leary's friends were deluded into thinking that he no longer actively participated in the secret movement, Dublin Castle made no such mistake. From the day in January 1885, when he landed once more on Irish soil, he was shadowed daily by a member of the G (detective) division of the Special Branch of the police. O'Leary himself soon became aware of this practice and derived some amusement out of leading his shadower by devious routes through Dublin city, finally to end up at a bookstall on the quays —near which the detective often had a long wait before following his charge home again to Rathgar. When in the late 1880s the Special Branch was re-organised and the lists of suspects divided into three categories, the Castle paid O'Leary the compliment of placing him on the 'A' list, comprising men constantly followed.

Following is one thing; ascertaining what went on at meetings is quite another. When ultimately the police found it necessary to intensify their efforts towards this end, the Supreme Council was obliged to hold its meetings outside Ireland. On one such occasion in 1887, a conscientious detective followed a group of leading IRB men as far as the French city of Rouen where the party, aware of his presence, decided to give him the slip. P. N. Fitzgerald, acting as decoy, accosted the detective early one morning in a lane and, with the aid of a revolver, persuaded him to take a rest. That night a peaceful meeting was held in the seclusion of a Paris hotel.

O'Leary was not at this meeting; but it may be assumed that most of his regular trips abroad were for the purpose of attending IRB conferences. When he went to London he stayed openly in the house of Dr. Mark Ryan, another Supreme Council member, and Scotland Yard placed a man outside Ryan's surgery. When O'Leary visited Paris he went round in public with John O'Connor, later secretary of the Council. There is a record of a mysterious trip by O'Leary to Amsterdam in the early 1890s, and at least one journey to Scotland, where a small but loyal branch of the IRB continued to function. At intervals also he visited Belfast, always staying in the home of Robert Johnston, for many years Ulster's delegate to the Council.

All the time, even when public support for the Parnell movement was greatest, the views of the physical force party were kept before the public. Meetings like those addressed by O'Leary in 1885 were periodically held, and in literary and social societies frequented by nationalists, men who were known to have been active in the days of James Stephens, or men who had since pointedly held aloof from all constitutional movements, were always prominent.

In the Gaelic Athletic Association, to mention only one such body, so strong had the IRB element become by 1887 that a split occurred, the climax to which was a stormy convention in Thurles in November of that year at which the physical force party, led by P. N. Fitzgerald, secured control of the organisation in the face of fierce opposition from the moderate nationalists, who then left the meeting in a body. This led to the withdrawal by Archbishop Croke of his support and to the exertion of pressure by the IRB on Fitzgerald to end the schism. After two months' negotiation the two sides were re-united to the satisfaction of both the Archbishop and the Supreme Council. O'Leary attended the final of a series of meetings in Thurles on 30 October 1887, apparently held to avert the split—but did not go with the Fitzgerald party to see Croke.

Just as the constitutional agitations of the 1850s had ultimately foundered and been succeeded by Stephens's organisation, the movements led by Parnell and Davitt would, the IRB leaders argued, come to grief and leave the field free for advocates of physical force. Just as England's difficulty was to be Ireland's opportunity, so the misfortunes of constitutionalism were to mark the revival of separatism.

Shortly before Christmas 1889 a petition for divorce was filed in the O'Shea case; it was November 1890 before the action came on for hearing. Most of these eleven months O'Leary spent in London, where it is certain he picked up some gossip about the forthcoming matrimonial proceedings involving Parnell. Parnell, as is now well known, had been living for eight or nine years with Katharine O'Shea, a non-Catholic who was the wife of one of Parnell's own MPs, a Catholic. In November 1890 she was divorced by her husband, Parnell being cited as the co-respondent; some months later she married Parnell.

When eventually, shortly before Christmas of 1890, O'Leary saw the possibility of Parnell's being thrown overboard by Ireland, he decided at once to do what he could to prevent this from happening. Returning to Dublin, he took rooms in 53 Mountjoy Square, and almost immediately plunged headlong into the violent controversy that had already begun. 'I went straight for Parnell, and dead against the Davitts, Healys, Tanners, and the like; and straight I mean to go with him as long as he goes for an Irish parliament with independent powers.'

The line O'Leary took was not original; it was simply that of the Parnellites themselves during the twelve bitter months before Parnell's death. What Parnell chose to do in his private life had, O'Leary argued, nothing to do with his position as a public leader. Moreover, to dismiss him now because English public opinion professed to be shocked by his private life was to allow the course of Irish affairs to be dictated by British politicians.

O'Leary went further. While insisting that he was not, and would never be, a follower of Parnell, he regarded him as the only hope of success through constitutionalism. To O'Leary, Parnell was not merely the central figure in the struggle for Home Rule, he was an essential part of it; the attempt to displace him O'Leary interpreted largely in terms of the ancient struggle between the two nations. He saw Parnell as the general and his party in Westminster as his army; and he made no secret of his view that in the case of this particular general there was no other to take his place.

What the famous 86 do now is unimportant. They did not make Parnell and therefore they cannot unmake him. . . . The question is not the leading of the 86 but the leading of the Irish nation . . . Parnell . . . is not only the fittest man intellectually to lead but, so far as we know, the only fit man, and it would be simply stupid and cowardly to abandon him because Mr. Gladstone screeches and his followers howl.

The Parnell Split was to act as a mental tonic to O'Leary. 'The Parnell struggle,' wrote Katharine Tynan twenty-five years later, 'made O'Leary young again. It gave him new life, bracing up the energies which the loss of his sister had all but broken.'[1] In public and in private he threw himself enthusiastically into the fight to retain Parnell as leader of the Irish people. After all his years holding views that were unpopular with the majority, it delighted O'Leary to find himself once more on the popular side after thirty years, and still at peace with his own conscience.

That O'Leary, who all his life eschewed constitutional agitation, should participate so prominently in the political crisis caused by the Parnell divorce case may at first glance seem odd. But he was far from being the only IRB leader to do so. From one end of the country to the other, members of the IRB became overnight staunch supporters of Parnell and remained so until his death in October 1891.

The story of Parnell's last year is well known—how, undaunted by the secession of forty-five of his MPs, he announced his intention to fight on for Home Rule no matter how small his parliamentary support, and how he defiantly and symbolically appealed, over the head of his now hostile colleagues at Westminster, to the Irish people, calling on them not to desert him in his struggle on their behalf for legislative independence. His provocative public statements during 1891, designed to win the support of the physical force party, naturally dismayed men like Davitt and Dillon, who had come to regard Parnell as committed to constitutional agitation. They were shocked to hear him justify his drastic course by denying that he had ever expressly accepted parliamentary agitation as the only road to Irish freedom.

How the hillside men, as their sneering critics referred to the IRB, responded to this call has never been fully told. When, with Gladstone's demand for his resignation, Parnell's greatest crisis had come, he found that his own party had acquired a vested interest in constitutionalism, and that the militant spirit needed to meet the situation no longer existed—as it did twenty years before, with so many IRB men in the party. But that spirit was adequately supplied by the IRB itself, whose members everywhere temporarily abandoned their underground activities and publicly rallied round the man who had for so long been accepted as the leader of Irish nationalism. In this dramatic turn of events O'Leary figured most prominently.

Men who for years had scoffed at constitutional methods found themselves sitting on committees with Parnellites. Men who had never spoken publicly in their lives found themselves on the same platform as members of the Irish Party. Men who had taken to the hills on a snowy night in March 1867 found themselves acting in concert with men who had sneered at them ever since.

When in December 1890 it became evident that a prolonged struggle was about to develop for the leadership of the parliamentary party and of the Home Rule campaign, a Parnell Leadership Committee was formed. Its personnel showed at once how deeply involved the IRB had become in the outcome of the Parnell Split. A substantial minority of this Committee were known members of the IRB and remained so for the rest of their lives; others were recognised sympathisers of the physical force movement either then or afterwards.

Of the original Executive of the Parnell Leadership Committee, James K. Bracken of Templemore, John Wyse-Power of Naas, and Fred Allan and Henry Dixon of Dublin were IRB men. Wyse-Power was then and for many years afterwards on the Supreme Council, of which Allan was later secretary. Later O'Leary and P. N. Fitzgerald, both also on the Council, were co-opted to the Committee.

It was the same story in branches of the Committee all over the country. In Belfast the local committee was under the chairmanship of Robert Johnston, then and for many years later on the Supreme Council. In Tralee the local secretary was Maurice

Moynihan, the IRB centre for Kerry. In Ennis the local secretary was Patrick McInerney, centre of the IRB in Clare. Across in London one of the vice-presidents of the London committee was Dr. Mark Ryan, another member of the Supreme Council and a close associate of O'Leary since the 1870s.

Nor did the IRB support of Parnell in 1891 end with mere committee work or letters to the press. In several parts of the country its members spoke publicly from Parnellite platforms. In the Kilkenny by-election campaign in December 1890, the most bitterly fought of three such elections, P. N. Fitzgerald addressed many public meetings. Some months later Robert Johnston spoke from Parnellite platforms in the Carlow campaign, bringing with him a team of IRB men from the north to assist him. 'There are men from Tipperary, South Cork, Clare, Waterford and Dublin, all fenians and advanced nationalists, assisting the Parnell party,' said a police report from Kilkenny made, during the election campaign, to the Crime Special Branch in Dublin Castle.[2]

That the Catholic hierarchy became concerned about the strength and source of Parnell's support during this eventful year in Irish history is evident from public statements of several Irish bishops. In May 1891 when a Parnellite rally was planned for Mullingar, Bishop Woodlock of Ardagh and Clonmacnois warned his flock of the dangers of secret societies and said he had reason to believe they were spreading under the guise of sports organisations.

A week later, when Parnell was in Kildare, Bishop Lynch of Kildare and Leighlin told his flock that membership of secret societies left them open to excommunication, betrayal by informers and the processes of the criminal law. On 6 June the Bishop of Down and Connor, in a letter read in all the churches of that diocese, declared that Catholics were unfit to receive the sacraments if they were members of a Parnell Leadership Committee.

There was alarm in Dublin Castle also at the apparent revival of Fenianism, so long moribund. As police reports came in from the various districts they confirmed that in many parts of the country IRB men were active as supporters of Parnell. It was discovered that such bodies as the Young Ireland societies and the branches of the GAA had been infiltrated by known advocates of physical force, and that in places where Parnellites were weak the IRB was actually organising support for Parnell.

As the year 1891 progressed, however, O'Leary's enthusiasm for the Parnellite cause appears to have diminished. By the summer his public statements had become noticeably fewer and less dogmatic; and early in the autumn he went abroad for several weeks, allowing himself to get wholly out of touch with Irish affairs for some time. On his return in mid-September he wrote a striking letter to the *Freeman's Journal*, which suggested that his earlier assessment of the split had been modified but made it clear that he still placed the cause of physical force above all else. He agreed with Parnell that it was time to stop talking of leadership, and that the real issue between the two sides was one of principle rather than of persons.

The man will lead who shows himself fit to lead, and whom the Irish people choose to follow. The question is where we are going and not whom we are following, and if Mr. Parnell were dead to-morrow, I and men like me, who are above and before all things Irish Nationalists, should never dream of following the party of clerical dictation and compromise with England. We go with Mr. Parnell as long as he goes and in so far as he goes for Irish freedom. . . .

Within three weeks of this statement Parnell was dead, and O'Leary showed how far he and those he spoke for had gone with the dead leader. As the biggest funeral Dublin has ever seen wended its way through the city streets, many citizens cannot have failed to observe the position occupied by the IRB. In front of the bier came the Executive of the Irish Party; behind it followed two carriages with Parnell's relatives and one containing the clergymen.

Next, before the Lord Mayor and the representatives of any public bodies, came a solitary carriage in which sat John O'Leary, James Stephens (recently home from exile) and P. N. Fitzgerald. And on both sides, with upturned hurleys, marched the men of the GAA, who some months before had come out as a body in favour of Parnell.

A fortnight later O'Leary made his last statement on the controversy that had divided Ireland for over a year. 'Regarding the present political crisis, I believe that the least said is soonest mended.' He took no part in the squalid squabbles that followed Parnell's death and which were to last for a decade. What was needed now, said O'Leary, was 'thinking and acting, not . . . talking'.

Exactly why the IRB decided to come out in the open for this brief period will probably never be fully known; for secret societies do not keep minutes. To Devoy, watching events from the United States, it was a united front 'against the coalition of British politicians, Irish bishops and reactionary Irish MPs'. But this is surely an over-simplification; so, too, is the theory, held by some members of the Special Branch in the Castle, that the IRB's motive was simply to ensure the collapse of the parliamentary movement and so pave the way for a new physical force era.

More likely it was that the Supreme Council of the IRB hoped that, by responding to Parnell's appeal for support, they would

detach him from Westminster and find a new leader for the still
occasionally mooted policy of planned abstention. Certainly, if
one were to take at their face value some of his utterances during
1891, Parnell entertained this idea also. But with his death it died
too; and the IRB once more went underground.

2

GAVAN DUFFY ONCE SAID of J. P. Leonard that for years he had
acted as if he were Chargé d'Affaires in Paris of an Irish government. Later, during his fourteen years in that city, Irish nationalists had an unofficial ambassador in France in the person of John
O'Leary. By the early 1890s O'Leary had reached a position of
even greater prominence in Ireland. The long-drawn out proceedings of the *Times* Commission had focused public attention on the
activities of the various sections of extreme nationalism; and his
part in the Parnell Split soon afterwards made O'Leary a national
figure.

Of all the original leaders of the IRB, he alone still adhered to
his early principles and was still resident in Ireland. Even after the
death of Parnell and the withdrawal from public affairs of the
IRB, O'Leary remained in the public view. His arrivals in Ireland
and departures from it, and his occasional illnesses, were announced
in the social columns of the daily papers; his most trivial statement
on public affairs found a place on the main pages; his letters were
accepted by journals which abhorred his views.

Not merely had he, while still only in his early sixties, become the
Grand Old Man of Irish nationalism; he was now also a public
figure in his own right. In a city even then famous for its wits and
conversationalists, for its eccentrics and characters, O'Leary more
than held his own. Some of his views and sayings became famous
in late Victorian Dublin. Of Maud Gonne, before and after a close
friend, he remarked, when he heard that she had gone down to
support the tenants of New Tipperary, then engaged on their no-
rents campaign: 'She is no disciple of mine; she went there to show
off her new bonnet.' His contempt for teetotallers was well known.
'No man of intellect can possibly recommend total abstinence for
these countries because of the climate.' When reminded of Cardinal

Manning, he smiled and remarked: 'I ought to have said "no man of the higher intellect".'

Some of the most commonly quoted of his sayings were generalisations about Irish affairs. To a man so fond of quoting Davis's statement that 'freedom comes from God's right hand', his own rule that 'there are things that a man may not do, even for the sake of saving a nation' was but a corollary to this. And when distinguished supporters of constitutional agitation, or the prominent advocates of a dynamite policy, were mentioned in argument, he would contemptuously dismiss them by remarking that 'there was never a cause so bad that it was not defended by good men for what seemed to them sufficient motives'.

Once, shortly after John Redmond had said something in public that irritated him, O'Leary overtook Redmond in the street. Redmond, who at this time might be mistaken for his brother Willie, was unprepared for O'Leary's strategy. When asked abruptly why his brother John was making such an ass of himself, Redmond innocently pulled O'Leary up. 'Why, Mr. O'Leary, are you not mistaking me for my brother Willie?' Unabashed, O'Leary strode on: 'Oh, good God, good God, I was, I was; but what the devil do you mean by looking so like your brother?'

His imprecations often shocked the refined company O'Leary found himself in. 'God God in heaven' was a frequent exclamation of his, and when uttered in his booming Tipperary accent had a startling effect—as intended. When in a club or house he had to listen to someone expound a view with which he totally disagreed, O'Leary would sit in silence, showing his impatience by constantly crossing and re-crossing his legs, until finally he would sit bolt upright and launch into the speaker in a most aggressive way. If the topic was literature, the man would probably be told that he was 'faultlessly ignorant'; if he was a mild nationalist, he might be adjudged bereft of national morale, or guilty of contributing to lowering it.

On the Parnell divorce case and its aftermath O'Leary was particularly explosive. His favourite comment, intended to end all discussion on the subject, was: 'You can't depose a man for gallantry.' At times this was replaced by a series of more acid comments. 'God God in heaven, while he was ruining the morals of the country (an allusion to the Land War) they were all with him; but now that it is only a question of his own morals, they are all against him.'

Towards women O'Leary was a model of chivalry. His handsome appearance, his noble head and features, his formal manners, his treatment of members of the opposite sex as intellectual equals to those of his own—all made him a favourite with women acquaintances. Indeed, women when arguing with him had an advantage over men; for O'Leary would never be rude to a woman. On the contrary, on such an occasion he relaxed many of his otherwise strict rules for discussion. He held a high opinion of any woman who dared to disagree with him, and was even inclined to defend her from more critical members of the company.

The poet Padraic Colum has often remarked on the gaps in the human experience of some of the Fenian leaders whom he met as a young man. He found that they had little knowledge of women, were shy of discussing love or related topics, and that some of them—Devoy is the most obvious example of this—had deliberately refrained from marrying, lest it interfere with their work for the cause.

Apart from the fact that he never married, none of this criticism is valid in the case of O'Leary, who of all the IRB leaders was best known to Colum. From his student days O'Leary had mixed freely with the opposite sex. Probably as a result of having lived with an unmarried sister, he had long since come to take females for granted in a way that was unusual for his time. He was genuinely surprised, not to say embarrassed, to find himself the constant subject of their admiration, and at times of their adoration; for he himself was then completely devoid of romantic ideas.

To a few close friends, who wondered why he had never married, O'Leary now confided that, when a young man, he had had a love affair that had not been successful. He and a friend had found themselves in love with the same girl, and she, unable to choose between them, had entered a convent. Asked by Katharine Tynan how he had taken this decision, O'Leary frankly admitted: 'For a good while I was in hell.'

It is almost certain that O'Leary's intended bride was none other than 'Mary' of the *Nation*, the Cork poetess, Ellen Downing, whose other suitor was Joseph Brenan, the 1849 leader. Only after O'Leary's death was it publicly reported that he and a fellow-revolutionary had once fallen in love with the same girl, who had resolved the crisis by entering a convent; one inaccurate version identified the rival as James Stephens.

Confirmation of Katharine Tynan's account comes from a letter (now lost) written shortly after her death by Ellen O'Leary, and published in 1913 with the vital name omitted. 'John lost his best chance (of marrying) in ——. God had chosen her for a higher bridal.' That Ellen Downing was the person is strongly suggested by an otherwise cryptic remark by O'Leary himself in his memoirs, where he quoted a poem of her's in a chapter on the *Irish People*: 'It may not be easy for the reader to see how I can associate "Mary" or her verses with my recollections of Fenianism. But the reader must guess.'

We have seen how, in the exciting days of 1849, O'Leary and the Cork journalist had been close associates in the revolutionary movement. Ellen Downing and Brenan had been engaged but had broken off the engagement by agreement, Brenan having to flee to America in October 1849, after the failure of the rising the previous month. That same month Ellen Downing entered the North Presentation Convent in Cork; she was to remain a nun for less than a year, and after many years of ill-health died in 1869. Brenan became a successful journalist in the United States, where in 1851 he married a sister of John Savage, but died tragically in 1857.

While it cannot be suggested that this theory of John O'Leary's only love affair is proved beyond doubt, there is nobody else to whom all the known facts point so directly as 'Mary'. Other evidence also tends to connect her with the story. D. J. O'Donoghue, an intimate friend of O'Leary in old age, appears to have deliberately omitted all references to the affair in both editions of his *Poets of Ireland*, although between the first and second editions he had discovered (perhaps from O'Leary) the identity of Miss Downing's fiancé.

O'Leary fully exploited his reputation in Dublin in the 1890s, but always for the purpose of furthering the cause of Irish nationalism. Then as today literary Dublin knew no distinctions of class or creed or politics, and O'Leary gladly accepted invitations to visit clubs and houses where he was certain to meet men whose political outlook totally differed from his. He became an accepted, indeed, almost an essential, figure at parties and receptions in some of the city's fashionable residences, where the presence of one with such extreme political views would otherwise have created a stir.

His knowledge of English literature and European history gained O'Leary many new friends at this period. But he never felt inhibited from launching into a full-blooded political discussion at such functions; and by degrees his conversational powers, and his generally conservative view of what a free Ireland should be like, won some notable converts to nationalism. In particular, his constant attendance at the Contemporary Club, where he could dominate the discussion at will, resulted in many men connected with Trinity College gaining a new appreciation of the nationalist case.

About his personal appearance at this period O'Leary was so concerned that even some of his friends considered him vain. Once during a conversation in the Contemporary Club on Dublin's handsome men, O'Leary, when asked for his view, calmly replied: 'Well, after myself, I think —— is the best-looking.' A few years later, when honouring Sara Purser with one of his voluminous postcards, he mentioned a portrait of himself that had appeared in a London periodical and 'which I think is not at all as good as the one in the book'. But it is arguable that such remarks are evidence, not of vanity, but simply of his frank manner of speaking, or of a subtle humour.

Vanity would seem to have been out of place in such a man and it is likely that any care for his own appearance sprang from a different cause altogether. O'Leary would have realised that to members of non-nationalist Dublin society he represented a particular class of Irishman, and he would naturally have been anxious to ensure that he did not let down the side he stood for.

As a result his conduct at public functions was impeccable. In dress, in manners and at table he was above reproach. In some respects he was in advance of what contemporary society regarded as fashionable; for, as a direct consequence of his fourteen years' residence in France, O'Leary was inclined to follow continental practices both in dress and in food.

It is clear in any event from many contemporary references that O'Leary made a most favourable impression on strangers and political opponents. The list of notable figures with few Irish connections who were numbered amongst his acquaintances in the 1890s is unique for any Irish nationalist. It included York Powell, the unconventional Oxford professor of history; James Louis Garvin, the distinguished journalist (then on the *Newcastle Chronicle*); Lionel Johnson, the poet (who dedicated a poem to O'Leary); Sara Purser, the artist; General Sir William Butler; Oliver Elton, the critic and authority on English literature; Andrew Lang, the poet and novelist; Sir William Percy Bunting, the social reformer and editor of the *Contemporary Review*, and Ernest Rhys, the originator of Everyman's Library.

The early years of the last decade of the century passed slowly and eventfully for O'Leary. On his return to Dublin in 1890 he had settled in rooms in 53 Mountjoy Square, not far from where he had stayed thirty years earlier when editor of the *Irish People*. Here, and later in 17 Temple Street, he held his informal morning receptions, as, dressed in a frieze dressing-gown, he strode from room to room, a glass of lukewarm milk in one hand and a slice of cold toast in the other.

From here later in the day he wandered forth to rummage in the quayside bookstalls, whence, later still, he would make his way on foot to the Contemporary Club or to whatever house he had been invited to for dinner, or perhaps to a committee meeting of the National Literary Society. And when life in Dublin threatened to become routine, there were those periodic visits, either abroad to London or Paris, or not so far afield to Belfast or Tipperary.

All this time O'Leary continued to work intermittently at his memoirs, putting aside his manuscript when his friends ceased to urge him on or when some good excuse, such as the non-arrival of notes from America, presented itself. When he once again got into the swing of writing, he toyed for a time with the idea of writing for a living, presumably to augment his now precarious, if not meagre, financial resources. Perhaps the presence of Willie Yeats, with whom for a period in 1892 O'Leary shared rooms in an old mansion in Clontarf (Lonsdale House, St. Lawrence Road), revived his interest in the practice of journalism.

At this stage O'Leary succeeded in getting into print. A few book reviews in Irish and English periodicals were followed by a couple of articles in the *Academy*, a theatrical critique in *United Ireland*, and—most noteworthy of all—a biographical sketch of John O'Mahony for the *Dictionary of National Biography*.

But that was all. Whether O'Leary himself or his friends felt that he would be more profitably employed in concentrating on his own book, or whether it was simply that his improved financial position brought on his old indolence, cannot be said. Certainly by 1892 he ought not to have been any longer short of money. The committee sponsoring his book succeeded in collecting over £100 and, early in 1892, with New Tipperary almost forgotten, the sale of his niece's shop realised £450, of which her uncle got the biggest share. All this represented wealth to a man of O'Leary's Spartan habits.

By 1894 he had completed his memoirs; but it was well into 1896 before they appeared. Published in London by his Waterford friend, Edmund Downey, O'Leary's *Recollections of Fenians and Fenianism* ran to two volumes. A work that had long been awaited, it was well-received on the whole. Most of the leading journals in Ireland and England reviewed the memoirs favourably, and the book was serialised in the *Weekly Independent*, as well as in the *Newcastle Chronicle*, which thus made up for its rejection of O'Leary as a correspondent eight years before.

To the student of Fenianism, or of Irish affairs generally during the period covered by O'Leary's memoirs, they usually produce a feeling of disappointment. There is no chronicle of events in the movement either in Ireland or the United States, and no sensational disclosures about either the leaders or the movement itself. The author, too, often strays off into discussions of side issues, and far too frequently hurls his own views at his readers on topics that, even by 1896, were stale.

No secrets of the IRB are disclosed, and the whole account ends abruptly with the writer's conviction in 1865. Even in the long section on the *Irish People*, which takes up most of Volume II, the fortunes of the paper are nowhere discussed, and the reader is left to try to assess for himself the impact of the paper on the movement and its place in its history.

All these faults are the result of the reader's having, without justification, expected too much from the memoirs of a man who, by the 1890s, was the most distinguished of the surviving leaders of a movement that had gone close to altering the course of Irish history. The book, as its title implies, is nothing more or less than the random memories, by an IRB leader, of the men and the movement as he encountered them.

Anyone who had read, even occasionally, O'Leary's speeches and letters to the press ought to have expected him to write a discursive book. Such a person should have anticipated the tilts at the parliamentarians, the land agitators and the clergy. He ought also to have bargained for the book's literary bias, for the liberal sprinkling of French and Latin phrases (there are no less than sixty in all) and for the absence of any references to the writer's five years in jail.

All this is, perhaps, merely to say that his *Recollections* are a typical product of O'Leary. For him the IRB movement ended in 1865; for him all the violence in Irish politics since then was directly traceable to the land agitation. Not for him the so-called Union of Hearts between Ireland and England which, at the time he was writing his book, was so fashionable; to him Gladstone was not the big-hearted English statesman who had been converted to Irish self-government, but the party politician who some time before had treated political prisoners as thieves and pickpockets.

The student of modern Irish history who reads more carefully may find O'Leary's memoirs more satisfactory. They reveal more of the character of their author, for example, than do Devoy's much more factually informative recollections. In their detailed treatment of the management of the *Irish People* and in their analysis of the material it contained, they deal with an aspect of the IRB movement ignored everywhere else.

Because of their penetrating portraits of Stephens (gallantly defended to the end) and Luby, they form an essential source of study for two of the early leaders of the movement. Taken as a whole, the countless criticisms of the other political movements of nineteenth-century Ireland comprise a formidable argument for physical force as the most effective instrument for achieving Ireland's separation from England. And in a hundred minor ways the 514 pages of these two volumes form a mine of information about political and literary matters in mid-nineteenth-century Ireland.

As a commercial venture O'Leary's memoirs were a failure. The price, £1, was prohibitive, especially to the class of Irish reader which would have been most anxious to buy them—though it is

fair to point out that both Downey and O'Leary had hoped to
bring out a cheaper edition, as had been done in the case of Mitchel's
Jail Journal. Furthermore, the necessary legal steps were not taken
in time to prevent the book from being pirated in the United States;
and no attempt appears to have been made to serialise the book
in that country. His monetary reward for what must have been
a tedious task was little more than £250, excluding the £100
originally collected by the sponsoring committee. But £250 went
a long way with John O'Leary.

3

THE PARNELL SPLIT marks a turning point in modern Irish history.
The once united Irish party at Westminster broke into three groups,
each with its own daily organ and each outdoing the other in
washing the other's dirty linen in public. With the parliamentary
movement thus crippled, many patriotic Irishmen lost interest in
party politics and Home Rule was temporarily forgotten. Instead,
educated men of patriotic meaning became increasingly interested
in the literary revival, with its emphasis on Irish culture and its
study of the nation's glorious past. Gradually the Union of Hearts
with England was replaced by a revival of separatist ideals.

In view of its part in the events of the year preceding Parnell's
death, one might have expected the IRB to have exploited the lull
in Irish affairs from 1892 onwards. It was not in a position to do
so; for the fortunes of the Brotherhood probably reached their
lowest point during the period between 1891 and 1898. On the
death of Parnell it transpired that by no means all of the prominent
IRB figures had been in favour of open action in support of a
parliamentary movement, C. G. Doran of Cobh and Michael
O'Hanlon of Downpatrick in particular taking a strong line on this
matter. However, the Parnellite majority appears to have for some
time entertained the hope of continuing to support the Parnellites;
if police records for the period are reliable, a nebulous secret force
called the Army of Independence (doubtless a recruiting ground for
the IRB) was established with the connivance of John Redmond.

In addition, the split in the Irish-American revolutionary movement, originating in the mysterious death in Chicago in 1889 of

Dr. Cronin, murdered (Devoy claimed) by the followers of Alexander
Sullivan, had spread across the Atlantic, so that by 1890 there were
Sullivanite wings and Cronin or Devoy factions in several counties.
P. T. Hoctor, the GAA official, was said to be a Sullivanite; so was
Dr. Mark Ryan of London, who by 1894 was organising an Irish
National Brotherhood as a rival to the IRB. There was even, the
Castle believed, a remnant of the Invincibles still operating in
Dublin, which kept the police busy with its mysterious doings.

With this bewildering multiplicity of divisions in the physical
force movement, it is not surprising that sincere nationalists who
eschewed parliamentarianism should seek an outlet for their activities
and aspirations in literary societies. It was to the work of young
men of this type that the ultimate revival of separatist ideals are
to be traced. Indeed, the real origins of the Sinn Féin movement
are to be found in this period, when the names of men like Arthur
Griffith and William Rooney appeared with increasing frequency
in nationalist journals.

Griffith about the time of Parnell's death had founded the Leinster
Literary Society, of which Rooney soon became a member. In
1893, because of internal dissensions, Rooney established the Celtic
Literary Society, to which Griffith soon transferred his allegiance.
Superficially, the objects of this body, of which O'Leary was an
early sponsor, were confined to Irish literature, history, language
and music; but examination of its early records shows an undoubted
bias in favour of physical force, with discussions on such topics
as Fenianism, Kickham, Fintan Lalor and '98.

O'Leary, as if realising the futility of the struggle between Parnell
and his party, had even before Parnell's death been thinking along
the same lines. At a meeting in the Rotunda on 18 September
1891 at which he presided, there was formed a body called the
Young Ireland League, itself a typical example of how literature
and politics had come to encroach one on the other at this period.
The speakers at the Rotunda included W. B. Yeats, Anna Johnston
(the poetess Ethna Carberry), George Coffey the antiquarian and
members of the Sigerson family. In their speeches in regard to
the new body's aims the emphasis was on such matters as the
provision of local libraries, the study of the Irish language, the
encouragement of Irish music and the reform of the primary school
system.

However, the attendance also included Arthur Griffith and Fred
Allan, as well as Michael Cusack (the founder of the GAA) and
William Redmond MP, both then on the fringe of the extreme wing.
Amongst the first members of the new League were P. N. Fitz-
gerald, William Moore Stack and Henry Dixon. It is safe to assume
that for these men such objects of the League as 'the encouragement

of self-reliance . . . in politics amongst Irish youth', 'the carrying into effect of the Young Ireland movement' and 'independence in Irish politics, freed from English dictation' were of more immediate importance than the study of language or music.

Meanwhile O'Leary busied himself with other projects. At his instigation the first selection in book form of writings of Fintan Lalor appeared in 1896 in the Shamrock Library. The editor was O'Leary's fellow-bibliophile, D. J. O'Donoghue; O'Leary wrote the introduction. With the completion of a monument over the grave of Kickham, plans (originally formulated by the Young Ireland Society in the late 1880s) to erect a statue of Kickham, were revived by O'Leary, Dixon and other IRB men.

The outlook for Irish nationalism in the 1890s continued to remain bleak. Things would doubtless have gone on indefinitely in this unpromising manner had it not been for an ingenious idea conceived early in 1897 by some of the leaders of the Young Ireland League. Exactly who was the originator of the scheme will probably never be known. But its subsequent history strongly suggests the IRB element, and it is safe to assume that O'Leary was in on the secret from the start—if, indeed, his was not the master mind.

On 5 January 1897 a meeting of the League's Council decided to call a public meeting of nationalists in the City Hall, Dublin, on 4 March, Emmet's birthday. This conference was to be asked how best the centenary of the rising of 1798 should be celebrated, and to approve plans for such celebrations. With O'Leary in the chair, the City Hall meeting was duly held. Attended by several shades of nationalist thought, it proved a success and formed the '98 Centenary Provisional Committee, charged with planning '98 celebrations. O'Leary, put at the head of affairs, made a magnanimous appeal for support from all parties and guaranteed that the new body would be non-political and non-sectarian.

So began what a close associate of Arthur Griffith called 'the beginning of all modern efforts towards a return to ideals of independence'. All over the country '98 clubs, affiliated to what came to be called the City Hall Committee, were formed, and nationalists of all camps spontaneously united to make the movement a success. At the suggestion of P. N. Fitzgerald the Dublin body was called the '98 Centenary Organisation; at the suggestion of the poetess Alice Milligan (seconded by Peadar Doyle of Inchicore, later a TD and Lord Mayor of Dublin) the principal aim of the body was fixed as the erection of a national memorial to Wolfe Tone and the United Irishmen. Soon there were branches in Britain, the United States, even on the Continent, in Australia and in South Africa.

Alone of prominent non-loyalist bodies the Gaelic League, then

29. John O'Leary and Major John MacBride (who was executed in 1916) at Fontenoy, Belgium, 1905

30. John O'Leary with the Carew children,
Kilkenny, October 1906—five months before his death

strictly non-political, held aloof. Its absence was more than compensated for by the fact that up and down the country IRB men had infiltrated into the '98 clubs to such an extent as to control the whole centenary movement. Centres of the IRB transformed themselves *en bloc* into '98 clubs; in Dublin one powerful centre had a member specially deputed to act as chairman when it met publicly as a '98 club. The City Hall Committee even survived a threatened split led by prominent MPs, aided by the Hoctor faction and supported by the anti-Parnellite press; eventually the nomination of leading parliamentarians to the Committee brought peace.

When 1898 eventually came the IRB was probably surprised itself as to how efficiently but unobtrusively it had done its work. Physical force men, both wings of the parliamentary party, as well as leaders of cultural, religious and labour bodies, all participated in the celebrations, which took place in every county and lasted throughout the whole year. The country got the injection of national enthusiasm it so badly needed to recover from the shock of the Parnell Split.

Nationalist Ireland welcomed the centenary year of 1898 with impressive torchlight processions on New Year's Eve, 1897, through the streets of Dublin, Cork, Limerick, Belfast, Derry, Sligo and other towns. Within a week a meeting of prominent Irishmen resident in London planned corresponding celebrations. Michael Davitt and J. F. X. O'Brien MP took a leading part in this work, and W. B. Yeats was elected president of the '98 Centenary Committee of Great Britain and France. A fortnight later a mass meeting was held in Piccadilly.

While the public meeting, addressed by public figures from all parties, became the most popular method of '98 celebration, it was by no means the only one. In many places national monuments were erected commemorating historic events in Irish history; visits to the sites of victorious battles by Irish armies were arranged; plaques were unveiled at the birthplaces of patriots and headstones over the graves of others.

A special liner was chartered by Irish-Americans, who planned to visit Ireland in large numbers, headed by the veteran O'Donovan Rossa; but the project was abandoned on the outbreak of the Spanish-American war. English and Scottish cities witnessed celebrations by their Irish communities. At the other end of the world 200,000 people lined the streets of Sydney and 50,000 packed the square outside the cathedral, as Cardinal Moran, who earlier had frowned on the '98 centenary movement as savouring of French republicanism, presided at the re-interment of the bodies of the hero of '98, Michael Dwyer and his wife. Two months later there were more celebrations in Auckland, New Zealand.

In all the principal events in Ireland during that year O'Leary played a leading part. The Executive Committee met weekly in the City Hall, Dublin, reviewing progress and planning future events. Alice Milligan has left some amusing impressions of O'Leary presiding at these proceedings. Liable to make the most capricious rulings (which were never questioned), he invariably interrupted discussions to take his periodic coffee. For the most part he listened in silence and endured a variety of opinions.

O'Leary was not prepared merely to act as chairman in committee. He also considered it his duty to attend and speak at the more important public functions. And if he now mostly said what was expected of him, his presence added to the occasion; and he could be relied on to get across the viewpoint of the extreme nationalist wing without interruption.

On 13 March a monster demonstration was held in the Phoenix Park, Dublin, each of the four provinces having its own platform. O'Leary presided on the Leinster platform, the theme of his address being that 'until we come, in more senses than one, to be United Irishmen again, there is little hope of Emmet's epitaph being written'. Three months later he unveiled a tablet at 151 Thomas Street, where Lord Edward Fitzgerald was arrested; this time he spoke on Tone and his message. A few days later he presided at Tone's grave in Bodenstown, where he placed a bust of Tone on the grave.

By far the biggest and most impressive meeting of the year took place in Dublin on 15 August, when O'Leary laid the foundation stone of a Wolfe Tone monument at the entrance to St. Stephen's Green. Months of careful preparation preceded this event, which was planned as the climax of the '98 centenary year. All business in Dublin closed, the day being declared a municipal holiday by the Corporation.

On 15 August Dublin was packed with tens of thousands of people, who came by special trains from all over the country. Delegates from affiliated societies in the United States (including a bishop from Boston), Britain, France, and South Africa arrived. The ceremony at the top of Grafton Street followed a slow parade through the city by a circuitous route which took in such historical places as Tone's birthplace, Emmet's execution place and the old Parliament House in College Green.

At the site of the ceremony the customary round of speeches began, with orations from O'Leary, John Dillon, John Redmond, W. B. Yeats, a French delegate, William Rooney (who spoke in Irish) and the Lord Mayor, Alderman (later Sir) Thomas Pile. That night at a banquet in the Mansion House O'Leary again spoke, bluntly disagreeing with Pile's view that Irishmen could best rule themselves under English law, receiving warm support from Dillon.

For O'Leary, however, the most moving occasion of all in 1898 came on 27 November, when in a triumphant return to his native Tipperary he unveiled a statue of his old associate, Charles Kickham, before a great gathering of nationalists from all parts of the south. Special trains ran from many parts of Munster and, in addition to O'Leary, speakers included T. D. Sullivan MP, P. N. Fitzgerald, John Daly (the Limerick IRB leader recently released after fifteen years in jail) and the mayors of Cork and Clonmel.

The statue, one of the finest works of John Hughes, the sculptor responsible for the statue of Queen Victoria which stood in front of Leinster House until recently, and for the statue of Provost Salmon in Trinity College grounds, was the culmination of a decade of committee work by a small group of Kickham's admirers, chief amongst them O'Leary himself. The striking life-size bronze figure of Kickham depicts him in a sitting posture, holding paper and a quill in his hands.

However, said O'Leary in his address to the assembled thousands, 'this statute is erected not in honour of the literary man . . . but mainly . . . in honour of the patriot and politician'. After touching on his own associations with Kickham, O'Mahony, Stephens and Luby thirty-five years before, O'Leary said that the time had now come to 'lift the veil and tell an ignorant world that Charles Kickham had been the leader of the new Fenianism' from his release from jail to the day of his death thirteen years later. [3]

The overall effect on Irish nationalism of the '98 centenary celebrations cannot be exaggerated. After seven years of bickering the two parliamentary camps were brought together on a neutral platform, and spokesmen of both made sincere appeals for unity in the Home Rule campaign. The hierarchy remained in the background; but the movement obtained their support and in some places clergymen sat on '98 committees.

To a generation that had gradually become more anglicised, the local demonstrations served the beneficial purpose of reminding them of their nation's historic heritage. At a time when Irish history was rarely taught in the schools then controlled by the British, the '98 centenary movement took the place of a popular twelve-month course in this neglected subject for adults and young people alike. Most important of all, the celebrations awakened in many Irishmen a desire to become a separate nation from England. To the mass meetings and parades, to the unveilings of monuments and plaques, and to the visits to battlefields and patriots' graves many who later took a prominent part in Irish affairs owed their first patriotic urge.

For the leaders of the IRB it had been a year of well-directed

energy. In addition to O'Leary, Fred Allan and Henry Dixon
had worked tirelessly in the City Hall, Dixon as president and
Allan as treasurer of the Executive Committee. So too did P. T.
Daly, for many years afterwards a prominent IRB figure. At public
meetings all over the country P. N. Fitzgerald, P. T. Hoctor, C. G.
Doran and John Daly addressed enthusiastic audiences. On the
platform at the Dublin meeting on 15 August was Captain Charles
Underwood O'Connell, a leading Cork IRB man of the 1860s then
on a visit home from the United States, as well as James Stephens,
who with Maud Gonne went to Manchester in November for a
demonstration which 100,000 attended. In London Dr. Mark Ryan
and John Ryan of Chelsea, both leading IRB men for thirty years,
were on the local '98 committee.

The IRB, which had been the mainspring of the whole '98 centenary movement, failed almost entirely to exploit the upsurge of
separatist feelings which the events of that year had produced.
Two main factors accounted for this failure. Despite a number of
favourable omens, the IRB remained split into two factions as the
year 1899 began. Ironically, it was to take a war on the continent
of Africa to bring the two sides together. In addition, it is now
obvious that the leadership of the IRB in the 1890s was not of the
quality required for the consolidation of the gains of 1898. The
Supreme Council had degenerated to the level of a convivial club,
whose members were intellectually inferior to those hitherto on the
Council; it was to take a younger generation to shake the Brotherhood out of its lethargy a decade later.

But if the IRB as a body was unable to render adequate service
to the separatist cause, some of its members, including O'Leary,
were not content to remain idle. Back from two years' exile in
South Africa came Arthur Griffith in October 1898; and out of
English jails after fifteen years came Thomas Clarke in the same
month. By the spring of 1899 Griffith's first weekly paper, *United
Irishman* (called after Mitchel's organ of the 1840s) had begun to
appear; some months later Clarke emigrated to the United States,
where under Devoy he at once began to work for the rejuvenation
in Ireland of the physical force movement.

Griffith's paper became the principal medium of expression of a
new, if slow, revival of separatist and republican ideals. Supporting *United Irishman* was the Supreme Council party of the IRB,
now gradually growing in strength with the infusion of new rank-
and-file members recruited from a number of '98 clubs scattered
round the country, which had remained in operation and which
now also helped to push the sales of the new paper. From across
the Atlantic came money grants from Devoy and Clarke to extricate
Griffith and Rooney from the periodic financial crises into which

they ran. From London more financial assistance came, significantly from Dr. Mark Ryan, for years a supporter of the Sullivan wing of Clan na Gael.

From its first issue the *United Irishman* had the enthusiastic support of O'Leary. He might—indeed did on several occasions—cavil at some of Griffith's views on literature; for the proposition that a national literature should be subservient to politics was one with which O'Leary never fully agreed. After so many years of organs of the various wings of the constitutional movement, the appearance of a paper which preached so many of O'Leary's own ideas—that Irishmen were wasting time remaining in Westminster, that Irish culture in all its forms deserved to be fostered, and that anglicising influences of all kinds must be sternly opposed—must have delighted him.

That the *United Irishman*, although edited and managed by a comparatively unknown group of young men, should from its inception have attracted some of the more promising Irish writers may be attributed in part to O'Leary's support. Amongst those who contributed to Griffith's paper were J. B. Yeats and his son W. B. Yeats, George Moore, John Eglinton, Oliver St. John Gogarty and AE. When in September 1903 *United Irishman* turned itself into a public company in order to weather the latest financial storm, O'Leary's name was first on the list of directors of the paper after that of Griffith, its managing director. The others were Maud Gonne MacBride, Thomas Kelly TC, Henry Dixon and Seamus MacManus the Donegal writer and husband of Ethna Carbery, so that three of the six directors (O'Leary, Dixon and Griffith) were IRB men.

Just as, nine years earlier, the Parnell Split had spurred O'Leary into activity again, so the outbreak of the Boer War in October 1899 acted as a mental tonic on him. From Griffith, who had spent nearly two years among the Boers, he would have learnt much about this sturdy race with its unconcealed anti-British feelings. As news reached Ireland of the spate of initial Boer military successes—Mafeking, Stromberg, Magersfontein, Colenso and Spion Kop all inside a month or so—O'Leary became increasingly elated: 'My God, my God, this is the greatest news since I came out of prison.' Moreover, as the British, in the face of a growing volume of world opinion sympathetic to the Boers, continued to fight with a ferocity not seen for decades—this was the war which witnessed the origin of concentration camps and the scorched-earth policy—O'Leary became convinced that the British were becoming decadent and that the end of the Empire was in sight.

To other Irishmen, however, the series of British reverses in South Africa served as a reminder of the old advice—'England's

difficulty Ireland's opportunity'. Little could be achieved until the
split in the IRB was healed; but early in 1900 both wings came
together and the Supreme Council was reconstituted under the
presidency of John O'Leary. The question then arose of how best
to assist the Boers. An Irish Brigade under Major John MacBride
was in the field but, since Ireland was part of the United Kingdom
and thus officially at war too, direct military assistance by Irish
nationalists seemed out of the question.

There was, however, no law forbidding the dispatch of medical
aid; so, with O'Leary as its president, an Irish Transvaal Committee was formed for the ostensible purpose of sending an Irish
ambulance corps to the Boers. Once again O'Leary played his now
accepted role of presiding at committees; once more this veteran
of earlier movements preserved harmony amongst spokesmen of
diverse interests. Here, for example, he again met the young labour
leader James Connolly, who in 1898 had formed a '98 club out of
his Irish Socialist Republican Party, and who was now doubtless
anxious to play his part in frustrating the commercial aims of
British capitalism in South Africa. Others on the committee were
Griffith, Maud Gonne, Yeats and P. T. Hoctor.

Although there is no evidence that an Irish ambulance corps
ever reached South Africa, this campaign did not mark the end of
the Transvaal Committee's work. It remained in existence, doing
all it could to encourage sympathy for the Boers and understanding
of the Boer cause. It also issued public notices setting out the law
on recruitment for the British army, and did its best to discourage
Irishmen from enlisting to fight a struggling nationality.

As the climax of its campaign of defiance of the British Government, the Transvaal Committee sent to Paris an Irish deputation
to bring to President Kruger, then in Europe seeking aid, the good
wishes of the Irish people. An illuminated address was drawn up
in Irish, French, Dutch and English and signed by O'Leary. In a
dispatch to the *United Irishman* from Paris on 1 December 1900,
the future classical scholar Stephen MacKenna described how
Kruger received the Irish party, headed by the septuagenarian
O'Leary and including Major MacBride, in the State reception room
of the Hotel Seine, where O'Leary addressed the Boer leader in
French.

Meanwhile in Dublin the new separatist movement, spearheaded
by the *United Irishman*, lacked direction and cohesion. It took
over a year before advice, offered by Griffith in an article in the
issue for 2 April 1899, entitled 'A National Organisation', was
accepted. On 23 November 1900, in the rooms of the Celtic Literary
Society, was held the first annual convention of the Cumann na
nGaedheal, a federation of some twenty existing literary, political

and athletic societies, which was planned by Griffith in O'Leary's rooms in Temple Street and in Maud Gonne's house in Rathgar. O'Leary was elected president, a post he held until his death; MacBride and Robert Johnston of Belfast became two of the vice-presidents and William Rooney was appointed treasurer.

It was to Cumann na nGaedheal, at its third annual convention in 1902, that Griffith first enunciated his Hungarian policy of abstention from Westminster, a policy which became the official policy of the organisation in 1905 and became the basis of the subsequent separatist movement. And it was Cumann na nGaedheal which, having in the meantime absorbed other nationalist bodies such as the Dungannon Clubs and the National Club, became in April 1907 the Sinn Féin League—a fortnight after the death of the first president of Cumann na nGaedheal, John O'Leary.

4

FOR THE LAST TEN YEARS of life left to him John O'Leary led a full and satisfying existence. From the moment early in 1897 when the '98 centenary celebrations were first advocated to the day of his death a decade later, the direction which Irish affairs were taking was to O'Leary's liking. For the first time for thirty years a separatist movement flourished to which he could give his unqualified support, and in which he felt he could participate without prejudicing his own principles.

To the young and inexperienced leaders of the new movement O'Leary's support was not only welcome, it was also badly needed. For to win public support men like Rooney and Griffith, whose names meant little to Ireland, had to compete with men like Dillon, Redmond and O'Brien, whose names were by now known in the humblest Irish cottage. Alone of the leading figures of the now distant 1860s O'Leary was still true to his separatist ideals, had never gone over to parliamentarianism, was still alive and resident in Ireland, and still active in the physical force movement.

Little wonder then that from 1897 onwards he found himself enthusiastically accepted as the titular leader of the new Irish separatism. For every public demonstration, for each new literary or political group, for the latest gesture of defiance of the Castle, the extreme nationalists of the late 1890s looked to one man as their figurehead, 'because there was in him', said Padraic Colum, 'a virtue, an integrity that gave a spiritual value to words and programmes'. And O'Leary revelled in his new position of honour.

Now in his middle sixties, past an age at which a man could be expected to render much service to a national cause, much less to lead a national movement, O'Leary found himself regarded as the symbol of resistance to British rule in Ireland. He who for most of his life had been an inveterate critic of almost every nationalist movement now found himself called upon to preside at assemblies at which every shade of nationalist thought was represented; his became the task of keeping harmony between them all for the sake of advancing the cause of Irish nationalism.

Characteristically, O'Leary rose to the occasion. He quickly developed a style of chairmanship which satisfied everybody and still permitted business to be efficiently transacted. Considering that the interests represented on such bodies as the City Hall Committee of 1898 ranged from the mildest constitutionalists to the socialists, it is a tribute to O'Leary that harmony prevailed. There are no records of wrangles of the type he introduced into the New Departure negotiations; no McCarthy Teeling besieged the City Hall.

In the early 1890s, when Irish affairs reached their lowest ebb since the days of Sadlier and Keogh, the periods of depression which O'Leary had experienced in Paris in the 1870s returned occasionally. 'I feel as if 'twere probable that I'll die without seeing much more life in the old land . . . What hurts me most . . . is a sense of my own helplessness, at least for the time being.'[4] But with the success of the '98 celebrations and its invigorating effects on all nationalists, O'Leary's pessimism disappeared as all his gloomy forebodings were proved wrong.

Enthusiastically he took on his new role. When Ramsey Colles, a Castle hack and a literary acquaintance of O'Leary, made insulting references in his society journal to Maud Gonne and was pursued in the criminal courts by her, O'Leary it was who accompanied her to court and followed the proceedings to their successful conclusion. When in April 1901 James Stephens died in Dublin, O'Leary it was who delivered the graveside oration: 'The acts of James Stephens speak for themselves . . . . Fenianism was in its time a great power in the land, and James Stephens was . . . the greatest power in Fenianism.'

When in the same year Irish nationalists desired to express their appreciation of the action of John MacBride in fighting British imperialism in South Africa, it was O'Leary who on their behalf led a deputation to Paris to present to MacBride an address and a sword of honour, just as a year earlier he had headed the deputation to President Kruger in the same city. In 1903 when the centenary of Robert Emmet's rising was celebrated in Dublin, it was O'Leary who presided and spoke at the principal ceremony on 20 September, at the site of Emmet's execution outside Saint Catherine's Church, Thomas Street.

I am not here to talk. Emmet desired that his epitaph be not written until his country was free, and the best way to honour his memory is to strive to bring about the time when his epitaph can be written. I have nothing more to say. But we all have much to do.

Not surprisingly, perhaps, there were times when O'Leary felt that the role of figurehead ill fitted him and he insisted in taking part in the formulation of new policies and decisions. It is apparent that on such occasions his influence on the younger men was still strong and that they were glad, indeed, often anxious, to seek his advice. When in October 1902 Griffith was shaping his Hungarian policy, O'Leary was one of the first he discussed the idea with; it is a matter for speculation whether O'Leary's partiality for a constitutional monarchy influenced Griffith's theory of a dual monarchy for Ireland and Britain.

The visit to Trinity College early in 1900 of Joseph Chamberlain showed that, at nearly seventy years of age, O'Leary still retained much of his old fire when presented with an appropriate challenge. To permit the nationalists of Dublin to mark their disapproval of the visit of the man who had sabotaged Home Rule in 1886, the Transvaal Committee arranged a public meeting in the square behind the Custom House for the night of Chamberlain's arrival. An imposing list of speakers, which included O'Leary, Davitt, William Redmond, Maud Gonne and James Connolly, was published; at this stage the police banned the meeting.

Despite the last-minute defection of Davitt and Redmond, it was decided to defy the Castle. O'Leary was against the idea because it might result in defenceless citizens being batoned by the police; but as usual he loyally accepted the majority vote. At the hour fixed for the meeting a horse-brake, driven by Connolly and containing a 'frail, venerable figure . . . looking very happy . . . his grey beard blowing in the wind', drove down Abbey Street and broke through the police cordon in Beresford Place. As O'Leary rose to open the proceedings fierce fighting broke out between the crowd and the police, who skilfully led the vehicle round the corner into the yard of Store Street police station—its distinguished platform still aloft.

Realising that the crowd outside was expecting more excitement,

Connolly persuaded an embarrassed sergeant to open the gates. Out came the brake again, down through the crowd, on to O'Connell Street and over the bridge followed by thousands of cheering people. Outside the closed gates of Trinity College the speeches began again, but the police kept the brake moving. With Connolly ensuring that the horse moved at a walking pace along Dame Street, the speeches continued to the delight of the crowd.

Exhilarated by his success, Connolly turned to his companions as he reached the top of Dame Street: 'There are only two sentries at the Castle gate; shall I drive in and seize the place?' But the chance of a great sensation was missed, and the brake continued down to the quays and back to O'Connell Street with mounted and foot police now in (literally) hot pursuit as Connolly quickened the pace. 'We drove O'Leary back to his lodgings. He was tired but satisfied; we had held the banned meeting . . . and no one could say Dublin was loyal to the British Empire.'

In retrospect it seems a pity that all this enthusiasm could not have been repeated three months later when Queen Victoria visited the city. Her coming caused a split in the Supreme Council of the IRB, a narrow majority voting in favour of permitting their secretary, Fred Allan, who also happened to be secretary to the Lord Mayor, to carry on his official duties. When the minority refused to attend meetings, plans for a demonstration fell through.

In many respects O'Leary's daily routine in these last years of his life differed little from what it had been for close on fifty years. He still spent the morning cutting the papers, posting the cuttings and arranging his books. In the afternoon he still rummaged round the quayside bookstalls, where he became one of the city's best-known figures. It was at this time that he became friendly with one Michael Hickie, an astute bookseller of Bachelor's Walk who was known to all Dublin bibliophiles as 'Tricky Micky Hickie'. O'Leary discovered to his delight that Hickie was well read, a Tipperary-man and a former member of the IRB; what more could a man want in a friend?

O'Leary and Hickie would spend many hours in friendly argument about the value of some book O'Leary wished to buy. Finally the matter would be settled by the toss of a coin, which inevitably became lost amongst the precarious piles of books. Many a customer was puzzled as he entered the shop to find two elderly, bearded men crawling round the floor searching for a coin, itself often worth more than the book.

To the end of his life too O'Leary made at least an annual visit to London, staying with Dr. Mark Ryan, calling on friends like Stopford Brooke or Richard Barry O'Brien, poring over some books in the reading-room of the British Museum, even—as he did as late as 1904—presiding at some public meeting. Paris too saw him periodically, if less frequently; so did Belfast, Kilkenny and, above all, Tipperary.

Until confined to bed in the last few months of his life, O'Leary never missed a meeting of the National Literary Society. Weekly he would climb the six flights of stairs to the society's rooms in College Green; until 1903 he was a member of the Executive Committee, often coming near the head of the poll in annual elections. Every Sunday afternoon he would dine at Sigerson's in 3 Clare Street, where a literary group regularly assembled. It was here one day that Willie Yeats found a crystal ball and was excitedly telling the company of the giant letters and the god-like figure in white garments which he saw in it, until Dr. Sigerson abruptly pulled him up to point to the window-cleaner at work in his shirt-sleeves outside the chemist's shop on the opposite side of the street.

At every literary gathering O'Leary would dominate the company, as he moved through the crowd seeking converts to the cause of nationalism from among the young people and studied the new members of the various nationalist bodies. 'He always wanted to see and know the men who were working for Ireland in any sphere of labour,' said Alice Milligan. 'He was always on the look-out for a man or boy, or perhaps even a woman, who would be worth something to Ireland, and when he had found such a one he looked him or her in the face with those keen, searching eyes of his, before passing judgement. . . .'

At this period O'Leary's personal appearance became even more striking than before. His snow-white hair grew longer and his beard reached half-way down his chest; he had, as Colonel Arthur Lynch MP put it, 'assumed the aspect of an Old Testament prophet'.[5] He still clung to the formal frock coat, but now topped it with the prominent wide-brimmed 'wide-awake' hat, which had become the mark of a Dublin IRB officer. O'Leary for several years sported a pure white 'wide-awake', as if to distinguish him from the rest. At public functions he insisted on being introduced as a representative of extreme Irish nationalism and, if his new acquaintance was an Englishman, was always anxious to know if he had made a favourable impression.

It is to some of the young people who attended these gatherings that we owe the pen portraits of O'Leary at this period. To his rooms in Temple Street on many a Sunday morning came the young Padraic Colum, to sit through hours of discussion on poetry as O'Leary renewed glass after glass of warmed milk from a saucepan that sat on the burning coals. Around the walls the books were piled high; they lay on tables and chairs too, and even outside on the floor of the landing.

In the house of her own father, a loyal Orangeman, or more frequently in that of Robert Johnston, an equally staunch IRB man, the poetess Alice Milligan first met O'Leary. As usual with a lady, she was able to penetrate deeper into his personality than were many of his male acquaintances. She found that he had an almost hidden sense of humour and that, up to a point, he loved to be drawn into argument with people holding views diametrically opposite to his on a given topic. Only thus could one rouse him; 'without losing his temper he gave forth scathingly his opinions of men and things'.

Towards womenfolk and children he was still as chivalrous and gentle as ever. In his mid-seventies he would courteously but firmly insist, when they had alighted from the tram together at Parnell Square, on seeing Alice Milligan to her door at the far side of Mountjoy Square. She was almost forty years younger than he but, as he would remark with a smile: 'At this hour of the night it isn't at all nice for you to cross the square alone.'

When he called on the Rollestons he would encourage the children to climb on to his knees and would tell them stories well past normal bed-time. When he visited his own relatives the Carews in Kilkenny, or his old friend Dr. John Byrne Hackett in the same town, he would display remarkable energy as he played with the younger folk of both families in the garden.

As old age caught up with him, O'Leary mellowed in many ways. He no longer saw anything wrong in sitting on the same platform as F. H. O'Donnell, a critic of the physical force party with whom O'Leary had quarrelled violently at the time of the New Departure negotiations. He even struck up a genuine friendship with T. D. Sullivan, going so far as to insert in his memoirs an explanatory and half-apologetic footnote regarding a passage critical of A. M. Sullivan.

Like many advanced nationalists of the pre-1900 period O'Leary was apathetic towards the Irish language, which he did not consider to be an essential element of Irish nationality; Douglas Hyde never forgave him for some deprecatory remarks on the language which O'Leary made as far back as 1886. Nevertheless, although he ignored the Gaelic League, O'Leary's attitude was not one of hostility to the language movement, and he became a regular attender at the annual Oireachtas festival. He was once even persuaded by Maud Gonne to attend a concert for a charitable purpose. On another occasion when, in February 1900, Alice Milligan's play *The Last Feast of the Fianna* was on in the Gaiety Theatre, O'Leary (with Rolleston and George Coffey) walked on to the stage in the appropriate role of an ancient Irish warrior.

Although several pencil sketches of him had existed previously, not until his old age was O'Leary persuaded by J. B. Yeats to sit for his portrait; the result can be seen today in two of the best Yeats paintings in the National Gallery of Ireland. Oliver Sheppard the sculptor also did a notable bust of O'Leary, now in the Municipal Art Gallery, Dublin. When one of the Sigerson girls wanted to complete a figure of Father Time it was the head and face of O'Leary she sculpted.

But while he remained mentally alert as ever, O'Leary's physical health began to deteriorate round the turn of the century. By 1901 he was suffering periodically from fits of giddiness and dyspepsia, and in the spring of 1902 he had to remain in bed for several months. Gradually his already thin frame became leaner, and the thinner he became the more difficult he found it to remain warm in the winter months.

Friends in Tipperary kept him supplied with home-knitted woollen clothes; but he had to resort to greater consumption of whiskey and was then caught in a sort of vicious circle of ill-health. He was, said James Joyce, like a 'figure from a world which had disappeared. He would often be seen walking along the river, an old man dressed in light-coloured clothes with a shock of very white hair hanging down to his shoulders, almost bent in two. . . .'[6]

From time to time also he became saddened by the death of relatives and old friends; to D. J. O'Donoghue he once confided that he found the only sorrow of old age to be the constant loss of old friends and the feeling one was being left alone in the world. In June 1898 his eldest half-sister, Eliza, wife of William King, a merchant of Tipperary, died; she appears to have been the last of his brothers and sisters. Three years later, in August 1901, William King himself died at the ripe age of eighty-six, having lived the last ten years of his life in extreme poverty, possibly a victim of New Tipperary. Finally in 1906 came the death of O'Leary's lifelong friend, Dr. Jeremiah Dowling of Tipperary, a Young Irelander, scholar and poet.

From the United States also came periodic reports of the passing of old IRB associates. In September 1900 Dr. Denis Dowling Mulcahy died; he and O'Leary had been associates since the days of the 1849 movement and had corresponded with each other for half-a-century. Perhaps the hardest blow of all came in December 1901, when a long and touching letter from his son James in Jersey City described the last days of Thomas Clarke Luby, O'Leary's dearest friend, who had died at the age of seventy-nine the previous month.

Some time early in 1906, possibly because the majority of his close friends resided on the other side of the city, O'Leary moved from Temple Street to 11 Warrington Place, off Mount Street, a fashionable street then the residence of well-known barristers and judges. He had been contemplating this move for some time but had hesitated because of his books, which now numbered 10,000. Gradually, however, he reluctantly accepted the advice of D. J. O'Donoghue and, having picked out the more treasured ones for himself, sent the rest to be auctioned. Then he moved.

It was some time before anyone learnt what became of the library. O'Donoghue, puzzled like several others by the apparently low price O'Leary said he had obtained, made private inquiries and discovered that O'Leary had bought in most of them himself. Embarrassed to admit this to his friends, he had had them stored in a room over the offices of the United Irish League (of all bodies), where he could consult them privately when necessary.

From Warrington Place O'Leary continued to sally forth daily except in the wettest weather—down to the bookstalls, thence to the National Literary Society's room or perhaps to the National Club in Parnell Square (always a haunt of Dublin IRB men), returning home by tram in the evening if he had not been invited out to dinner. Although as late as June 1905 he was fit enough to attend the unveiling of a monument to the Irish Brigade on the historic battlefield of Fontenoy in Beligum, by the autumn of 1906 he had become 'very feeble, worn almost to a shadow, but his piercing eyes still lit up his face with vitality' as he erupted on one of his favourite subjects.

'Are you one of those dreadful people called teetotallers?' he asked scornfully of the actor Joseph Holloway one Sunday evening in Sigerson's. The following Sunday he dined at Sigerson's again. It was pouring rain, and he had been soaked to the skin. Having taken the tram from Mount Street bridge, he had allowed himself to be carried on past Sigerson's near the corner of Lincoln Place to the stop further down, beyond Kildare Street. Muttering imprecations at the tram driver, he trudged back in the rain. It was his last time out of doors.

What began as influenza developed first into pneumonia and then to bronchitis. Persuaded to take to his bed, O'Leary allowed a favourite grand-niece, Eily Carew, to come and keep house for him and to nurse him. Gradually he began to sink and as Dr. Sigerson, who attended him, told his friends that O'Leary was unlikely to recover this time, they began to call at the house. The constant stream of callers seemed to keep O'Leary's spirits up.

Around Christmas 1906, after several calls by Father Thomas Finlay SJ, O'Leary at last became reconciled to the Church. He had not been to Mass for half-a-century; one would like to have a record of the conversation between him and the Jesuit. By February 1907 bulletins about O'Leary's condition began to appear regularly in the Dublin newspapers. Still he lingered on, enjoying long periods of consciousness and retaining his mental faculties to the end.

On 11 March a memorial to the Manchester Martyrs was unveiled in his native Tipperary. As in the case of the Kickham statue nine years before, the occasion was turned into a public demonstration by the IRB. O'Leary, faithful to the end, sent a message regretting his inability to be present. A day or two later he was anointed by Fr. Finlay and on 16 March, at 5.20 p.m., in the presence of his niece and the priest, he died peacefully. He was within three months of his seventy-seventh birthday.

O'Leary's passing was regretted by organs of all shades of nationalist opinion, and by several journals not normally sympathetic to anything Irish. 'Single-minded, incorruptible, a scorner of flattery . . . John O'Leary was a man amongst men, ever and always . . . a valiant upholder of the right,' commented the *Irish Independent*.[7] 'Never did he by any formal act renounce the doctrine that Ireland's rights can only be fully vindicated on the battlefield,' said the *Irish Catholic*.[8] His bitter opponents in the *Freeman's Journal* had no editorial comment, but in a brief letter to its editor J. B. Yeats said that '. . . to tell the unwelcome truth to one's own countrymen and one's own friends. . . . John O'Leary possessed this courage. But for him and his like the nation would have perished.'

Arthur Griffith in *Sinn Fein*, which carried mourning rules on every page of the next issue, wrote:

. . . John O'Leary was a man who lived by his conscience, who never spoke but what he held to be the truth, and who never feared to proclaim the truth. Such a man when he combines intellect with character is obnoxious to usurped authority, and so John O'Leary lived and died obnoxious to the Government which prevails in Ireland, and its enemy to the last. . . . The British Government in Ireland has failed because Ireland can still bring forth men who hold their honour dearer than their lives. Such a man was John O'Leary.[9]

D. P. Moran in the *Leader* said: 'The hearts of the Irish people in every land, whatever their shade of nationalist views be, will do homage in spirit to his memory and breathe a prayer for the soul of the dead Fenian.' And in *Inis Fail* P. S. O'Hegarty, after quoting O'Leary's saying that 'I never had much hope, but I went into the Fenian movement because I knew it was right', commented: 'That was the keynote of his life, politically and intellectually.'[10]

To the *Pall Mall Gazette* Katharine Tynan contributed some touching memories of O'Leary. Most striking of all, the *Daily Telegraph,* long regarded as the popular semi-official organ of Tory

England, published a long appreciation of O'Leary, attributed to Harry Meltzer, in which he described O'Leary as 'an ardent and incurable revolutionary—gentle but persistent in his fanatical gospel, rigid, consistent, incorruptible, as modest in desire as in means'.

Across the Atlantic John Devoy devoted a large part of the next issue of his paper *Gaelic American* to tributes to O'Leary and sketches of his career, many clearly from Devoy's own incisive pen. 'No man of his generation and no man of the last 100 years has left a brighter example of steadfast adherence to principle and purity of life.' To Devoy also six weeks later came a long letter from Harry Meltzer, alleging in effect that the *Daily Telegraph* had stolen his appreciation, and then going on to add some recollections of 'the noblest and the purest man I ever met . . . gentle as a woman, invariably unselfish . . . chivalrously generous'.

In the American *Donahoe's Magazine* O'Leary's devoted disciple Alice Milligan wrote: 'He stood for principle against compromise, and . . . denounced the methods of continental anarchy . . . in a few instances . . . introduced into the Irish struggle. He was not very sanguine of immediate success, had seen enough of failure to daunt the bravest heart; but he taught us that in spite of failure we should not surrender.' And in Trieste, James Joyce, commissioned to write a series of articles in Italian on the evils of empire, used O'Leary's death as a peg on which to hang one of his contributions and revealed some enthusiasm for Sinn Fein.[11]

'The rebel can reckon upon nothing in life; he is sure to be calumniated; he is likely to be robbed, and may even be murdered; but let him once go out of life and he is sure of a fine funeral.' Thus O'Leary had commented in his memoirs eleven years before. Ironically, in his own case he was to be proved wrong. Down the years, since the death of O'Connell, Irish nationalists had used funerals of great patriots to stir up popular feeling, and the two wings of Fenianism had brought the practice to a fine art. Now, as if indicative of the weakness of the IRB in the first decade of the new century, they were to reveal, on the death of O'Leary, a degree of inefficiency unusual for that body.

In fairness it must be admitted that the fates conspired to make it difficult to organise a public funeral for O'Leary. He died on a Saturday, and the following Monday was a Bank holiday, so that normal means of communication were not fully available. On top of this, O'Leary's few remaining relatives objected to a public funeral from the start. And, as if to complete the sequence of unfavourable events, torrential rain poured down on Dublin for the whole of the day on which he was buried.

In the circumstances he got as impressive a funeral as could have been expected—but not the one he deserved. The '98 Centenary Committee, still in existence, took charge of arrangements but altered their published plans at least once to add to the confusion. Finally it was decided to defy the wishes of O'Leary's relatives.

A large crowd braved the elements as the coffin was borne from Westland Row church to the hearse by four old comrades of the IRB—James O'Connor MP, P. T. Daly, Major John MacBride and John O'Hanlon. The coffin was then covered with the green flag with which O'Leary had been presented by New York admirers in 1898, and, followed by thousands of nationalists, the cortege moved off through the centre of the city to Glasnevin cemetery.

Members of the various extreme nationalist organisations marched in groups—the '98 Committee and the '98 clubs, the Old Guard Union of IRB men of the 1860s, Cumann na nGaedheal, the GAA and the Parnell Commemorative Association. Amongst prominent IRB men present were Fred Allan, John Wyse-Power, John Daly, Arthur Griffith, Henry Dixon and Anthony Mackey of Castleconnell. The Parliamentary Party was present in force too; John Devoy was represented by the Honourable James Sullivan of the Connecticut State legislature, while from O'Leary's native Tipperary came a strong contingent led by the veteran Dr. John O'Ryan.

At the entrance to the cemetery a large crowd watched as the coffin was again shouldered by O'Connor, MacBride, Daly and O'Hanlon, and carried to the grave along a route lined by 200 men with hurleys raised. After prayers in Irish burial took place, without an oration, near the Manchester Martyrs' Plot and beside the grave of James Stephens.

O'Leary's admirers had purchased the grave from the representatives of Davitt, who had originally acquired the plot on the death of Stephens. Two years after O'Leary's death, in a simple ceremony, again without speeches, a memorial in the form of a Celtic cross was unveiled over O'Leary's grave by an old IRB man from Antrim, Neil John O'Boyle, in the presence of Griffith, MacBride, Allan, Daly and a small assembly. Two months later again an almost identical monument was erected over the grave of Stephens.

When they came to settle his affairs, O'Leary's friends discovered that for all practical purposes he had died penniless. By his will dated 21 March 1905 he left his father's 'insurance policy' (there were in fact two, of £500 each) to his grand-niece Eily Carew, and the balance of his property, principally his books and pictures, on trust for the National Literary Society of Ireland.

The policies when cashed came to some £1,180, from which was deducted the mortgage to Dr. Mark Ryan, the remaining £875 going to Miss Carew. The National Literary Society selected the best of his books and sold the remainder for an undisclosed sum.

Although O'Leary is known to have received out of Land League funds as recently as 1905 compensation for the Tipperary property, by 1907 he owned not a single piece of property. Thus with his death ended the O'Learys' connection with Tipperary, where they had settled a century before.

Romantic Ireland's dead and gone,
It's with O'Leary in the grave.

By a single quotation from Yeats is O'Leary remembered by many of his countrymen sixty years after his death. It is appropriate that, if he is to be remembered by them at all, O'Leary's name should be linked with that of Ireland's outstanding figure in modern literature. To suggest that, but for O'Leary's influence, Yeats would never have become a great poet would be wrong. Rather is it that Yeats's career, both as a writer and an Irishman, is a permanent reminder of O'Leary's broadminded concept of Irish nationality, a concept which, from his own conversion to Irish nationalism in 1846 until his death sixty-one years later, he preached incessantly to Irishmen of all creeds and classes. Ever faithful to the message of Davis and Young Ireland, his tone remained to the end (to use his own pun) 'the tone of Wolfe Tone'.

Despite his lifelong interest in literary affairs, however, O'Leary deserves a place amongst the leading figures in his country's struggle for political independence. That he is still almost unknown, even to a generation taking a growing interest in nineteenth-century Ireland, is probably due to the fact that O'Leary's name—unlike those of O'Connell, Davitt and Parnell—is not associated with any success in the nationalist struggle. To many Irishmen of the mid-twentieth century Fenianism connotes events such as the disastrous rising of 1867 and the series of terrorist activities in English cities in the 1880s. The origin and impact of the New Departure are often forgotten, and the revolutionary beginnings of the Land League frequently overlooked.

That the ideas of both the Irish and American wings of Fenianism were often woefully unrealistic is undeniable; that their methods for long periods were sadly inefficient is equally true. But to O'Leary and his associates more than to any other group of Irishmen is due the credit for ensuring that, though Irish separatism was at times moribund, it never expired. If England failed to kill Home Rule with kindness it was a handful of amateur conspirators like O'Leary who ensured that failure. Out of the early IRB grew Butt's Home Rule League, Parnell's united party at Westminster and

Davitt's Land League. To the later IRB can be ascribed the foundation of Sinn Fein, the 1916 rising and the series of spectacular successes achieved by Irish separatism between 1918 and 1922.

The IRB of the 1860s and the IRB of the post-1898 period were, in almost every respect but in name and aim, two wholly different bodies. In both one man only, John O'Leary, occupied a position of prominence and influence. When a student in his twenties he sacrificed the prospect of a promising professional career to join the revolutionary movement because he conceived it his duty to his country to do so. Aristocratic in bearing and in outlook, though never class-conscious, he considered a constitutional monarchy the ideal form of government for a free Ireland. From the age of nineteen he was implacably opposed to any form of agrarian agitation before the attainment of political freedom. He was unsympathetic to the Irish language movement, not regarding it as essential to the nationalist campaign.

It is a measure of O'Leary's stature that, notwithstanding these views, he became a leader of a movement that was unavowedly republican in outlook and had socialist leanings from its inception, a movement to which may be traced the origin of the Land League and a movement which ultimately included in its objects the restoration of the Irish language. No greater tribute could be paid to O'Leary than his associates in the separatist cause thus paid to him for over half-a-century.

SOURCES AND NOTES

NOTE: The following abbreviations are used in the following lists and notes:

Denieffe — Denieffe, Joseph: A Personal Narrative of the Irish Revolutionary Brotherhood (New York, 1906).
Devoy — Devoy, John: Recollections of an Irish Rebel (New York, 1929).
FJ — *Freeman's Journal*.
FP — Fenian Papers in State Paper Office, Dublin.
GA — *Gaelic American* (newspaper, New York).
II — *Irish Independent*.
NLI — National Library of Ireland.
O'Leary — O'Leary, John: Recollections of Fenians and Fenianism (London, 1896), Vols. I and II.
SPO — State Paper Office, Dublin.

General Sources

O'Leary.
O Donoghue, D. J.: John O'Leary and his Friends, a series of twenty articles in the *Sunday Independent*, 22.6.1913 to 2.11.1913.
O'Donoghue, D. J.: John O'Leary and his Friends, MS–786, NLI.
O'Leary Papers, NLI, MSS 5925 to 5927, 8001/1 to 8001/56, 8002 and 8752.

CHAPTER ONE

Principal Sources

Parliamentary Gazetteer, 1846, Vol. 3.
Pigott's Directory, 1824.
Slater's Directory, 1846.
St. Michael's Church, Tipperary: baptismal and marriage registers.
Public Record Office, Dublin: certified copies of wills.
O'Leary, Ellen: Lays of Country, Home and Friends (Dublin, 1890).
Quane, Dr. M.: The Abbey School, Tipperary, in *Journal of Cork Historical and Archaeological Society,* Vol. LXV, No. 201, pp. 40-76.
Erasmus Smith Schools (High School, Dublin): records.
St. Patrick's College, Carlow: records.
MacSuibhne, Peadar, PP: The Beginnings of Carlow College, in *Capuchin Annual,* 1960, pp. 290-299.
Knockbeg Centenary Book (Carlow, 1948).
Comerford, Rev. M.: Collections Relating to the Dioceses of Kildare and Leighlin, Vol. 1 (Dublin, 1883).

Notes

[1] Webb, Compendium of Irish Biography (Dublin, 1879), p. 159.
[2] O'Leary, Vol. 1, p. 230, note.
[3] SPO, FP (Series 1), Box 23, file 291; *Irish People* (New York), 19.8.1871.
[4] *Clonmel Chronicle*, 21.7.1877.
[5] *II*, 20.3.1907.
[6] *FJ*, 18.3.1907; *Clonmel Chronicle*, 20.3.1907; *Nationalist and Leinster Tribune*, 23.3.1907.
[7] Doyle, William S.: More Fragments (Tipperary, 1960), p. 5.
[8] Dowling, J.: An Irish Doctor Remembers (Dublin, 1955), p. 21.
[9] Devoy, p. 286.
[10] Kehoe, L. J., PP, in *Nationalist and Leinster Tribune*, 17.3.1934.
[11] Brenan, Rev. M.: Schools of Kildare and Leinster (Dublin, 1935), pp. 427-428.
[12] *Dublin Evening Post*, 24.7.1817.

CHAPTER TWO

Principal Sources

SPO, Chief Secretary's Office, Outrage Reports, Co. Tipperary, 1848 and 1849.
Gwynn, Denis: Young Ireland and 1848 (Cork, 1949).
St. Patrick's College, Carlow: records.
O'Neill, T. P.: Fintan Lalor and the 1849 Movement, in *An Cosantoir*, Vol. X, No. 4.
Fogarty, L.: James Fintan Lalor, Collected Writings (Dublin, 1947).
Luby, Thomas Clarke: memoirs in *Irish Nation* (New York), for 30.9.1882, 28.10.1882, 30.12.1882, 19.1.1884, 5.7.1884.
McCarthy, Justin H.: quoted by T. P. O'Connor in The Parnell Movement (Dublin, 1886), p. 299 et seq.
Kiernan, T. J.: The Irish Exiles in Australia (Dublin, 1954), pp. 93, 132, 172, 175.
Ormsby, Lambert Hepenstal: Medical History of the Meath Hospital and County Dublin Infirmary (Dublin, 1888), pp. 283, 287.
Queen's College, Galway: records.
Queen's College, Cork: records.
Denieffe, pp. 3, 46, 48.
Yeats, W. B.: Autobiographies (London, 1955), p. 212.

Notes

[1] *II*, 18.3.1907.
[2] As[1]; also *Evening Telegraph*, 8.3.1913.
[3] O'Leary, Ellen: Lays of Country, Home and Friends (Dublin, 1890), p. 13.
[4] *GA*, 11.5.1907.
[5] *GA*, 23.3.1907.

[6] MacCarthy, Justin: preface to Poems of 'Eva' of the Nation (Dublin 1909), p. xiv.

[7] *Irishman*, 10.5.1862.

[8] Public Record Office, Dublin.

[9] O'Sullivan, T. F.: The Young Irelanders (Tralee, 1944), pp. 153-155.

[10] Ó Néill, Tomás: Fiontán Ó Leathlobhair (Ath Cliath, 1962), p. 115.

[11] Dictionary of National Biography, Second Supplement (1910-11), p. 33.

[12] Devoy, p. 272.

[13] *Irishman*, 6.2.1875.

[14] Recollections of an Irish National Journalist (Dublin, 1882), p. 58.

[15] O'Donoghue, D. J., in *Sunday Independent*, 22.6.1913.

[16] Hurley, James: Old College Record Books, in *Cork University Record*, No. 27, Easter 1953; *Southern Reporter*, 25.10.1849.

[17] O'Leary, Vol. II, p. 164.

[18] *Evening Telegraph*, 4.4.1907; *FJ*, 20.3.1907.

[19] As[11].

[20] J. B. Yeats (sen.) in *FJ*, 20.3.1907; Tynan, Katharine, Twenty-Five Years' Reminiscences (London, 1913), p. 196.

[21] Macken, Mary: *Studies*, Vol. 28, pp. 136-141; Hinkson, Katharine Tynan, in *Pall Mall Gazette*, quoted in *GA*, 20.4.1907.

[22] *Daily Telegraph*, 12.4.1909.

[23] SPO, FP (Series 1), Box. 22.

[24] Letter to author from Very Rev. James Rice PP, Ballyhea, Co. Cork, 23.4.1963.

[25] Gooch, G. P.: The Second Empire (London, 1960), p. 74.

[26] Luby Papers NLI, MS 331-333.

[27] As[26].

[28] Rossa, Jeremiah O'Donovan: Rossa's Recollections, 1838 to 1898 (New York, 1898), pp. 268-281.

[29] *GA*, 23.3.1907.

[30] As[23].

[31] *Irishman*, Christmas Number 1874.

[32] *Irishman*, 26.12.1874.

[33] SPO, FP (Series 1), Box 30, manuscript note on *'Phoenix'* of 20.8.1859.

[34] *Irish News* (New York), 7.5.1859.

[35] *Evening Telegraph*, 30.3.1907.

[36] SPO, FP (Series 1), Box 30.

[37] As[26].

[38] Archives of Catholic University of America, Washington, DC.

CHAPTER THREE

Principal Sources

Irish People (Dublin), 1863-65.

Nation, 1865.

SPO, FP (Series 1), Boxes 15, 21-23, 29-31.

Irishman, December 1874; series entitled 'Fenianism Photographed'

by Firinne (James O'Connor), together with subsequent correspondence.
O'Donoghue, D. J.: *The Shamrock,* Vol. XXX, January–April 1893, series entitled 'The Literature of '67'.
O'Donoghue, D. J.: The Poets of Ireland (London, 1892-93).
Denieffe.
Corish, Rev. Patrick J.: Cardinal Cullen and the National Association of Ireland, in *Reportorium Novum,* Vol. 3, No. 1, 1961-62, pp. 13-61.
MacSuibhne, Rev. Peadar: Paul Cullen and His Contemporaries (Naas, 1961 and 1963), Vols. 1 and 2.
O'Mahony Papers (1863-1877), Catholic University of America, Washington, DC.
Stephens, James: diary of 1859 US tour, in Public Record Office, Belfast, also NLI, MS 4148.

Notes

[1] Rossa's Recollections, 1838 to 1898 (New York, 1898), p. 203; O'Kelly, J. J.: series entitled 'The Dawn of Fenianism' in *Irish People* (Dublin), Sept. 1899 to May 1900.
[2] *Irishman,* 10.7.1875.
[3] Devoy, pp. 33, 41 and 46.
[4] *Irish Nation* (New York) 28.1.1882.
[5] *GA,* 23.3.1907.
[6] Church of Saints Michael and John, Dublin; marriage register.
[7] J. J. O'Kelly, as [1].
[8] *Irish Book Lover,* Vol. XXXI, October 1921, p. 26.
[9] *Irish Freedom,* May 1911, p. 5.
[10] As [8].
[11] Devoy, p. 44.
[12] As [11].
[13] Devoy, p. 45.
[14] Special Commission report (see Principal Sources to Chapter 4).
[15] O'Sullivan, T. F.: The Young Irelanders (Tralee, 1944), pp. 115-122.
[16] Sullivan, A. M.: New Ireland (paper-covered edition), p. 431.
[17] As [5].
[18] Kickham, C. J.: Sally Cavanagh (Dublin, 1869), p. x.
[19] Devoy, p. 42.
[20] As [19].

CHAPTER FOUR

Principal Sources

FJ, August 1865–January 1866; March–June 1870; January–December 1869.
Irishman: February 1874; December 1870; January 1871.
Evening Mail, 26.6.1867.
Irish Times: 27.6.1867; 7.3.1889.
Nation: September–December 1865; 29.6.1867.

Report of the Proceedings of the Special Commission for the County of the City of Dublin, held at Green Street, Dublin, for the Trial of Thomas Clarke Luby and others, for Treason-Felony (Alex Thom, Dublin, 1866).

O'Donovan Rossa: Irish Rebels in English Prisons—A Record of Prison Life (New York, 1882).

Report of the Commissioners appointed to inquire into the Treatment of Treason-Felony Convicts in English Prisons, Vols. I and II (HM Stationery Office, London, 1871).

SPO, FP (Series 1), Boxes 15, 21, 30 and 31.

Devoy, pp. 48, 49, 54, 55, 69, 70, 278, 295, 296, 322.

Denieffe, pp. 94, 104, 107, 119.

Notes

1. *Irish People* (Dublin), 30.12.1899.
2. SPO, FP (Series 1), Box 29, file 291.
3. *Irish Nation* (New York), 31.12.1881.
4. Devoy, John, in *Irish Freedom,* March 1913.
5. *Daily Express,* 4.1.1866.
6. *Nation,* 26.3.1864.
7. Kickham, C. J.; Sally Cavanagh (Dublin, 1869), p. viii.
8. *GA,* 29.12.1906.
9. Devoy's Post Bag (Dublin, 1948), Vol. 1, p. 14.
10. *The Times,* 7.6.1869.
11. *Irish American* (New York), 4.8.1866.
12. *GA,* 23.3.1907.
13. O'Donoghue, D. J., in *Sunday Independent,* 22.6.1913.
14. *Irishman,* 26.8.1866; letter from Ellen O'Leary.
15. *Irish American,* 15.8.1866; letter from Thomas Duggan.
16. *Irishman,* 30.11.1867; *Irish American,* 15.8.1868; *Irishman,* 25.4.1868, 8.8.1868, 29.8.1868.
17. Original in possession of Bourke family, Greenrath, Tipperary; copy in NLI.
18. Yeats, W. B.: Autobiographies (London, 1955), p. 211.
19. *The Times,* 15.3.1869.
20. Brodrick, Hon G. C.: Memories and Impressions 1831–1900 (London, 1900), pp. 167, 168.
21. *Irishman,* 8.4.1871.
22. *The Times,* 19.12.1870.
23. As [12].
24. *Irish People,* (New York) 18.3.1871, letter from John O'Leary.

CHAPTER FIVE

Principal Sources

Irishman: 1870–1; October–December 1878.
Irish Citizen (New York), 1872.
Irish Nation (New York), 1881–1883.

Irish People (New York), 1871.
GA, 23.3.1907, 20.4.1907, 11.5.1907.
SPO, FP (Series 2), Box 91; Green File 39 (file A612); Chief Secretary's Office, Crime Department, Cartons 44 and 50.
D'Arcy, Rev. W., OFM CONV.: The Fenian Movement in the United States, 1858–1886 (New York, 1947), Chapter X.
Devoy's Post Bag, ed. Ryan and O'Brien (Dublin, 1948 and 1953), Vols. 1 and 2.
Devoy, pp. 280–286, 305, 308, 312–316, 344, 370.
Devoy, John: Davitt and the Fenians, in *GA,* June–November 1906.
Devoy, John: Parnell and the Fenians, in *Chicago Journal,* 24.3.1899.
Ryan, Dr. M. F.: Fenian Memories (Dublin, 1945).
O'Kelly, J. J., MP: The Dawn of Fenianism, in *Irish People* (Dublin), September 1899 to May 1900.
Moody, T. W.: The New Departure in Irish Politics, in Essays in British and Irish History, ed. H. A. Cronne and others (London, 1949).
O'Brien, R. Barry: The Life of Charles Stewart Parnell (London, 1899), Vol. 1.
O'Donnell, F. H.: A History of the Irish Parliamentary Party (London, 1910), Vol. 1.
Davitt, M.: The Fall of Feudalism in Ireland (London and New York, 1904).

Notes

[1] Letter from F. F. Millen to George Cahill, 14.8.1871, in archives of Boston College Library, Boston, Mass., USA.
[2] As [1].
[3] *Irishman,* 28.3.1874 and 3.4.1875.
[4] Denieffe, p. 46.
[5] Denieffe, pp. 201 and 225.
[6] Hone, Joseph: The Life of George Moore (London, 1936), p. 55.
[7] Colum, Padraic: *The Dubliner,* summer 1963, pp. 84–86.
[8] Downey, Edmund: Twenty Years Ago (London, 1905), pp. 111–114.
[9] Devoy, John, in *Irish Freedom,* May 1913.
[10] *Irishman,* 18.7.1874.
[11] *Irish Nation* (New York), 17.2.1883.
[12] *Irish Nation* (New York), 4.9.1875.
[13] *Irish Nation* (New York), 27.3.1875.
[14] *Irish Citizen* (New York), 18.11.1871.
[15] SPO, Chief Secretary's Register 1877, file 5572.
[16] *Irish Freedom,* April 1913.
[17] *Tipperary People,* 22.2.1878.
[18] *Catholic Bulletin,* Vol. IX (1919), p. 646.
[19] Dowling, J.: An Irish Doctor Remembers (Dublin, 1955), p. 24.
[20] Yeats, W. B.: Autobiographies (London, 1955), pp. 358–359.
[21] O'Brien, William, MP: Recollections (London, 1905), pp. 139–141.
[22] Harris Papers: letter from John O'Leary to M. Harris, MP 30.6.1879.
[23] SPO, FP (Series 2), Green File 157.

²⁴ Harris Papers: letter from Michael Davitt to M. Harris 10.7.1880.
²⁵ As ¹³; also *Irish Daily Independent*, 1.3.1895.
²⁶ SPO, FP (Series 2), Green File 39, file 492S.
²⁷ *Tipperary People*, 22.6.1883.
²⁸ Tinsley, W.: Random Recollections of an Old Publisher (London and Bournemouth, 1900), Vol. 2, pp. 326–327.

CHAPTER SIX

Principal Sources

FJ: 1884, 1885, 1886; 21.9.1888.
Tipperary People, 1885–6–7.
Tipperary Nationalist, 26.10.1889.
Hammond, J. L.: Gladstone and the Irish Nation (London, 1938), pp. 376, 378, 381, 382, 386, 418.
Gavan Duffy, Sir Charles: Mr. Gladstone's Irish Constitution, in *Contemporary Review*, May 1886.
Gavan Duffy, Sir Charles: The Price of Peace in Ireland (Dublin, 1885).
O'Leary, John: What Irishmen Should Know (Dublin, undated), lecture in Cork, February 1886.
O'Leary, John: How Irishmen Should Feel (Dublin, undated), lecture in Newcastle-on-Tyne, 17.12.1886.
Tulloch, Jessie: Some Recollections of John O'Leary, in *Irish Monthly*, Vol. 38 (1910), pp. 151–158.
Tynan, Katharine: Twenty-five Years (London, 1913).
Tynan, Katharine: The Middle Years (London, 1916).
Yeats, W. B.: Letters to the New Island, ed. H. Reynolds (Harvard, 1934).
Yeats, W. B.: Autobiographies (London, 1955).
Yeats, W. B.: Letters to Katharine Tynan, ed. R. McHugh (New York), 1953.
Hone, Joseph: W. B. Yeats 1865–1939 (London, 1942).
Wade, Allen: The Letters of W. B. Yeats (London, 1954).
McHugh, Roger: Yeats and Irish Politics, talk to Kilkenny Literary Society, 13.2.1961.
Boyd, Ernest A.: Ireland's Literary Renaissance (New York, 1916).
Macken, Mary: W. B. Yeats, John O'Leary and the Contemporary Club, in *Studies*, Vol. 28 (1939), pp. 136–142.
Dublin University Review, 1886.
Dublin Magazine, Vol. 1, p. 521.
The Bookman, Vol. V, (October 1893–March 1894), article by Katharine Tynan on pp. 13–14.
Irish Book Lover, Vols. VIII (pp. 89–90), X, XII (p. 103), XIII (pp. 21, 25–27, 52–54), XXVII (pp. 245–249).
Celtic Literary Society minute book, NLI, MS 200.
The Liberal Union of Ireland: The Plan of Campaign—the Smith-Barry Estate, Tipperary (Dublin, 1890).

Notes

[1] Originals of both addresses in office of Tipperary Urban District Council.
[2] O'Brien, R. Barry: The Life of Charles Stewart Parnell (London, 1898), Vol. 2, p. 68.
[3] *Dublin University Review,* December 1886.
[4] Fisher, H. A. L.: James Bryce (London, 1927), Vol. 1, p. 211.
[5] Fogarty, Canon P.: Tipperary's GAA Story (Thurles, 1960), p. 22.
[6] Ryan, W. P.: The Irish Literary Revival (London, 1894), p. 127.
[7] Public Record Office, Dublin; probate of John O'Leary's will.
[8] *FJ,* 19.3.1891.
[9] *FJ,* 8.1.1891.
[10] *FJ,* 26.6.1891.
[11] Curtis, L. P., junior: Coercion and Conciliation in Ireland (London, 1963), pp. 255–260.

CHAPTER SEVEN

Principal Sources

FJ, November–December 1890; 1891, 1897, 1898; 21.9.1903; 1907.
Weekly FJ: 1897, 1898; 15.3.1913.
Evening Telegraph, 1907; May to July 1909.
Evening Mail, 1907.
Evening Herald, 1907.
United Ireland, November–December 1890; 1891.
United Irishman, 1899–1906.
GA, March–April 1907.
The Times, 16.9.1891, p.7.
Irish Book Lover, Vol. XIII (October 1921), D. J. O'Donoghue on pp. 25, 52–4.
Irish Monthly, Vol. 24 (1896), p. 102.
Catholic Bulletin (Vol. IX), 1919, pp. 646–648.
Celtic Literary Society minute book, NLI, MS 200.
National Literary Society of Ireland, minutes, NLI, MS 645.
Public Record Office, Dublin: copy will and probate of John O'Leary.
SPO, FP (Series 2), Box 77; Crime Special Branch reports 1890–1, Boxes 1–5; Crime Special Branch, file 523W/10,953; District Inspectors, Crime Special Branch, reports 1887–1895.
Colum, Padraic: Arthur Griffith (Dublin, 1959).
Colum, Padraic: A Revolutionist of Another Age, in *Irish Statesman,* Vol. 3 (8.11.1924), p. 274.
Colum, Padraic: John O'Leary, talk on Radio Eireann, 17.8.1958.
Holloway, Joseph: diaries for 1900 (p. 71) and 1907 (pp. 176–7), NLI, MS 1798 and 1805.
Holloway, Joseph: Some Recollections of John O'Leary, in *Evening Telegraph,* 21.6.1913.
MacBride, Maud Gonne: A Servant of the Queen (Dublin, 1950).
Milligan, Alice, in *New Ireland,* 16.3.1918.

Milligan, Alice: *Donahoe's Magazine,* May 1907.
Ó Lúing, Seán: Art Ó Gríofa (Dublin, 1953).
Lyons, F. S. L.: The Fall of Parnell (London, 1960).
Lyons, George A.: Some Recollections of Griffith and His Times (Dublin, 1923).
Lyons, George A.: Two articles in *The Leader,* 1.1.1948 and 15.1.1949.
Lyons, George A.: Article in *Forum* (Dublin), January 1950.
Rolleston, C. H.: Portrait of an Irishman (London, 1939), pp. 27, 141.

Information supplied to the writer from the following persons on the subjects mentioned: Messrs. Denis McCullough, Dublin; Bulmer Hobson, Clifden; the late Piaras Beaslai, Dublin, and the late Dr. P. J. McCartan, Greystones (on the IRB in the early 1900s); Mrs. Bronson Alberry (formerly Miss Una Rolleston), London; Ald. C. M. Milligan, Bangor, County Down; Miss Maureen Carew, Fleet, Hants.; Mr. Norman Carew, Elanora, New South Wales; and the late Miss Florence Hackett, Kilkenny (on the life, habits and health generally of John O'Leary in his old age).

Notes

[1] Tynan, Katharine: The Middle Years (London, 1916), p. 25.
[2] SPO, Crime Special Branch 1890–1, file 2267.
[3] *Tipperary People,* 2.12.1898.
[4] Tulloch, Jessie: Some Recollections of John O'Leary, in *Irish Monthly,* Vol. 38 (1910), pp. 151–158.
[5] Lynch, Arthur, MP: Ireland—Vital Hour (London, 1915), p. 28.
[6] The Critical Writings of James Joyce, ed. Mason and Ellmann (London, 1959), pp. 187–192.
[7] 18.3.1907.
[8] 23.3.1907.
[9] 27.3.1907.
[10] 23.3.1907.
[11] As [6].

INDEX